A Journey

taken by

Ann Atkinson

ISBN: 978-0-244-32491-9

BIOGRAPHY

Ann Atkinson lives with her husband in the Oxfordshire Cotswolds but she calls herself one of the last Colonials having lived in Aden, Northern Rhodesia and Basutoland when they were all part of the Empire. She then lived in South Africa for many years and eventually returned to live in England. Her career in the travel industry in Aden, Africa and England included visits to many parts of the world and it was only after she retired and came under the spell of Oxford academia that she commenced eight years of study at the University of Oxford gaining assorted certificates and diplomas and eventually a Master of Science degree. This journey from her earliest memory during the London Blitz of 1940 to the present day is in response to the request from her daughters -

'you must write it all down'.

DEDICATION

To Damian who has been my loving companion on these later stages of my journey
To my daughters
To my sister Mary and other family members
To all the friends who travelled with me
Thank you for making this journey worthwhile.

CONTENTS

THE FOUNDATIONS

'You have lived such an interesting life you must write a book' so say the family and friends who want to know the ins and outs, warts and all of several decades of me. It may have been interesting to me but perhaps not to others, however where do I start to write the story of my life? Commonsense says start at the beginning and progress through to now, in other words chronologically - I was born in.... lived in.... went to school... got married and again and again...and here I am retired but that is not how I view my life in retrospect. A succession of flashes appear with no thought to chronology. A jumble of blue and white pottery on a bomb site, a picnic basket with a fried egg sandwich, the push in my back as Concorde flies through the sound barrier, a blue knitted duffle coat on a chubby baby daughter, lying on a beach as Concorde flies over my head at seemingly zero feet, a bottle of Here XVII for Dutch courage before going on stage, shopping with Grandma in Oxford Street on a Saturday morning, my Mother dying in my arms, Rod Stewart on stage at Sun City and Queen and Elton John. Gradually my life is flashing before me in this series of pictures, feelings and remembrances, they come with no thought of where or when, not constrained by chronology, just an unraveling of the storage space in my memory bank.

In order to make sense of all this a timeline provides the railway track for my life, there will be trucks loaded with reminiscences and branch lines to cope with deviations in the story and stations where interesting stops will be made. I will be as truthful and open as possible but bearing in mind the grandchildren perhaps it will be more blemish free than 'warts and all'. A subtle distinction perhaps but there must be some things that a gal keeps to herself.

A railway track needs a solid base and this was provided by my ancestors. They have given me my genes and DNA so their history is my pre-history and their lives may prove to be far more interesting than mine - I leave it for you to decide.

Having set the foundations the track will take me through my childhood with forays into World War II and schools, onwards to the Empire or rather my part as a Colonial child, travels with my parents, more school and then approaching the minefield of adolescence into adulthood. A major station en route is Aden which played such a significant part in my life and here I will branch off into boyfriends (strictly censored) clothes and my first jobs. Back on track I encounter marriage, children and more travel into what remained of the Colonies. There are bumps along the way and upheavals and deviations before approaching the final stations in my journey.

My memory bank has been helped by letters that appeared in boxes having been hidden away for decades, by my sixty-six photograph albums which start in 1947 and continue to this day and by the arrival and departure date stamps and visae in my many passports. Now with an open-border policy in many countries these stamps are rarely used and I do wish the UK border control had thought to stamp the passports of her citizens as they came and went, it would certainly have helped with the timetable of my journey.

So here goes, the engine is fired up and we are off.........

CHAPTER 1
Laying the track

'We're all ghosts. We all carry inside us, people who came before us'
Liam Callanan

After my Mother died in 1996, and spurred on by the stories of the family that she had passed on to me I commenced years of researching the family's history and this was before the digitalisation of all records, now a quick search through computerised records will take you into births, deaths and marriages, censuses, travel and immigration, burial indexes and so on, but when I started in 1997 it was a question of visiting County and London Record Offices and man-handling large volumes of records on and off shelves in search of that elusive piece of information to add to the jigsaw of my ancestors' lives.

The ritual of the weekly journey to London became part of my life, leaving home early and wondering what new details the day would bring forth or would today be a wasted journey. I felt that in handling the volumes of records I was a step closer to my ancestors and that digitisation has made family research more impersonal. One of the highlights of waiting on the steps of Myddelton House where the records are kept and waiting for the doors to open, was listening to comments from others in the queue - each person trying to outdo the other in how clever they had been in their research.

So whose genes do I carry, who are the ancestors who are part of me? If my life proceeds along a railway track then these ancestors have provided the fuel to get me going!

On my maternal side are Harbournes and Thatchers and on the paternal side Emerys and Berrymans. I will introduce you to some of the more interesting characters and the stories relating to them, they are all fairly ordinary so don't expect any lords or ladies or stories of wealth and importance. As is common for a great number of the population in England we are mostly descended from the ubiquitous ag-lab - where would England be without its agricultural labourer, the backbone of the country!

Harbournes

This is the side that my mother was interested in, her own mother was Harriet Harbourne, and she had many stories to tell which had been passed down to her via her Grannies.

According to family tradition Adam Adams was a soldier who served with the Duke of Wellington, he was one of the 'Blind Half Hundred', was injured in battle and as a result had a pension which bought him a new pair of boots every year from Yapps, the Bootmakers in Sloane Street and there was enough money left over for his daughter, Mum's Great Granny Harriet Daisy Adams also to have a pair of boots made annually. He was a Chelsea Pensioner and when he died he was buried in the grounds of the Royal Hospital, Chelsea, alongside what is now Chelsea Bridge Road. When the road was being widened Mum's Granny would be there to ensure that the grave was not disturbed. Some of these details are true, some not. Stories as they are passed from one generation to the next can change subtly along the way as in the game of 'whispers'.

The facts are that my ancestor was not Adam Adams (1803-1866), but his brother James Adams (1789-1854)) who was with the 50th Regiment of Foot, the Blind Half Hundred, from 1806 when he was 16years old to 1812 when he was discharged because he had 'fractured leg by a fall in Portugal' – the story of the boots was obviously true, paid for by his pension. In 1835 he asked for an increase in his pension, I don't know if he ever received it. His discharge records show that he was born in Chereton Hants his occupation was a labourer, an ag-lab of course, he was 5ft.6 ½ ins tall, had hazel eyes, a brown complexion and brown hair. Just for the record the other soldiers discharged at the same time had complexions variously described as ruddy, dark and fresh! The hazel eyes, brown hair and brown complexion have passed me by. The family are now blue-eyed with hair of various hues!

You may wonder at the name of the regiment, 'Blind Half Hundred', half hundred as they were the 50th Regiment and during a campaign in Egypt in the early 1800s the soldiers suffered badly with opthalmia while there, earning the nickname the Blind Half-Hundred. The regiment was later called the Dirty Half Hundred because the soldiers wiped their faces with the black cuffs of their jackets and the dye came off onto their skin!

What of the story of Adam Adams, or James Adams as we now know him, being buried at the Royal Hospital Chelsea? Only In-Pensioners were buried there, that is retired soldiers who gave up their pension in exchange for living in the Royal Hospital and we know that James was in receipt of a pension for his boots. Does the story of the Granny who stayed by the graveyard as Chelsea Bridge Road was being widened have any basis in fact? In spite of my own research in the late 1990s I could find no evidence of James's burial, but Jill Davis, who is distantly related by marriage to the Harbournes eventually came up trumps. Corporal James Adams was living in the Royal Hospital in the 1851 census, he died age 64 and was buried on 13 January 1854 in 'The Burial Ground of Her Majesty's Royal Hospital Chelsea'. This was used for In-Pensioners until later in1854 when their burials were located to Brompton Cemetery. These dates would tie in with the widening of the road and the building of the new Chelsea Bridge.

I can imagine Harriet Daisy standing in Chelsea Bridge Road amidst the clamour of horse drawn carriages and navvies who were working on widening the road making sure that nothing was done to disturb the burial place of her father, James. The first Chelsea Bridge was proposed in the 1840s as part of a major development of marshlands on the south bank of the Thames and was intended to provide convenient access from the densely populated north bank to the proposed Battersea Park. The opening of the bridge, initially called Victoria Bridge, was delayed because of work on the Chelsea Embankment and did not open until 1858. What a change from the marshlands of the south bank in the 1850s to the urban development of the South Bank by the 1950s

James, his six siblings and his wife Mary Cleverley were all born in Hampshire as were his father also James (1751-1825), grandfather John Winkworth(1712) and great-grandfather Thomas Winkworth (1680).

Our ancestors live on in the memory and stories of them told by our contemporaries and this is true of Harriet Daisy Adams (1817-1876) she who stood in Chelsea Bridge Road and her daughter Charlotte (1845-1930) who was my mother's Granny and of whom she had a fund of stories. Harriet was born in Hampshire, Charlotte in Pimlico, London, this movement from country to city being common in the early 1800s.

The 19thC was a period of great upheaval, the Great Agricultural Depression of the 1870s was responsible for many ag-labs and yeoman farmers seeing their livelihood disappear but this was long after Harriet Daisy had moved to London. What could be her reason for leaving her family behind and starting a new life in the big city? We can speculate that the pull for the move would have been opportunity and freedom but the push is much easier to define. Agricultural changes were taking place in the countryside from late 18thC in the form of enclosures of previously open strip field farming resulting in amalgamation of small farms into larger properties and the subsequent reduction or even loss of livelihood. In the Warnford area of Hampshire where the Adams family lived, enclosures took place in the early part of the century and although their occupations are not known they must have been connected with farming. Add to this the Railway Mania of the 19thC and the opening of the London and South West Railway in 1838 the lure of London must have been strong indeed to Harriet Daisy. In 1841 she was living in Kensington with her injured father James and mother Mary and then by 1851 Harriet now Palmer was (presumably) married and a dressmaker living with her mother and daughter Charlotte aged 6 in Drury Lane.

My mother's memory from her Granny Charlotte is that Harriet Daisy married William Palmer, a Frenchman whose name was originally Palmure but no record of this marriage exists. He worked at the Royal Court Theatre as a carpenter and family legend has it that when their daughter Harriet Mary (1871-1951) was born she was kept in one of the large baskets in the dressing rooms of the theatre. Our sewing gene comes from Harriet Daisy and Charlotte, they were both dressmakers and Charlotte worked on Queen Alexandra's wedding dress (1863) which was made by the London dressmaker Mrs James of Belgravia. In order to get to the facts about this wedding dress I wrote to the curator at Windsor Castle to ask for information. It was apparently made by a dressmaking establishment called Mrs James of 2, Hanover Square in 1863, (Charlotte lived in Hanover Square in '66) and after the wedding the dress was altered for a painting and the alterations were done by Mme Elise of 170 Regent St. Both Mrs James and Mme Elise employed a team of

dressmakers, so Charlotte and her mother could have been part of these establishments.
Charlotte, my mother's Granny, taught her to sew, everything had to be made by hand, the thread from tacking stitches was not discarded but kept to be used again and the stitches small and duly inspected. Even in her 80s my mother's stitching was amazingly small and neat. When I made my own clothes Mum would turn to the inside of the garment to inspect the hem and seams, all had to be as neat inside as out. Remember that in the later 19thC all clothes were still made by hand and I marvel at the photos of Harriet and Charlotte in their crinolines and the time and care that it must have taken to make their own clothes as well as those for clients. Charlotte and Harriet also made clothes for the children of Coutts the bankers. I also wrote to Coutts who could not help. Thomas Coutts had three children, all of whom died in the 1830s and 1840s, they were daughters all of whom married so none of their children were Coutts by name. So I can only assume that the Grannies made dresses for these Coutts grandchildren – the story goes that Queen Victoria saw the Coutts children and asked who had made their dresses. So this could be right ..or not.

Charlotte lived a scandalous life! Did her children and grandchildren know? Certainly no word was ever mentioned by my mother or even my grandmother, Charlotte's daughter, of any irregularities regarding Charlotte's marriage. There was however a mystery concerning her 'husband' Edward Harbourn(e) (1842-1902) which has been passed down through the family. It is said that he was illegitimate, and having the Harbourn spelt with an 'e' and without was the clue to illegitimacy or not. There was a story of him coming from a rich or titled family but as I discovered this is all rubbish. His parents were John Harbourne and Ann Bolas, John was a railway porter in Birmingham where Edward was born, and his brothers were all ag-labs. Where do these stories originate? There is often a grain of truth somewhere as in the Adam Adams and James Adams story but it is not to be found for Edward - unfortunately. However maybe he <u>was</u> an illegitimate child of a rich and titled family and was adopted by the Harbournes, we will never know.

What do we know of Edward? He certainly never married Charlotte. I spent many an hour lifting those heavy volumes at

Myddleton House looking for a marriage certificate using different spellings of their names and finding nothing, why? Because he was married to someone else!

Charlotte had five children with Edward between 1866 and 1878. The various census returns that I found gave details of Charlotte and her children and her mother Harriet, but never a mention of Edward so I decided to pay a professional researcher to delve into the Army records to find out anything about this chap who appears on his children's birth certificates as variously – Sergeant, Grenadier Guards, and Commercial Traveller. I gave the researcher his probable birth date, and the details from the children's birth certificates, plus the name of his wife, Charlotte. The researcher eventually came back with a pile of interesting details of Edward's army career. His research confirmed Edward's birth date in Birmingham and that he was a Sergeant with the 3rd Battalion, Grenadier Guards from 2 January 1860 to 18 January 1881, and after completion of 21 years service he was transferred to the 4th Battalion Worcester Regiment where he stayed until 18 January 1891. His records give his intended place of residence on departure from the regiment as Norton, Worcester – more of that later. His wife's name is given as Emma Spencer and two children are also mentioned. I checked with the researcher that he hadn't found another Edward Harbourn(e) but he assured me that there was only one on the muster rolls of the regiment, and he apologised for having to tell me that my grandmother was illegitimate. We see on his Army discharge records that Edward was a butcher by occupation, was 5ft.9ins. tall, had black hair, grey eyes and a dark complexion (on his Army engagement papers in 1860 his muscular development is given as 'middling', obviously not a strapping chap!)– his fellow soldiers being discharged had complexions variously described as fresh, sallow, fair and dark.

Well I thought, thank heavens Mum is not around to hear this, but of course it explained why I could not find a marriage certificate.

Edward married Emma in 1866, she died in 1879, and they had seven children, two born in Dublin in 1868, 1869, and five in London in 1870, 1874,1876,1878,1879. He married Elizabeth Maria in 1879 and moved to Worcestershire and she died in 1896, and

Susan in 1897 in Worcestershire. His children with Charlotte were born in London in 1866, 1870, 1872, 1874 and 1878. Two months after he married Emma his first child with Charlotte was born, then Charlotte had a break whilst he was in Dublin with Emma for two years and as soon as he returned to London both Emma and Charlotte had children within two months of each other.
Did Charlotte know of her husband's other lives? I think she did as evidenced by how she stated the father of her children on their birth certificates. `

1866 Winkworth Harbourn, father Winkworth Harbourne Palmer
Sergeant Grenadier Guards born Ebury St. Pimlico
1870 Harriet Mary father Edward Harbourne
Sergeant Grenadier Guards born Sloane Square
1872 Eveline Charlotte father Edward Harbourn
Commercial traveller born Sloane Square
1874 Laura father William Harbourn
Commercial traveller born Chelsea
1878 Frank no birth certificate found

Charlotte lived near the Chelsea Barracks where Edward was stationed so it would have been easy for them to meet.

The story of Charlotte's liaisons does not end with Edward who had moved away from London in 1879. She went on to have five more children with Robert Hall (1832-1907) and the birth certificate for Alice Maud born 1880 gives the father as Edward Harbourn, Commercial Traveller although Robert was definitely her father and Charlotte and Robert never married. Fortunately Mum left me a family tree which she had prepared giving the names of the Harbourne and Hall children otherwise I would have been in the dark.

Returning to Edward, for years during my research I thought that he only had one wife, Emma (plus Charlotte) but then a dramatic turn of events which make researching family history so worthwhile. My sister Mary and I went to St James Church in Norton juxta Kempsey to look for Edward's grave as we knew from his death certificate that he had been buried in Norton, but after a fairly good search could not find it so we went on to the Worcester Records

Office to try to find out information and details from the census and parish records of Edward's stay in Norton. From his soldier's retirement records I knew that he was living in Norton so we found the 1891 census for Norton and there he was with his wife Elizabeth Maria!!!! not another one….and some younger children who had been born in Claines, Worcs to Emma. Then I looked through the wills for Worcestershire on the off chance that he had made a will – and yes he had, with various bequests of paintings to his children, which reconfirmed that the names I had were correct but of course no mention of his children with Charlotte, and a final bequest of the residue of his estate to his wife Susan (who he married in 1897) – well Mary and I were flabbergasted to put it mildly. We returned to the churchyard in Norton and found his grave almost on the path, I don't know how we missed it before and you can see from the inscription on the tombstone that he was buried with his wife Elizabeth Maria.

Edward died aged 60, having had three wives plus Charlotte, and 12 children as well as a career in the Grenadier Guards. He was born in Birmingham, served as a soldier in London and Dublin, then returned to Norton, not too far from Birmingham, for his last few years. Charlotte outlived him by 28years, I wonder if she ever knew when he died, or indeed of the other wives and children.

Edward's bequests in his will - *to my son Arthur Edward two oil paintings of a Duckwing Cock; Brown red cock and hen to my son William; oil paintings of Duckwing Cock and Hen and a Black red cock and Hen to my daughter Elizabeth Ann (Pussy) my oil painting Farmyard and Landscape to my daughter Charlotte Carew and my print of Her late Majesty receiving the Crimea wounded; to my son James Bolas; my picture by Captain Eaton of a Black red cock*

Thatchers

When I started to research my mother's paternal ancestors they seemed grey and characterless as I did not have as many handed down stories as on the Harbourne side, but having pieced together the facts from Mum's stories, and from visiting the villages and the graveyards where the Thatchers lived and finally ended their days I can put together a picture of them through the generations. When I returned from Africa in 1986 and went to live in Oxfordshire Mum told me that her father's family had come from Oxfordshire, oh really says I, why didn't I probe further, although I think she would have told me if any place names had been familiar to her when we had picnics and excursions together in the Oxfordshire countryside.

From the early 18thC through to the mid 19thC the Thatchers were Oxfordshire families in the village of Charney Bassett. They first emerge as characters worth exploring with Samuel Thatcher (1776-1831) and his wife Elisabeth Povey(1760). The church in which they were married was St Peter Le Bailey, all that remains now of this church is the tower which is right in the centre of Oxford at Carfax, on the crossroads of Queen Street, Aldgate Street, Cornmarket and The High. The rest of the church was demolished in the late 19thC for road widening. I cannot say for certain that the birth and death details that I have for Elisabeth are correct. I do have a concern in that she was 16years older than her husband Samuel but as her mother's name was Harriet, this could show that this is the right connection as Harriet is a family name

However finding the details for Samuel Thatcher has been very rewarding as the parish register and monumental inscriptions book for Charney Bassett yielded much information. Samuel came from a huge family but with such a sad history. He was one of 16 children of whom 10 died in infancy as commemorated in the monumental inscriptions in Charney Bassett graveyard. Why did they die? It is worthwhile noting the births of all those children.

October 1773/ September 1774/ August 1775/ July 1776/ *October 1777 /August 1778/ August 1779/ August 1780*/ August 1781/ *August 1782/October 1783/ October 1785/ August 1786*/ July 1789/ July 1790/ July 1792
Only the babies born in 1774/ 1775/ 1776/ 1781/ 1789/ 1790 survived past infancy.

The churchyard at Charney Bassett where James, Giles, John, Sophia , Charles and Samuel (and a Samuel from a preceding generation) are buried and the 10 infants commemorated, is just 30 minutes drive from where I live in Witney. When Mary and I visited in early 2000 the gravestones were already very hard to read, one almost impossible if you did not have the sun shining in the right direction to cast a shadow on the stone. Perhaps one day when we win the lottery we can have new headstones carved for the family. At this period in history families did not move from where they lived due to lack of transport and also they stayed where the work was available and at Charney Bassett there was a mill on the river and also the Manor House both of which would have provided work. The great-great grandfather of the children mentioned above died in Charney Bassett in 1772 and his extensive will is a family researcher's dream giving as it does names and relationships of family members.

In the name of God amen; I Samuel Thatcher of Charney in the County of Berkshire,(now Oxfordshire) *yeoman being in a bad state of health but of sound mind do make this my last will and testament in manner following (that is to say) First, I commend my soul into the hands of Almighty God my Creator hoping for eternal happiness by and thro the precious death and merits of my Lord and Saviour Jesus Christ and my body I desired may be buried in a decent manner And I desire that the sum of three pounds and three shillings may be expended in any coffin which I desire to be lined And I also desire that my Executor hereinafter named will get six Paul* (sic) *bearers to hold up the paul for whom and the Minister who shall attend my funeral I order silk scarves and gloves and to such of any neighbours as shall be invited to my funeral I order plain Hatbands and Gloves And I order my Executor to distribute five pounds amongst the poor of Charney aforesaid on the day of my funeral And I desire my Executor to put up a pair of Grave Stones in memory of me with a plain stone between the head and feet stones and I order three pounds and three shillings to be expended for that purpose*.(these still stand in the graveyard) *And after my temporal state I dispose thereof in manner following (that is to say) I give to my Brother Thomas Thatcher ten pounds and to his sons Thomas and Richard thirty pounds apiece And I give to his daughters Elizabeth Mary – Jane Rachael and Ann ten pounds apiece. I give to my Brother William twenty shillings to his son Giles fifty pounds and to his daughter Elizabeth wife of Richard Beasley fifty pounds I give to my nephew John and Richard (sons of my late Brother John Thatcher) ten pounds apiece and to Hester Christian Elizabeth Rachael and Ann (the daughter of my said late Brother John Thatcher) ten pounds apiece I give to my sister Elizabeth Strainge ten pounds I give to the said Richard Beasley his Executors and adminori three shillings weekly and every week during the natural life of my sister Margaret Capon In Trust that the said Richard Beasley his Executors and adminori do and shall weekly and every week towards her support and maintenance whose ..... from time to time shall be sufficient discharge to the said Richard Beasley his Execs and Admori for the said weekly sum of three shillings And I do order my executor to pay the first weekly sum of three shillings on the Saturday that shall happen next after my decease. And I give to Edward Capon the husband of my said Sister Margaret one shilling and to her children William Edward and Elizabeth five pounds apiece Also I give to Charley Joseph Elizabeth and B..... the Children of my late sister Mary Hughes five pounds apiece I give to my kinswoman Sarah Pryor now living with me the yearly sum of ten pounds for four years now and next ensuing and forty pounds at her age of twenty one years Also I give to my Maidservant Ann Kent ten pounds. All which legacies I order and direct to be paid within twelve months after my decease (except the yearly sum of ten pounds and forty pounds given to the said Sarah Pryor) And as to all the rest and residue of my monies Securities for money Goods Cattle Chattells and personal Estate whatsoever and wherever After and subject to the payment of my just debts funeral Expenses and the Legacies and sums of money hereinbefore given, I give and bequeath the same and every part thereof unto my nephew James Thatcher now living with me whom I do hereby and appoint the sole Executor of this my last Will and Testament And I do revoke all former Will or Wills by me made and do declare this only to be my last Will and Testament. In witness thereof I have hereunto set my hand and seal this fifth day of April in the year of our Lord one thousand and seven hundred and seventy two.*

Samuel died only 4 days after making this will. For all his wealth and it was considerable and given that he was a yeoman and a churchwarden, he could not write, and also it seems that he was not married as there was no mention of a wife or his own children. His bequests to his family members with their relationship to him put flesh on the branches of this side of the family tree.

Samuel's brother Thomas died in 1804 also in Charney Bassett *'being very sick and weak but of perfect mind and memory'.* Apart from bequests of money he leaves household items to his daughters and these give us a glimpse of the inside of an 18thC house.

First) I give and bequeath to my daughter Mary Saunders immediately after my Decease the following articles One Flock Bed and Bolster and a Bedstead belonging, A large brewing kettle, one brass pot. One Brass Skillet, Half a Dozen pewter plates marked with a single D on the back, Three Broad Brimmed Pewter Dishes And Two Flag Bottom'd Ash Chairs by her freely to be possessed and enjoyed forever.
Secondly) I give and bequeath to my Daughter Elizabeth Gleed (during her life) the following articles One Feather Bed and bolster, a Long Table and Three Joint Stools, A Dresser and Shelves. A Clock A Long Settle, A Warming Pan, A Pair of Dog Irons, Fire Shovel & Tongs, Half a Dozen Iron Candlesticks, Two Iron Spits and a Pair of Balance, A Large Brass Pot, Three Barrels a Small Table and Cubberd and the Brewing Tubs) And after her decease all and singular the aforesaid articles shall be the property of the aforesaid Mary Saunders her heirs and assigns forever.
Thirdly) I give and bequeath to my Son Richard Thatcher all my wearing apparel

A slim book *Charney Bassett Through the Ages* provided some details about our Samuel (1776-1831) the one who married Elizabeth Povey. In the parish accounts it mentions Samuel Thatcher as a Churchwarden and his payment to James Thatcher (his father) for sparrowheads, pole cats and hedgehogs, so our James must have been the equivalent of the local rat catcher.

The Thatchers stayed in Oxfordshire until the early 19thC when Samuel's grandson James (1830) made the move to Addlestone in Surrey and the succeeding generation moved even closer to London, and then they come within my memory. James's move away from the country occurred at the same time as Charlotte Palmer went to London and whereas she probably went on the new fangled railway James could have used either of the two main roads into London from the west. Why did he move? He had 11 siblings and his father was a labourer, so I guess he had to move away to make his own living as he became older and Nuffield where he was born was not far from one of the direct access roads into London. On a 1822 map the two roads into London from the west are exactly where the M4 and M40 are today, and from Nuffield to Henley and then on to what is now the M4 is a logical and easy way towards London with Chertsey and Addlestone en route.

James became a miller, so by moving away from Nuffield he was setting out to make his own way in the world and Coxe's Lock Mill on the River Wey where he settled in the 1850s must have been a thriving commercial enterprise with many opportunities for work. The railway had arrived in Addlestone in 1848 so the mill became even more accessible to young men seeking work. His wife was Elizabeth Badger and her father was a confectioner and pastrycook in High Street, Cheltenham, one of my Mum's stories was that her father's mother's family were from a well known family, the Badgers, that made sweets so this seems to have a degree of truth. By 1871when my grandfather George was born the family had moved to Battersea where James continued his occupation as a miller.

I have tried to come up with a reason why they moved away from Addlestone and the mill which then would have been very rural, to Currie Street in Battersea, an area which was becoming industrial and affected by the huge railway expansion that was going on a couple of miles away at Clapham Junction.

There were three flour mills on the River Wandle in the mid 19^{th}C but Currie Street was in the very industrial area of Nine Elms, right by the Gas Works and other large industrial works – however on Granddad's birth certificate James' occupation is 'miller' so presumably he continued with the family occupation and travelled by horse and cart to Coxe's Lock Mill to collect the flour and brought it back to Wandsworth to re-sell it. This is not pure speculation as I have a late 1880s photo of George and James with a horse and cart containing flour sacks.

My maternal ancestors made the move from country to London in the mid19^{th}C and their descendants now come within the compass of my memory, but what of my paternal ancestors? Were they Town or Country, ag-labs, millers or rat catchers. There has always been within the family a suggestion that this other side were further up the social scale, even in my time when it was a question of whether you were born north or south of the River Thames - a really stupid idea as with such a meandering river you could be born south of the Thames but actually be at a point north of the north side of the Thames. It sounds complicated but just look at a map of the river.

Emerys

Grandma B, Alice May Berryman née Emery, my father's mother, definitely thought that her family were higher up the social scale than my mother's family. She did have a point as her own father was a teacher, not in 'trade' but go back further and we come to those ubiquitous ag-labs yet again. For such an educated and articulate lady she had no stories to tell me of her family, maybe because I never asked. I remember mention of her father 'a kind and sweet man' but I only discovered after her death when delving into the records that she had a sister and two brothers so with no firsthand accounts of this side of the family what can the records tell us?

In the late 18^{th}C the Emerys lived in Malmesbury and were ag-labs. By 1861 my great grandfather, Charles Emery who started out as an ag-lab was a schoolmaster living in Crouch End, a suburb of London. He married Sarah Baker who came from Wells in Somerset and her father was a grocer - definitely one step up from working on the land. Charles was married in 1869 in Wells having given his place of residence Huyton, near Liverpool and occupation a school master, so he certainly travelled the country which was unusual for these times. It is interesting to ponder why Charles Emery left his family home in Malmesbury, Wiltshire and came to live so close to London, but his occupation gives us a good reason for explaining this move to Crouch End where he was master in the school from1870 to 1911.So from an agricultural labouring background we can say that this local farm boy made good.

Charles came from a large and extended family all living in Malmesbury; he had four brothers and a sister and his brothers all went on to have large families. His brothers married girls from nearby villages, Sherston and Rodbourne, both within a good walk from Malmesbury and Charles' mother Elizabeth came from Corston, again not far away. Malmesbury is not far from Tetbury, near Highgrove, home of Prince Charles, and it was at the Rattlesnake Inn in Sherston that Prince Harry was found to be drinking, tut - tut, in the summer of 2001!

Returning to Charles and his career as a school master, here are extracts from the *Testimonial to Mr Charles Emery* dated May 1911 that provide interesting reading.

At the end of July next Mr Charles Emery, having reached the age limit, after nearly forty-one years' service, retires from the position of Head Master of the Crouch End Council School and from the service of Hornsey Town Council.

Commencing in 1870 with about 90 scholars (boys and infants) the school has so grown that it now has on its rolls more than 1,200 scholars.....Throughout the whole period of Mr Emery's service the school has consistently earned the highest possible Government Grants and has built up and maintained, both in the public mind and in official circles, an excellent reputation for 'earnest and good work'.

It is notorious that even now teaching is by no means a highly paid profession, and that in the past the salaries of teachers have been miserably inadequate but we think it will surprise and pain many to know that the retiring pension to which Mr Emery is entitled after forty-one years of devoted work as Head Master is just over £34, apart from an annuity of about £4 purchased by deductions made by the Board of Education from his salary. In this matter Mr Emery is treated just as are other teachers under the Board (and does not complain) but the wrong thing is that there should be such a paltry pension scheme for teachers generally, no advantage being given to those who have occupied a responsible position of a Head Master. We feel that it would be a graceful act, and one that would give pleasure to many of his old friends, to raise a fund that would supplement Mr Emery's pension.........The amount raised will be presented to Mr. Emery by cheque or in the form of an annuity ....we may say that each sum of £10 subscribed will purchase an annuity of £1.

The value today (2017) of £34 is roughly £3600, and £1 is £106.

By the time that his wife Elizabeth died in 1914 they had moved to Bristol to live with his son Charles Herbert and his wife so hopefully his pension provided them with some quality of life in their later years.

Where possible I have always tried to find the final resting places of my ancestors, seeing a headstone with a familiar name somehow puts a tidy end to their life. My sister Mary and I have had some fruitful and sometimes exasperating searches in damp and overgrown churchyards, none more so than looking for Charles' parents, Richard who died in 1885 in Malmesbury and Elizabeth who died in 1900 in Hornsey, London.

I found in Grandma B's possessions a small sepia, dog-eared, photo of a headstone which was so faint that none of the inscription could be read. On the reverse of the photo Grandma had written ' my grandparents Richard & Elizabeth Emery' (*take heed from this and always write on the back of your photos because if Grandma hadn't done this heavens knows how long it would have taken to find this grave and who was interred in it).* But where was this grave and what were the dates and indeed the names? I sent the dog-eared photo to the company with specialised equipment and they were able to confirm the names and years of burial. Mary and I spent a freezing afternoon walking up and down all the rows of headstones in Malmesbury cemetery and not finding 'our' grave - lots of other Emerys as this is Emery country! So I had to get directions from the Malmesbury Burials office and back Mary and I went. It was obvious why we had not previously found the headstone, many years ago it had fallen flat on its face and broken in half. Mary and I managed to lift the top half and place it on its back so that we could read the lettering - it had been a beautiful stone, marble, with real lead pinned letters, and because the face had been protected by being face down in the dirt, the marble and letters were in very good condition. We have had the stone repaired so Richard and Elizabeth hopefully look good for another hundred years.

After the war Grandma would go to stay 'with my doctor cousins in Westcliff-on-Sea'. This sounded very grand, doctors and Westcliff-on-Sea - definitely up the social scale. Her doctor cousins were Charles William and Frederick William Emery, both still alive and living in Westcliff long after Grandma had died. They also signed the death certificate of Louise Margaret, Grandma's sister. No mention had ever been made that Grandma had a sister, she died a spinster aged 52 in 1930. Her existence though unmentioned by Alice May is confirmed in three books with their inscriptions:

The English Hymnal	- handwritten inscription L.M. Emery
Poetry of Emerson	- handwritten inscription From Daisie with love. To Alice Christmas 1900
Poems of Matthew Arnold	Auntie Daisy With love from Mark. Christmas 1925

Another cousin to mention is 'Bert', Stephen Egbert Emery who Grandma lived with briefly when she was between homes in the late 1950s. He was a Registrar of Births, Deaths & Marriages in Chippenham, Wiltshire. Her stay there was not long as being a Londoner born and bred she missed the familiar surroundings and returned to Putney to end her days.

Credit must be given where it is due - in the time before the emancipation of women and long before they had the vote Grandma - Alice May, trained as a teacher in 1903 when she was 21 and went on to eventually have her own school in Woodside Park from 1910 to 1919 and was Principal at The Lady Margaret School from 1924 to 1934, both schools in north London.

The Emerys therefore followed the route from rural to urban living and from working on the land to becoming respectable middle-class families.

Berrymans

Alice May Emery, Grandma B, married well, remembering that in later life she considered her family a bit above the Thatchers. There are no ag-labs in the known Berrymans but 'trade' did figure as an occupation. Thomas Berryman (1773-1843) was a solicitor in

London, and his father-law a brewer, his daughter Ellen Sarah married Josiah Beddow who for a time was in business with Thomas' son Frederick (1819-1867), they were cloth merchants and various trade names appear for this Frederick and his son Frederick James (1853-1927) such as warehouseman, linen draper, cloth merchant, hosier, commercial agent. Frederick and Josiah Beddow appear in the bankrupt directory on 9 March 1841 with their occupations given as Scotch and Manchester warehousemen. Apparently this means they were wholesalers of linen and cloth made in the northern factories. I am sure Grandma never knew that her husband's father had been bankrupt! This Frederick married in 1843 Elizabeth Sarah Bell (1820-1899) whose father was a master mariner. Judging from all the prose and poems that he wrote about Sarah it was a happy marriage although he pre-deceased her by 32 years. In his journal there are three poems that he wrote to her on her birthday, 17th December, in 1837, 1839 and 1841.

There are 15 verses headed 'Stanzas to Lizzy', all of overly Victorian sentiment, a flavour such as this:

What means this fadeless love of ours!
This unison of soul?
O 'tis a light divinely fair
That gilds illumes the whole

And this is ours! The sacred love
That's purified by pain:-
The Blessed unity of soul

An oil painting survives of Sarah as a child with her mother Elizabeth Pullen, wife of James Bell.

Frederick's business must have done well after the bankruptcy as his will shows that he owned four London properties with a total value of £1000, today (2017) worth £109,000 and his total assets were valued at £2575 (£280,675)

Properties owned by Frederick Berryman and mentioned in his will of 1867 were 2,4 and 6 Florence Street East, Florence Road, New Cross. London.

As New Cross is south of the River and some distance from where the Berryman's had settled in North London the houses must have been bought purely for speculation and income. In the mid 1800's this was an area of very high density houses, there was much scope for employment in the area, nearby was Deptford Creek, busy with shipping and leading to the River Thames and the shipyards at Greenwich. There was a corn mill at Tide Mill in Church St just streets from Florence Street operated by the tidal waters of Deptford Creek which had been operating since the 14^{th}C. Not far from Florence Street was an extensive brick-field. There were also several local foundries casting both iron and brass and a number of small independent breweries. So if you owned three properties in Florence Street East you would have no difficulty in letting them, Also from the Ordnance Survey map of the times you can see that the size of the properties in Florence Street East were larger than those in Florence Street and Florence Road. Added to this the whole area was crisscrossed by railways and tramlines which would have provided easy transport for workers if they had to travel further afield.

He also owned 5 and 7 Warwick Road, Gordon Road, Stoke Newington, London. Stoke Newington is north of the Thames and very close to where the Berryman's lived in the 19^{th}C. Stroud Green, Muswell Hill, Finchley Park are all not far away and Abney Park Cemetery, opened in 1840, where Frederick and other members of the family lie today is just a mile away from Warwick Road. Although these properties were small, the area of Stoke Newington and South Hornsey was far more up market than New Cross, and I think the same could be said today. I have records for this area for 1868 which shows that it was a predominantly middle class area with some of the surrounding fields not yet built over but there was rapid development in the next ten years and by the 1880's the number of houses in Stoke Newington had increased by 127%. There were many brick-fields to support this development. Neither the trams or railway had reached this area by the 1860's.

So whenever Frederick bought the houses he probably had no idea of the rapid expansion that was to take place and no doubt his investments gave the family a good income after his early death at the age of 48 in 1867. Since then these houses have been demolished and the sites have been re-developed.

Frederick and Elizabeth Sarah had two children, Frederick James (1853-1927), my grandfather, and Emily (1850-1872). Emily died, unmarried, of consumption and her mother writes in her journal the following lines:

If I do keep a poor little thing with all my life, it would matter, will it dear Mamma - so long as I keep with you
- one trial I shall have
-to give up getting married-I have had all along an impression I shall get better, and I don't believe God would give me that & then deceive me - it is a great trial of faith - He may bring me so low that I cannot move & yet restore me just to show His Power

What my darling one said to me shortly before her death
-precious - precious girl.

Elizabeth Sarah was by then a widow and lived a long life with her son Frederick James. Some of the poems that he wrote in his journals suggest that around 1883 she had a stroke which severely affected her remaining 15years.

Christmas Eve 1883 - To My Mother
Sleep deep sad heart, and shut the present out
Draw down the veil that hides thee from the morrow:-
Dreary and dim, life's pathway lies in mist
Rolling in clouds that rain but grief and sorrow

Since that dread evening when life's painful light
Trembled in agony and died in battling
Since he! Who fed thy spirit and my own
Heard o'er life's sea, Deaths wind the cordage rattling

Though drawn apart by times severe decreeing
And forced to live in seeming separation
Thy touch is still upon me, time will die!
Eternity will bring its reparation.
FJB

Frederick James has come to life from his poems and prolific writings in his journals. It seems to have been in the Victorian psyche to be obsessed by death and FJ had ample opportunity to record his thoughts through the deaths of his sister Emily, mother Elizabeth Sarah, and first wife Sarah. My daughter Sarah (yes it's a family name dating from the 18thC) writes her account of FJ based on the facts that we know and his journal entries.

'Thunderbolts & Palaces'
Frederick James Berryman 1853 - 1927

'There's not much difference between a suitcase and a coffin,' muttered Frederick James Berryman to himself as he hung his head and shoulders out of his bedroom window of 98 Downham Road, Hackney. He sucked in air, one rapid breath after another. He did what his sister Emily ultimately couldn't do. Consumption had extracted the breath out her.

He turned back into his bedroom and glanced at the small leather suitcase in the corner of the room. His gut shrank with the pain of the nineteen years of his life they had spent together and the loss of the future they would not have. Before the funeral he had gone to the institution where Emily had spent the last year of her life, kept apart from the family, in search of a cure, in protection and sanctuary. He had packed her belongings in that small case. Part of her lived on between those leather coverings.

Sitting on his bed he picked up the blank book his father had given him for his birthday. A black marbled hardcover book with feint lined pages and a small brass lock. Opening the first page he sat down and began what was to turn out to be fifty-three years of poetry and notes to himself.

Oct 3rd 1873
Wake not, beloved! Be thy sleep
Silent as night is & as deep

...

Four years after Emily died, FJ, as his friends knew him, married Sarah Nicholson in a blaze of middle class Victorian celebration and they moved to the more upper class residence of 54 Victoria Road in Finsbury Park. Emily's suitcase moved with them and was placed in the ample loft. A son, Laurence, soon followed along with another house move to Stroud Green. Factual records show an upwardly mobile family moving through Victorian society with increasing larger houses. FJ was a member of the Congregational Church, a participant in local society and as a relatively successful wool merchant represented a secure Victorian middle class.

However, despite these outward impressions FJ's diaries show a man fraught with insecurities and dilemmas.

July 1879

In this July weather I sit and shiver in unnatural cold, and my spirit seems to have been chilled in the very summer of my manhood. Single handed and solitary must I walk in the picture palace of my imagination and sigh to tell my joy to another whose heart is tuned to mine.

FJ threw himself deeper into his career as a wool merchant. His second son, Ernest Mark was born in 1881 and soon after the family moved again, to 91 Corbyn Street, Islington, though still within reach of his mother who was only a quarter of a mile away. Staying within easy reach of her turned out to be very important to FJ as he grew older. Also this move made FJ's commute into London much easier than it had previously been. However, the filth of the streets in London, the noise and the frantic construction works all stressed him and he struggled to keep focused on his developing business activities. For a few years he ended up playing a minor role in his business partnerships much against his better judgement. Set against the Victorian ideals of success, FJ was tipped into a deeper depression by some poor business decisions that meant he lost the three London houses that were left to him when his father died.

1884

A thunderbolt has fallen and shattered my prison house... That which I took for the sky was but the dim roof which hung over me in gloomy obscurity... I am forever shut out from regions which were possible before captivity came upon me.

Self doubt persisted throughout his life though this difficult period seemed to persist through most of his thirties. On his thirty-third birthday FJ sat in the garden at Corbyn Street and penned one of his birthday poems. Barely middle aged he was feeling the passing of time.

They say "Time flies", and when I was a boy
He seemed to soar so light
I scarce could hear his pinions beat:
Himself quite out of sight-
But now he's heavy footed grown, and walks
Upon the earth quite near
His measured tread keeps pace with mine
He whispers in my ear-

With his forties came a period of upheaval and FJ rode them like the North Sea waves he sailed on trips to Rheims in France to buy wool. At times he was sick and helpless, other times, deliriously happy.

FJ found himself consumed in a battle for his business interests, against losses and shady deals. In his marbled notebook he recorded verbatim discussions, minutes of meetings, as though the pen would resolve the difficulties. These business ordeals continued for nearly ten years. A distinguishing feature seems to be his desire to reach a compassionate conclusion, without being unkind to his business colleagues. However, he was aware and dissatisfied in coming off second best in the continuing negotiations.

Coming home from a trip to France in summer 1892 FJ was devastated to discover his son Laurence had run away from home, at the age of fourteen, having accepted a job at a theatre as a singer.

And must thou leave me, must thy music sound no longer in my ears, thy play be my recreation no more? In the silent hours, when the night makes a weird sound of its own stillness and thou art far away, when will the memory of our past lives come back to haunt me, and thee too I pray, not to sadden forever, as I must, but to strengthen the bonds now so cruelly broken – God help us both.

In the midst of both this personal trauma and the disturbing business dealings the family decided to move house again. Throughout his life, the house moves show a pattern of shifting and searching, as though trying to resolve and satisfy a need. This time FJ had much angst about whether to purchase the house or not. He worried about mortgaging it to the bank or whether borrowing from his mother would be the better option. In the end he purchased 31 Granville Road at Hornsey in 1891. They lived here until his wife Sarah died in 1906. A comfortable home, FJ started to write his poetry with freedom. His favourite was to reflect at the time of his birthday. Best of all was to do this in a familiar place, like under a tree or beside a soft light. As he reached his later middle age FJ spent more time concerned about what he wasn't achieving.

1901 aged 48

...

But the top of the hill is best
Though all is not what it seemed
In manhood's fullness are joys
Though not all the things I dreamed

...

His birthday poems also seem to capture a sense of regret, a feeling of not having quite done enough. This pattern of regret and worry underlies so much of his poetry and notes, especially regarding his children.

1902 aged 49

...

I turn my head to look behind
And watch the silent scene
As through me flash regretful thoughts
Of things that might have been

...

On later birthdays he had a greater sense of peace within himself. His fiftieth seems to have been a turning point. There is no mention in his diaries of a party and the poem suggests he was on his own as his fiftieth year shuffled to a close.

1903 aged 50
The clock has chimed the hour of twelve
And as the echoes cease
I close the fiftieth year of life
With hope, almost with peace.

...

In 1899 FJ stood in front of another horse drawn funeral procession for a woman. This time he was older. His mother's coffin was an elaborate affair, unlike the simple one for his sister Emily so many years ago. His grief was confounded by the loss of his mother as well as his personal loss of what might have been for himself.

Mother 1899

I stood beside my mother's grave
And pondered long upon the past
...
Her life was simple, pure and strong
And in my veins the same blood flows
But passion, with its ceaseless flow
Draws me forever to do wrong –
I should have loved another life
Inheriting her purer faith
And in remembrance of her death
Have been with evil, all at strife.

After his mother's death, FJ lost heart for writing in his notebook. The odd entry appeared through to his death in 1927. The notebook was found packed away in a suitcase.

There was happiness and some further sadness in Frederick James's life. In 1877 he married Sarah Nicholson and they had three children, Laurence (1878-1930), Ernest Mark Wilfred (1881-1950) and Henry Joseph (1882-1883). Henry Joseph's passing was marked by another lengthy outpouring of grief, in brief:-

My heart is all silent and lonely
Its chambers are dreary and dead
And out from its wide open windows
The angel of brightness has sped.

Ah! This is no short separation
For I wait his returning in vain
No more these dim cloudy recesses

Will make his bright chamber again.

He loved me and brought me all gladness
In days that are now past and dead
And little I thought how I'd miss him
Till now that his presence has fled.

To Laurence aged 7 he writes:

Sleep laddie sleep – little angels
Are hovering over thy head:
I whisper low, lest my presence
Should chase them away from thy bed.
...
Perhaps the kind angels that guard thee
May spare me a blessing divine
And tomorrow I'll wake with a feeling
That its passed through your hand, into mine

But all is not well in this household as a year later he writes:

O my little one my heart bleeds when I hear of your derelictions and I seek in vain for some remedy that shall survive my presence. In thy young blood runs the fire that courses through my own and I see as through an inverted telescope my own faults reduced but re produced- How can I train thee, my child, to love truth and obedience when my own poor life is so much removed from the calm quiet of acquiescence in a good providence. And yet I must – for thy good. I must assume a virtue if I have it not and try to bring thee back to love and honour the best and truest – heaven knows.

Only when his wife Sarah dies on 20 June 1906 do we hear of all that she meant to him. The following was written on 20 June 1907.

Night thoughts.

I wonder whether I can set down here a record of some of the thoughts that have sprung up during the day, without any attempt at polishing my sentences, but put them on paper just as they occur to my mind –

Today is our anniversary, full now of grief at the loss of her who made the first event possible – 30 years ago we joined our hands and made a bond that grew stronger as time went on, and now that it has become an invisible tie, it still links me in spirit to the dearest wife a man ever had – there have been times when our path was thorny & scenes were looked at with different eyes, but man and woman of any character can expect to always walk in the shade and never differ – I am only too thankful, now that she is gone, to remember how sweet were the reunions after our little estrangements, how loving and kind was her nature & how ready she always was to kiss and be friends – Ah: my heart swerved further away sometimes than she knew but over and above my selfish drives was she --- never to give her that heartache which could never be cured, and many a time she has brought me back to her side, ashamed to have strayed in thought from what I knew was right –

Today I have gone over many of the scenes of 1877 and seen many faces long, long ago lost in death or circumstance – I see my mother shedding tears as we say Good Life when we leave for our honeymoon, not selfish tears but still prompted by the feeling that I who was her all in all, had now another who comes first- How little they all know of my mother's nature, noble, good, simple & devoted.

14th July. I meant to write more often, but have not been in the right frame of mind – tonight it is different, I have sat above and in darkness on the balcony and tried to catch sight of her form as it wanders among the "shadows on the grass" tried to hear her voice calling me from some distant sphere and yet so close that I could answer – I often wonder whether, if we meet again as I most truly hope and almost believe, whether, I say, she will look once more into my eyes and tell me by that glance that she knows all I have been and have done since she left me!

30th Sept 1907 This is my second birthday since my darling went away! The first only since her person fled from sight but the second since she herself left the world of conscious thought (a stroke perhaps?) – *For from the awful moment when she was struck, she never came back, the bright unselfish, intelligent little woman that made her so dear to me and such a friend to all – Bravely she struggled to get back to life, but she was never more what she once was, never the true self that was taken away by the enemy of health.*

April 1916   Years have passed since I last wrote in this book but I still feel the loss of her dear self – I never knew how much she was to me while she lived, how her tender little hands shielded me from the rough touches of the common round –more than ever I now see how my happiness was the one aim of her life – this is a selfish way of looking at things, but I want to make it quite clear that I now know how good and kind & true she was – and that I now know as never before how much she loved and cherished me and that in her unselfish way she sought her own happiness only in trying to make me happy.

This last entry extolling the virtues of his late wife is written eight years after he married my grandmother Alice May Emery! But there is more to be said before we come to that event.

It is frustrating reading another person's journals and not know to what they are alluding. Frederick James says *Ah, my heart swerved further away sometimes than she knew*' and he mentions our '*little estrangements.* I would venture to suggest that he was very taken with the actress Mary Anderson.

Before the feelings depart from this too unrelenting heart, I must register the fact that I have seen a great and good actress – How beautiful is Mary Anderson and how pure, truth seems to shine through her eyes as the manifestation of purity within, and her lovely form the outward expression of a lovely mind.

Mary Anderson (1859-1940) was an American actress noted for her Shakespearean roles and after a distinguished career in the USA she toured Europe, eventually coming to England in 1883 where she stayed for six years performing at the Lyceum in London and the Shakespeare Memorial Theatre in Stratford-on-Avon. Her popularity was remarkable and on several occasions she was publicly crowned with flowers. 'In England her success was phenomenal and she was always favoured with large and enthusiastic audiences' *Prominent Men and Women of the Day,* Thos. W. Herringshow. This period from1883 to1889 was a bleak time for FJ, his mother probably had a stroke in 1883 and towards the end of the eighties there were financial problems at work. The stress both at home and at work may have caused him to stray with thoughts of Mary Anderson, perhaps mentally rather than physically.

It is worth mentioning some of the passages from FJ's journals concerning his problems at work. He devotes many pages to the financial position between himself as a commission agent with H.van der Beeck and the manufacturers of cloth and the silk and wool brokers.

'It is clear to me that he has been speculating on the Stock exchange weekly if not daily – and by his expression when receiving letters marked ' private' & which come quite regularly, and his half smothered exclamations of dismay when he opens some of them, I am convinced he has been losing- He is visited continuously by a man from some stock brokers who receive time and attention no matter when other business presses & who is no doubt the instrument by which the speculations are carried out.

The demands of our manufacturers for the settlements of a/cs which are already paid now quite frequent and show clearly that their money is not reaching them as it should. HvB told me that as he was being pressed from several quarters for advances, the arrangement between myself and him must be readjusted, as the profits of the Reims business had diminished enormously- that he could not stand any further expenses as ' he could not live, as it was'

On their financial matters I am never consulted, I mean the financial schemes which are undertaken superficially in the interests of our legitimate business & not those engendered as a set off against his private losses – My position does not exactly warrant my expecting to be asked whether they shall be undertaken, but at the same time, considering that they involve undue risks, merchant's risks without a merchant's profit, it is rather hard that as they are now undertaken principally to scrape money together by almost any means so as to stave off the day of reckoning, that I should be a sharer in losses brought about almost solely by reckless speculation.

And so the writings continue in the same vein with his commissions being reduced and more acrimonious exchanges with HvB. Is it any wonder that he may have turned to the delightful Mary Anderson on stage and perhaps in the flesh?

To return to the family: Ernest Mark Wilfred, son of Frederick James was engaged to Alice May. What happened between them we will never know. Other sides of the family have spoken of 'a mystery or scandal' regarding Alice and all she ever said to me was that she had been engaged to Ernest and then married his father in 1908. Perhaps it is not surprising that Ernest went to Canada in 1910 on the *Empress of Ireland* and was married there in1912.He is the only member of any of the family who served in the Great War, he was obviously just the right age whereas all the other relations were either too old or too young. Ernest served in the Canadian Expeditionary Force.

Frederick James and Alice May's son Frederick Mark (my father) was born in 1910, he was to be their only child. However after the war Ernest stayed with his father for a short while and wrote letters to Frederick Mark aged 8 who was at the seaside on holiday with his mother, the letter signed 'with brotherly love'. In 1923 Ernest went to live in the USA with his wife where he became a naturalised citizen and he died in1950 in California.

Photo albums show that Mark and his parents had a holiday in France and Belgium. This must have been a sentimental return for Frederick James to Rheims in particular to where he had conducted his earlier business dealings with silk and woollen merchants. The photos show the devastation of Rheims cathedral and the town of Albert, contrasting with happy family snaps on the beach.
Alice May was Principal of The Lady Margaret School in Willesden from 1924 to 1934. Frederick James died in 1927 leaving her a widow at 55. She found consolation with 'a gentleman' with whom she cruised in the 1930s. FJ had left her well provided for with the income from railway shares but the value of these diminished with nationalization in the '40s and her final years were in straitened circumstances. However she was a great influence on me in my childhood and I remember her with love and affection.

The track for the story of my life has been laid with strong foundations from an eclectic mixture of ancestors, so let's get the journey under way and see where the track takes me.

CHAPTER 2
Branch line through childhood

Childhood: the period of human life intermediate between the idiocy of infancy and the folly of youth.....
Ambrose Bierce

Although I said previously that I don't view my life chronologically I will start at the beginning of this journey with my earliest memory and then stop at the stations along the route, these will include the war, school and family and this line will join the mainline just before I enter my teens - the folly of youth.

In October 1940, I was 3½ years old and delving into a pile of rubble, bricks, wood, plaster, fragments of furniture and clothes - the detritus of war. When my father Mark Berryman joined the army in 1940 as an officer in the Royal Engineers we moved from our house in north London to a flat in Pentland Gardens, Wandsworth, just a few doors from my maternal grandparents, the Thatchers who lived in Pentland Street. Mum was working at Fulham Town Hall on some nights as an air raid warden so I was close enough to spend those nights with my grandparents.

It is fortuitous that one of her working nights happened to be 29October 1940 otherwise my journey would have come to an abrupt end. Pentland Gardens was hit by a high explosive bomb and our home was obliterated. So my earliest memory is of being chastised by my mother for bringing her fragments of her prized Cornish Ware pottery that I had recovered from the rubble. Since we were now homeless we moved in with Mum's parents in Pentland Street where we stayed until 1944. This house was damaged seven times from bomb blasts, the plaster on the front room ceiling came down frequently and for some reason the wooden slatted structure of the ceiling that was revealed was fascinating to a small child. During the period of The Blitz which lasted for a year London was bombed on 56 out of 57 nights from 7 September 1940.

Winston Churchill highlights the problem facing families who had lost everything -

He describes being at Ramsgate at an early point of the Blitz. He sheltered in a tunnel during a raid. When he emerged he surveyed the damage. A small hotel had been reduced to a 'litter of crockery, utensils and splintered furniture'. he recounts how the proprietor, his wife, and staff were in tears. What were they to do? He writes in his history of the War. "Here is a privilege of power. I formed an immediate resolve. On the way back in my train I dictated a letter to the Chancellor of the Exchequer, Kingsly Wood, laying down the principle that all damage from the fire of the enemy must be a charge upon the state and compensation be paid in full and at once. Thus the burden would not fall alone on those whose homes or business premises were hit, but would be borne evenly on the shoulders of the nation".[Churchill , pp. 371-72.] The Exchequer and the Treasury were very concerned about the potential liabilities involved. Eventually Wood devised an elaborate insurance scheme.

But recompense was not immediately forthcoming as shown by the following letters concerning my own home.

4 April 1941 Letter from Councillor Bonney to the Mayor of Wandsworth.

Re: Mrs. Berryman 7 Pentland Gardens.

It appears that Mrs Berryman lived in the upper floor of the above house which was practically demolished in the incident in October last. All her effects fell with the debris and were either smashed or covered, and it was not possible to recover anything at that time. Our Borough Engineer is now engaged in the demolition of the property. I hope that the case of silver referred to may be found during the execution of the work with anything else salvable........I suppose that in view of the new act (War Damage Act, 1941 (Part II) Private Chattels Scheme) Mrs. Berryman may now hope to receive compensation at a fairly early date'.

The value of the contents of the flat as assessed by my mother totalled £240, the full list is extensive as it covered the loss of everything that she owned. Here is a sample of the items:

Kitchen	1 set small saucepans	£16	11	0
	compete set Cornish Ware storage jars	3	0	0
	electric coffee percolator	1	10	0
	Food in store cupboard about	5	0	0
	1/2 ton coal	1	10	0
Nursery	Blue nursing chair from B&H	1	1	0
	Toy dog from Selfridges	2	19	6
	Clothes app,	2	10	0
Dining room	Oak table & four chairs	22	12	0
	Singer sewing machine treadle	19	15	0
	Best tea service 1 doz. of everything new from Selfridges	2	2	0
	Case solid silver cutlery	10	0	0
Bedroom	Oak bedroom suite	21	0	0
	Clothes not salvaged	10	0	0
Sitting room	Three piece suite	31	10	0
	Green carpet	11	0	0
	Electric clock	2	2	0

On 27 March 1942 a payment of £52.10.0 was made 'granted for distress or hardship' with the balance deferred and interest paid on this deferred amount until such time as the payment was paid. I am not sure when this balance was paid but a letter from my mother to the War Damage Claims department on 15 February 1944 indicates that she wanted to move from staying with her parents in Pentland Street into her own accommodation.

Since the date my flat was bombed my little girl and I have been accommodated - not very conveniently- in furnished rooms, but I have recently been asked to vacate these as soon as possible (I am sure this is not true but just said to enforce her requests). *I therefore feel that rather than seek other furnished apartments, I should like to start a real home for my child and myself, where my husband can spend his leave, whilst he is still in this country, without being made to feel an interloper.*

As a result of this letter on 21 March 1944 mother received a voucher to the value of 34 units of utility furniture and 1 curtain permit. A wardrobe was 12 units, bedstead 5 units, kitchen table 6 units, dining chair 1 unit and an armchair 6 units, plus of course the cost of the articles. By April 1944 we had moved into a very pleasant flat in Meadow Bank, in Putney where we stayed until 1947 and I remember it as well furnished. However the claim for further compensation went on into 1947 when we had already gone to Aden when a friend of the family, Geoff Foat, wrote to the War Office regarding increased payments that were being made after the end of the war. It is possible to see from this protracted correspondence just how stressful life must have been for a mother in wartime with a young child, having lost her home and with her husband serving in the army overseas.

Another aspect of War was the evacuation of children and families from towns and cities to the countryside where they were thought to be safe, the first evacuation being on 1 September 1939, the day Germany invaded Poland and this was two days before the British declaration of war. A register of the population was taken on 29 September 1939 along the same lines as the ten-year census and this shows that my mother and I were staying at the Black Horse Inn near Calne in Wiltshire but I was too young to have any memories of this. Apparently the widely expected bombing raids particularly on London did not occur so many evacuees returned home as I presume Mum and I did to the flat in Pentland Gardens until it was bombed in 1940. But I was evacuated again, this time on my own, in 1944. London and the south of England were being attacked by a new type of weapon, V1 and V2 rockets so this prompted another wave of evacuations and I was sent off to Buckingham. But before investigating my second experience as an evacuee I had started school.

At the age of five in 1942 I started at Burlington School near Shepherds Bush, a good hour on the bus and this for a five year old, what parents would let such a young child take this journey to school now, on their own, and in war-time? This was the school that my mother had attended which had then been situated in the much more up-market area of Cork Street in London. It was therefore deemed suitable for me however I lasted for only a term as apparently I came home with some really bad language! My grandmother - Grandma B, knew Ethel Strudwick who was High Mistress at St Paul's Girls' School and through her I then attended the junior school for SPGS known as Colet Court. Classes were held in Bute House on Brook Green, Hammersmith and across the road at No.93. Maybe bombing only took place at night as I don't remember any air raids during the day at school, but one of the 'pleasures' of walking from the bus stop in the morning was collecting pieces of shrapnel that had fallen from bombs the previous evening. A letter from me dated February1943 to *My Dear Daddie* says *I was put up today into the second form with the big girls...I have an allotment at school now and I am going to grow some beetroot seeds.*

'DIG FOR VICTORY', that was the phrase that brought under the spade acres of commons and gardens for allotments in which to grow food. During the war thousands of tons of shipping was sunk, ships that were bringing food into the country, and this resulted in food rationing which came into force in1940 in order to distribute the limited supplies fairly. Gardening became part of the curriculum in virtually all schools and I hope that my beetroot seeds eventually flourished. Actually I do have three memories of school lunches in Bute House, one is of hot beetroot in white sauce and the other is of gristly meat and of prunes, both of which ended up in the empty fireplace adjacent to the dining table.

It is hard to realise that rationing lasted until 1954, the amounts of groceries allocated to each person varied depending on availability and when looking at the some of the rations for an adult for a week in April 1945 you wonder how a housewife managed to feed a family: 2oz butter/4oz margarine/2oz lard/1 egg/4oz bacon/ 8oz sugar/2oz tea/2oz cheese/meat 1s.2d. and monthly 3oz toilet soap and 3oz soap flakes. I attribute my love of butter to Grandma B who was a diabetic and whose weekly ration was for 4oz butter and 8oz margarine so on any visits to her the butter was always spread thickly.

Returning to 1944, this seems to have been a period of upheaval for the family judging by the letters that I wrote. Father was away in the

Army, mother was working days here and nights there and I was looked after by various friends and relations until I was evacuated to Buckingham in the summer. This second evacuation of children was due to the increased bombing raids by the V1 rockets called 'doodlebugs'. They were very scary.

The period between June and August 1944, was like nothing experienced before or since. It has often been called the 'Doodlebug Summer'. People soon got used to the strange sound of the V1s clattering across the sky, The rasping grating noise was caused by the pulse jet engine which powered the missile. They soon realised that if this noise continued and went away in the distance that they were safe. However, if the engine cut out nearby then there was about 15 seconds before the missile came crashing down'.
www.flyingbombsandrockets.com

My mother kept all the letters that I wrote during 1944, so let this journey briefly leave the branch line and go into a siding to read some extracts written by a seven year old to her mother and father.

Dear Daddy 3rd April
I hope you had a lot of cards for your birthday.... I am liking my Music very much....if you don't send me a letter I will not answer another letter. Mummy has been going to bed very late and has been sleeping in the morning.
(Dad's birthday was on 6th April. Mum was an air raid warden at night at Fulham Town Hall and working during the day, at one stage at Nestlé's factory somewhere in London - she would bring home bits of broken biscuits, such a treat)

Dear Daddy postcard from Reading 24th April
I hope you enjoy yourself in Scotland. I wrote this in Reading and I am enjoying myself, lots of love from Ann
(This is addressed to Capt F.M. Berryman R.E., 654 A.W Coy.R.E., Morton Hall, Liberton, Edinburgh. Grandma B worked for the BBC in Sonning for a period during the war so I could have been staying with her)

Dear Mummy 25th April

I went out today and had tea in Peter Jones, I had an ice cream, bread and jam & a cup of milk. You never gave me my health certificate but Miss Hobson was alright about it.

(I must be back in London at school. Peter Jones is a large shop in Sloane Square. Miss Hobson was a horrible mistress at school. Mum must have been away somewhere.)

Dear Mummy and Daddy 28th April

I hope you are quite well. I have got to go to the specialist on Tuesday week the day which Daddy goes back on. I hope he will be able to come. I like school very much we have got 19 children and 20 desks. These are there (sic) names - Rosamund, Aelis, Jessica, Ann Crowther. I will have to tell you the rest when you come home. Margaret Mc., Ann C. and Norma C. have gone up to lower 3.

(Jessica, Rosamund, Eirlys and the others all went into St. Paul's Girls' School with me)

Dear Mummy 30th April

....I am wearing my school jumper, I am very cold in bed. I went to Ongar on Sunday we went on 9 trains altogether.

Dear Darling Daddy 25th June

....school is closed for a fortnight. Mummy said I have been a very good girl because I did all her shoping (sic) on Saturday June 24th. We have been having a lot of alerts but I slept through all the night raids.

(this would have been the start of the 'doodlebug summer')

Dear Daddy 11th July

Mummy thanks you very much for the German badges...

(Daddy sent from wherever he was stationed a complete set of German uniform badges - long since lost)

Dear Daddy 19th July

I hope you are quite well, we have had one air raid, mind the doodlebugs and shells...this is my new address Miss E.A. Berryman, c/o Mrs Hall, 33 Bourtonville, Buckingham, Bucks.

(I am evacuated away from London to Buckinghamshire)

Dear Daddy 24th July
Mummy will tell you if I am enjoying myself.... Mummy sent you a cake and 200 cigerites (sic) please write to me often.

Dear Daddy 3rd August
Mummy is coming down for her weeks holiday on August 13th, you still haven't told me when you will come home again......

Dear Mummy 5th August
We expect you down on Sunday the 13th. I haven't got the sweets yet. Are you sleeping in the Anderson yet?
(the Anderson air raid shelter was made from corrugated iron sheets bolted together, half buried in the ground with earth heaped on top to protect from bomb blast. There was one at the bottom of the garden at 14 Pentland Street so maybe Mum was staying there with her parents rather than at the flat in Meadow Bank. I do have memories of this horrid dark, damp place, and particularly of running to the kitchen early in the morning trying to avoid the chicken messes on the path and being chased by a fiercesome cockerel - hence my dislike of live chickens even to this day)

Dear Mummy 7th August
....I have still not got the sweets yet...these are the things I want, soap, pen, ink and writing paper
(all these letters are written in pencil except for the renowned one in green ink)

Dear Daddy 15th August
Mummy is going to buy a rabbit. Mummy is going to sell my bicycle and have the money for the baby.
(this letter is written in green ink and very smudged. I upset a bottle of green ink on the carpet and was threatened with being sent home. I don't think the rabbit ever appeared. As for the baby?? I know mother had a miscarriage but I thought it was in 1946, it was certainly after the war ended)

Dear Daddy postcard from Buckingham 16th August
....I have saved 3 shillings for the baby
(this is addressed to Capt. F.M. Berryman, 654 A.W. Coy R.E., British Liberation Army)

Dear Daddy 21st August
...I recieved (sic) the sweets...Mummy stayed down here for a week...

Dear Mummy 25th August
I recieved the sweets from Daddy. The Americans have got into Paris...
(up to date news from Buckingham! The German garrison in Paris surrendered on 25th August 1944)

Dear Daddy postcard from Wandsworth 26th August
....it is very hot in London..
(this is addressed to Daddy at 5C.T.E., 11 Avenue Road, Leamington Spa, Warwickshire. Mummy and I visited him there and I fell I the river from a slippery raft!)

Dear Daddy 29th August
...please don't send any more sweeties nor chocolate until I say so

Dear Mummy 29th August
...we heard you had no doodlebugs last night....

Dear Daddy 31st August
I have not seen you since 4th of June and wonder when we may be able to come over to France and Normandy. Daddy have you got any whiskers yet.

Dear Daddy 8th September
I hope these things are not too many and if I don't have the baby brother or sister could I have it for my birthday. kisses to father christmas.
(there must have been a list of Christmas presents required that was sent with this letter)

Dear Mummy 16th September
am very glad I am not coming home as it is so very nice down here....At night Auntie plaits my hair and in the morning my hair is quite curly, I expect you down on the 24th.

Dear Daddy 21st September
I am very glad you are Major and so you know Daddy after a major comes a General and then a feild marsal (sic)...

Dear Daddy 2nd October
Mummy said I could have a Christmas party and I want you to be home then. I am having...Ruth D. and Cosetta D., John Lines and Cynthia Lines my cousins, Tony and Margaret Northeast my cousins, Nanny and Grandad.... Daddy please tell me when you are coming home, don't forget to send Mummy a birthday card.
(Ruth and Cosetta were at Colet Court with me and Ruth went on to SPGS too. Cosetta lived on Putney Hill and Mum made dresses for her. John b.1935 and Cynthia Lines b.1939 were children of Beatrice daughter of Auntie Rose, sister of Nanny Thatcher. I don't recall the Northeasts.)

Dear Mummy 6th October
....I have made up my mind that I want to come back on October 31st the end of the month if I can go back to St Paul's at half term...

Dear Daddy 7th October
...Mummy says I am coming back when half term comes at St Paul's. Auntie bought me a new pair of shoes black lace up size one, they fit me very well...

Dear Daddy 27th October
Mummy said I am coming back on Nov.5th. Will you be home by my birthday Daddy. Here in Buckingham the trees are simply beutyfull(sic) I expect there are in France too...

Dear Daddy 10 Meadow Bank 10th November
I am glad to be home. Mummy curls my hair every night…I have got a new navy blue coat…
(evacuation ends!)

Dear Daddy Meadow Bank 15th November
….do you like being in Belgium, I hope you do. Could you send the tin helmet and badges please. Some German money please

Dear Daddy 10 Meadow Bank 10th December
…do you like Belgium, thank you very much for the two cards and the calendar written in Flemish, I did not ask Mummy to spell it. I have not been very well the last few days and I have to go to the childrens hospital on Tuesday at 9.15am for a few minutes because I have a pain in the bottom of my left foot.
(this was the start of many visits to Great Ormond Street hospital - I had flat feet and a related pain in my back and as a consequence I had to wear horrid built up shoes)

Dear Daddy Happy Christmas 28th December
Thank you very, very, very much for the cross and chain I only wear it at the weekends and thank you very, very much for the clogs I wear them every day and I am wearing them now. I had lots of presents for Christmas, 2 pencil boxes, 6 books, 1 chocolate shell, 3 boxes sweets, 1 Humpty Dumpty and lots of other things.
(the chain and cross were of platinum and the cross had a small diamond at its centre. The accompanying note from Daddy said 'may you live up to the purity of the diamond in the centre'. Sadly both note, cross and chain have disappeared. The clogs were part of a complete Dutch costume, striped wool skirt, bodice and bolero and hat which I said had ears).
All my letters were signed either Ann or Lizzie Ann which was how Daddy called me.

My 8th birthday party took place at the Wynnstay Hotel on Wimbledon Common where Grandma B was working as a housekeeper. Mum made me a pretty dress from two rolls of pink and rusty rose silk that Daddy had sent from France or Belgium. The rolls were narrow so the skirt was in broad stripes and the top and puff sleeves in the pale pink with darker pink bows around the neck.

Walking to the bus-stop and then taking the bus to school in Hammersmith every weekday I was able to see the devastation caused by bombing. It was in London, particularly the East End which experienced the worst of the bombing especially with firebombs where whole streets were demolished, in our part of London the damage was not so widespread but more contained. When the bomb landed on Pentland Gardens only three houses there were demolished although the effects of the blast were felt further afield with shattered windows and the plaster of ceilings coming down. During the eight months of the Blitz in 1940-1941 the bomb damage maps show that 24 bombs fell within a half mile radius of Pentland Street. During the doodlebug summer there were only two rockets that landed near Pentland Street, in All Farthing Lane and Heathfield Road and none near us in Putney.

Even as a child I found it intrusive to look into the skeletons of partially demolished houses, seeing the peeling wallpaper, empty fireplaces, tattered curtain remnants and sometimes broken furniture- where were the people who belonged in these houses, were they dead or injured, had the children lost all their toys?

Now for a brief pause to look at my maternal elderly relations, those who were a living reminder of the people we met at the beginning of my journey. Nanny (Harriet Harbourne) and Grandad (George) Thatcher, and Nanny's sisters Aunt Dolly, Aunt Laura, Aunt Rose and Aunt Maud. In mid 1940s they were all in their mid seventies and appeared to me to be very old and yet they were younger than I am now and I don’t consider myself 'very old'!

Nanny, Grandad and Aunt Dolly lived in 14 Pentland Street, the house was actually owned by Aunt Laura who was quite wealthy and a multiple property owner. Nanny had been a laundress in her working life and she was an expert at 'goffering'. This was a process of creating frills and ruffs on clothes in the late Victorian times with a special goffering iron especially on delicate fabrics. She was a quiet, loving lady with long white hair put into a bun, the ends of her hair still retained a smidgen of red, her original colour and I loved to brush her long hair. There was a fixed routine to household chores. Washing on Monday, drying on Tuesday, ironing on Wednesday and cleaning on Friday. Cleaning included black-leading the range which stayed in the kitchen until the '50s and whitening the front door step weekly in order to keep up with the neighbours.

Washing was a major event compared with today's wash-day where everything gets thrown into the washing machine and comes out almost dry a few hours later. Until the '50s the only way to heat water in large quantities was in a large construction in the scullery called a 'copper' water heater. It was built into the corner of the room with a wooden lid and a space underneath for a fire. Water was put in through the top opening and the fire was lit. When the water was hot enough clothes went into the top too and all were left to stew! Every now and again the mixture was stirred with a long wooden paddle called a dolly. Usually whites were washed separately from the coloureds which were put into the sink to soak and given a good going-over up and down the washboard to remove dirt and then put into the copper when the whites were taken out. Eventually the clothes were rinsed in the scullery sink with the whites having the Reckitts blue bag put into the water to keep them white and then put through the mangle which stood outside, in order to remove excess water. The drying process took place on airers around the range in the kitchen and in overhead racks on pulleys, or outside if the weather was clement.

An electric iron only came into the house in the '50s when the range was replaced by a fireplace, before that ironing was done with flat irons. These were made of cast iron and came in pairs - one in use and one heating up on the range. The backbreaking, lengthy process of housework in those days is well described with illustrations at *www.1900s.org.uk.*

I enjoyed going shopping with Nanny to Wandsworth High Street, there were no supermarkets or large shops in those days so we'd set off with a large shopping bag and go to the grocery shop and buy a slice of cheese, take a handful of biscuits out of a large glass jar, watch as the bacon was sliced, a couple of slices of corned beef, a chunk cut from a block of cooking salt and all put into paper bags. If rations allowed there might be some sweets too. We didn't need eggs of course but you could buy powdered egg which was useful for baking and was un-rationed. There wasn't much to buy in the butchers, perhaps scrag end of neck of lamb for stewing, or some offal. Just occasionally there was horsemeat in the shop which thank heavens Nanny didn't ever buy, it looked blueish, quite revolting.

In retrospect I realise I did a lot of walking with Nanny. She was an agent for an insurance company and she had clients all over Wandsworth that she walked to, to collect their weekly contributions of just a couple of shillings and all were meticulously recorded in small notebooks. I got to know Garratt Lane, All Farthing Lane, St. Ann's Hill, Geraldine Avenue and it must have been on these walkabouts that I saw all the bomb damaged houses.

What was Grandad doing whilst all this household activity was taking place, he would be sitting in his chair in the kitchen puffing away at his pipe. Early in the war he still had his horses and cart in the empty ground opposite the house but the haulage business faded with the war and he turned to chickens. I have explained about food rationing so he became an official supplier of eggs hence the large chicken run in the back garden. He was allowed to purchase feed for the chickens and his customers had to produce their ration books in order to purchase his fresh eggs. Spare eggs were pickled in a large glass jar. The chickens who were past laying were summarily dispatched by him with a tweezer-like contraption which was fitted on the wall by the outside lavatory.

Maiden Aunt Dolly lived upstairs, she had her own room and at her wish without even the mod-cons of the day. No electric light, only two lamps lit by gas where the mantles had to be changed frequently and a small coal fire in the Victorian tiled fireplace which was forever burning. Many a good piece of toast I have had from that fire produced at the end of a toasting fork, then we would sit by the fire and see what pictures we could see in the coals. She had a cat called Monty whose food was cooked in a saucepan over this fire and a jolly awful smell it made in the rest of the house. Some Sundays she would drag me off to Chapel to listen to fire and brimstone sermons. If I could have told her then that she, along with all her siblings, was illegitimate, that her mother Charlotte had never married her father, I think she would have died of shame.

Aunt Laura who owned the house lived nearby in St. Ann's Road, she had had polio as a child and wore calipers, Aunt Ethel 'talked funny' at least it sounded funny to me as a child as she had no roof to her mouth. I saw much more of Aunt Rose who was grandmother to John and Cynthia Lines who were invited to my birthday party and whose mother Beatrice was a great friend of my mother.

Aunt Rose and Uncle George lived at 2c Peabody Buildings at Clapham Junction. The Peabody Estates which could be found in various areas of London were an early form of housing association and the Clapham site was built in 1936 during the inter-war economic depression. The type of accommodation provided would be unacceptable today, there was no bathroom, the bath was in the scullery and covered with a wooden board. As a child this made a memorable impression on me as it contrasted particularly with the modern conveniences in our flat at Meadow Bank. I often walked from Pentland Street across Spencer Park and Wandsworth Common to Clapham to play with John and Cynthia.

Back on track the journey continues into 1945 when the war ended and Daddy was awarded the MBE. His commendation is dated 4 July 1945 and appeared in the London Gazette on 24 January 1946.

This officer has displayed great capacity in organising engineer work rapidly and efficiently throughout the period 30 Sept. 44 to the conclusion of the campaign. His cheerfulness and tact in dealing with up to 15 units under Command, with his formation Headquarters and many outside British and Allied Units requiring engineering assistance has been outstanding. He has also been of great service in getting work done by local civil engineer authority for re-opening roads, bridges and canals.
He has discharged these abnormal responsibilities with success. His ceaseless devotion to duty constituted a valuable contribution to the development of the military working of the Port of Ghent which was a valuable factor in the maintenance of the Allied Forces.

Ghent had been occupied by the Germans during the war but it was liberated by the British 7th 'Desert Rats' Armoured Division on 6 September 1944 so presumably that was when the process of rebuilding the roads and re-opening the port started.

Although the war ended in June 1945 Daddy was not demobbed until early 1946. It must have been difficult for all couples to come to terms with living together after six or seven years apart.

But on this occasion my parents managed it! Daddy started working for Wimpey, the house builders, and we moved from Meadow Bank in Putney to a brand new house in Harlington near Hayes. It is during this time that I thought my mother's miscarriage occurred but I might be wrong. However, a summer holiday ensued, the first since before the war and together with Grandad Thatcher we set off by car for Angle in West Wales. My mother documented the journey times:

Harlington to Angle 31 August 1946

Harlington 7.25am: Uxbridge: Denham: Beaconsfield: High Wycombe 7.55: Stokenchurch 8.5: Tetsworth 8.15: Wheatley 8.25: Headington 8.30: Oxford 8.50: Woodstock 8.55: Chipping Norton 8.10: Chastleton 9.20: Stow on the Wold 9.25:Toddington 9.50: Tewksbury 10.5: rest for 15 mins: Ledbury 10.55: Hereford 11.30 petrol 12/-:Whitney 11.55: Hay 12.0: Glasbury 12.10: Brecon 12.30: rest for 30 mins: Senny Bridge 1.20: Llandovery 1.40: Llanwrda 1.50: Llandilo 2.5: Llangoed 2.20:Carmarthen 2.30: St. Clears 2.45: Kilgelly 3.10: Carew Cheriton 3.20: Lower Nash 3.25: Pembroke 3.30: rest 5 mins: Castle Martin 3.45: Angle 4.0

The journey took 8½ hours, in the 21stC I doubt it would take less time as the benefits of motorways and ring roads around the towns would be offset by increased traffic.

My mother was a great one for keeping lists and in the same notebook as the journey times to Angle are several weeks of shopping costs for the household. One for the week commencing Friday 15 November is fairly typical.

	£	s	d	
coal		19	3	
milk		3	10	1/2
bread		1	5	1/2
grocer		15	6	
dog's meat		6	4	
butcher		12	10	
greengrocer		8	7	1/2
ann's fares & p.m.		8	3	
fish		3	0	

50 cigs Fri.		4	4	1/2
flowers		7	0	
fares			10	
scones & tarts		1	5	
cigs Sat.			10	1/2
	£4	**13**	**7**	**1/2**

In spite of my father having a job and mother not working at this time there must have been some dissatisfaction with life in general which prompted the move that was to have such a momentous effect on my life. I was not aware of this and my schooldays continued to be enjoyable. Whatever it was the winter of 1946 to 47 must have been the last straw.

It was the harshest winter ever then known with heavy snow all over the country, no coal for the power stations so there were electricity shortages, food was in short supply and vegetables froze in the ground. I am surmising here that it was a combinations of factors such as this weather, probably an unfulfilling job, the loss of the baby, cost of living and generally mean and hard living conditions that drove my father to apply to the Colonial Office for a position overseas, or maybe there was an advertisement that he answered for Civil Engineers in overseas territories - for whatever reason the result was this journey made an unexpected change in direction.

CHAPTER 3
Mainline station - Aden

'Of the gladdest moments in human life...is the departure upon a distant journey into unknown lands'
Richard Francis Burton

This quotation from the explorer Richard Burton seems appropriate for my journey. In 1855 Burton met John Hanning Speke in Aden where they discussed their forthcoming and successful expedition to find the source of the Nile; surely the ultimate distant journey into unknown lands?

The Barren Rocks of Aden were part of my life for the next eight years, I came and went during that period but this strange place influenced me in so many ways, I will take branch lines into school, work, friendships and loves, a rocky journey sometimes but always memorable.

The worst winter ever in England was over and my parents were preparing to set forth on a new adventure; this must have been almost like going into the unknown. The Crown Agents, who looked after the Overseas Territories issued prospective Civil Servants with a list of essential clothing requirements for the tropics. I presume no clothing coupons were required as my father purchased from the Army and Navy Stores in London a trunkful of items including a solar topee, khaki and white long trousers, shirts and jackets, a black evening dinner suit, mosquito boots, a mosquito net, portable canvas wash basin and folding canvas chair.

These items were redundant, he never camped so the chair and wash basin were not needed, there were almost no mosquitoes, a canvas sun-hat was more comfortable than a solar topee, and the khaki and white longs and jackets were far too hot. Instead, in common with all the other local Civil Servants, the Indian tailor in the back street of the market in Steamer Point made a far more sensible wardrobe of cool white shorts and short sleeved shirts, and khaki safari suits with both shorts and long trousers. For evening wear the standard attire was known as 'Red Sea Kit'. In the summer this comprised white trousers, white short sleeved shirt and a black cummerbund and in so called winter black trousers, long sleeved shirt and black cummerbund. Occasionally a jacket was called for, especially for Government House 'do's and the tailor made a white jacket in a light-weight material called sharkskin. Desert shoes were the standard wear for work and the local shoe maker made leather chappals (sandals) for us all to wear.

So with a trunk of useless clothes Daddy set forth from Liverpool on 2 April 1947 on the *SS Orbita* of the Union Castle Line. In the age of super liners it is difficult to imagine that this vessel was only 15,000 tons and yet had capacity for almost 900 passengers. By looking at the other passengers on this ship it is easy to see that ours was not the only family seeking a new, and hopefully warmer life. Of the 506 passengers on board most were bound for Mombasa which was the port for the East African territories of Kenya, Uganda and Tanganyika, only the RAF families of 33 persons continued to Durban where they went on to Southern Rhodesia, and 15 disembarked in Aden. There were 120 males on board all Government officials or in the Forces, 221 females who were either wives ,nurses or teachers and 165 children. This exodus of working men and women had a two-fold advantage, less mouths to feed and house in post-war England and a boost to the Colonial territories that had been neglected during the war.

It was probably a good idea that Mummy and I travelled later, at least it gave Daddy a chance to find his feet in a new job as Civil Engineer in the Public Works Department and to find us somewhere to live. We left Southampton on 29 April 1947 on *SS Empire Ken* of Royal Mail Lines. This was a small ship of 9000 tons and had a capacity for only 300 passengers. It had been a German Navy U-boat depot vessel and became a war prize and was converted into a troop ship in 1945 when it took its English name. There were 292 on board, just 29 disembarking in Aden and the remainder going on to East Africa, the majority of whom were Army families.

My own memories of the voyage are few. We shared a cabin with six bunks, my mother must have hated that, and why did I have a screaming fit one evening in the cabin which resulted in her dragging me along the corridor? In the canteen a large screen was erected and a film showed the deadly effects of mosquitoes and malaria with large drawings of the anopheles mosquito, this strange name etched itself on my childhood brain. I do hope that this proved more useful to the future African residents than to us in Aden. The 'bum boats' in Port Said provide another memory. The boats held items for sale such as baskets, pottery, cigarettes and tourist knick-knacks such as camel stools and carved replica sphinxes. The stewards on board would lower a basket at the end of a rope, goods would then be hauled up and inspected and either returned or accepted and money in payment placed in the basket for the seller, after much haggling..

Forget about the Aden of today, the area of unrest at the southern tip of Yemen with its battered buildings, lack of facilities and economic disasters. In 1947 this was a boom town! In the early 19thC it was of strategic importance as a coaling station for trade between England and India and was occupied by the British in1839 and with the opening of the Suez Canal in 1869 its importance was further increased until by the late 1950s the port was one of the busiest in the world.

The colony was only 74 sq.m although the Aden Protectorate was much larger, 110 sq.m. but I never went 'up country'. The colony consisted of separate areas basically determined by geography. Crater was as the name suggests the centre of an ancient volcano. Government offices and banks were here as well as a few houses for Europeans and a labyrinth of narrow streets with Arab housing and markets. There was the Sultan's Palace, the Anglican church of St. Mary on the Hill, the El Aidrus mosque, Civil Hospital and Sira Island topped by old fortifications. Further on was the lighthouse at Marshag and a few more houses. In Khusaf valley the Tawila water tanks and aqueducts dating from before the 7thC. Steamer Point had the harbour and port authorities and businesses, the Crescent of shops like Cowasjee Dinshaw, Bhicajee Cowasjee, the English Chemist and the Crescent Hotel, the latter to play an important part in my life.

Access between Crater and Steamer Point was via the Main Pass which lead to Ma'alla, then this was a long straight road by the water's edge with two small blocks of flats, one for B.A.T (British American Tobacco) staff and Cory Bros. the coal depot. Off shore was a flourishing dhow building area and a small island which was used for drying fish - very smelly! Onwards from Steamer Point were the RAF bases and RAF hospital, more blocks of flats, a couple of select houses including Lake House home of an early Governor (more on this house later), Government House on a promontory, the Cable and Wireless swimming pool and then onwards past deserted beaches till you finally come to the lighthouse at Goldmohur beach and the Bathing Club, centre of outdoor social life in Aden where so many afternoons and weekends were spent swimming and socialising over the years. All of these areas surrounded the peaks of a volcanic mountain called Sham Sham at a height of 1776 ft.

Joining these areas to the mainland was the sandy isthmus of Khormaksar, here was the airport, more RAF barracks and 12 white box-like houses in the grandly named Downing street, this was named after Roy Downing, a government official not the prestigious street in London. Windmills edged the 3600 acres of shallow salt pans between the road and the beach. 168,000 tons of salt were exported from Aden in 1959.

The road continued to a surprising oasis of greenery at Sheikh Othman where boreholes and wells were the main source of water supply for the colony. The small town was also the terminus for the camel caravans trading goods between the colony and 'up country'. Later in the '50s a causeway was built from Khormaksar to Little Aden where the oil refinery was to be built, but in 1947 Little Aden was just a complementary skyline to Sham Sham which was best seen from Goldmohur and was almost inaccessible other than by Land Rover. This then was where my father brought us to make a new life together.

Our first home was a large and airy double storey house close to the Sultan's Palace in Crater and overlooking Sira island. Coming from a London terraced-house this seemed like a palace with its large rooms, deep verandahs and black shiny tiled floors. The colour of these tiles seems strange but they deadened the glare from the bright sun outside although they must have been difficult to clean after a sandstorm. We were house-sitting for a family on long leave (Dr and Mrs Goodman) so we eventually had to move across the sand into a charming low rise house on various levels that had been the hospital in the '30s and here we stayed for the next two years.

The house was rambling, a large main room with three rooms off with half height louvre doors which we used as bedrooms. Two bathrooms had been added to the main building and the kitchen was away from the main house down a staircase.

A very large verandah surrounded the whole house and contained storerooms and the real joy was the garden, I think it was the only garden in Crater; soft silky soil had been brought in from somewhere, perhaps Sheikh Othman, and the mali (gardener) maintained runnels and small walls of soil around all the plants. There was a profusion of many different coloured bougainvilleas, jasmine and zinnias - it was a very special place amongst all the surrounding sand.

The interior features of these and the subsequent houses we lived in were similar. There were punkahs (ceiling fans) over the lounge and dining area and in the bedrooms. To a child the punkah over the bed was frightening as it rattled and shook and threatened to fall and decapitate you – or so I imagined. Air-conditioning in bedrooms became available in the '50s but my mother refused to have it saying it was unhealthy.

The furniture was the same, the chairs and settees made of wooden slats with cushions covered with your own material from the bazaar. This could have unforeseen consequences as when my mother went to her first dinner party at Government House and found her newly-made dress perfectly matched the seat covers! In the early days the beds were the local charpoys made from rope on a wooden frame with a mattress on top, they were supposedly cooler than a conventional bed. The best part of the 'hospital house' was the covered sleeping verandah on the roof where you could lie and listen to the sounds from the bazaar and even hear the sea. Although there was electricity for lights and punkahs, cooking was done on a paraffin stove and the fridge ran on paraffin too.

Shopping for fresh food was done in the bazaar by mother and our bearer Ali who accompanied her. Disgusting deep fried sheep's brains and lady's fingers were some of the results of shopping expeditions and it was only later I learned that lady's fingers were not animal but vegetable – okra. All vegetables and fruit had to be washed before eating or cooking in purple potassium permanganate and meat, chicken or lamb (perhaps goat?), was washed in vinegar to take away any 'off' smells. All this changed when the cold storage depot was built in Ma'alla, I think in the early '50s, and a wider range of food was imported – including delicious tinned butter and cheese.

Did we need so many servants to run these houses? The bearer was a superior fellow in his long whites with a red fez; he was in charge of the other servants and waited at table. The cook had an assistant, there was an inside and outside sweeper (a cleaner); when we had a garden there was a mali, a chowkidar kept watch from dusk till dawn and when my sister was born we had a tall and stately Somali ayah Fatima to look after her who was clad in dazzling white flowing garments.

My best friend Laura also lived in Crater and we both went to the Franciscan Convent School in Steamer Point. I had two other friends, Noreen who lived in Ma'alla and Gill who lived in a house at the Cory Bros. depot but they attended another school. There were very few European girls at the convent, mostly Indian, and they were so clever! However much I tried I could never come top of the class, this place was always, for every subject, reserved for Lourdes. I heard many years later that she was a doctor in London.

The uniform was a white dress with FC cross-stitched in blue on the bodice. The layout of the school was strange, it was one very large room in which there were four classes with no dividing walls, each being taught by a different Sister. Somehow it worked and we were able to concentrate on what our own particular Sister was teaching. I had extra-curricular piano lessons in the parlour of the Convent, and now any loud clock ticking reminds me of the metronome that sat on the piano and Sister's shouts when I couldn't keep time.

Piano lessons meant practising and as we had no piano at home I would spend one afternoon a week at the home of Padre and Mrs MacGuffie where I struggled to practice on their small organ. It was difficult enough to read and play the music as there were two large pedals to operate to get the organ going and a lever by the left knee whose function escapes me now. The best part of these visits was going to their flat in the back streets of Crater where I wasn't normally allowed to go and eating Mrs MacG's tiny meringues which she called 'kisses'. In spite of these attractions I still cannot play the piano – or organ.

After the frugal life that we had in London shopping expeditions even for a young child, were exciting experiences. The emporiums of Bhicajee Cowasjee and Cowasjee Dinshaw in Steamer Point had a selection of household goods and clothes and the English Chemist, run by Mr Rodrigues, stocked Elizabeth Arden cosmetics. But the best place to be whilst mother shopped was on the verandah of the Blue Bay Restaurant in the gardens under the watchful eye of a stature of Queen Victoria; here you could have a delicious watery ice-cream in a glass dish. There was a small dark shop like a museum where my father would take me to see two stuffed mermaids – dugongs – which I found horrid but fascinating and this reminds me that the parents had a Hungarian friend in one of the Ma'alla flats called Dr Holub and when we children visited he took out his glass eye and put it into his pink gin. Children remember the more macabre events!

During this tour and again in the '50s Mum sent back to England large parcels of food to Nanny and Grandad and Grandma to help with the rationing. Tins of butter, cheese and bacon, soap powders, cigarettes, sweets, biscuits, dates, coffee and tea were all packed in the large cardboard box which was then sewn into linen and labelled. It was then kicked around the room, with much glee by the children, before being shaken to hear if anything had broken.

School only lasted till lunchtime as we had to be home before the heat of the afternoon but my friend Laura and I spent our out-of-school hours exploring. She lived in what looked like a castle high on a hill in Crater looking down onto Sira, we met up in the afternoons and again during later school holidays before we both left Aden to begin our adult lives. It was a carefree time for us children, we could walk alone to Sira, past the Bottling Plant and climb to the fort. I wonder if the skeleton of a dog still lies in the moat. We rode polo ponies from the Khormaksar Club, sometimes along the beach and even in Sheikh Othman Gardens. On Sundays Laura and I would go to a church service held by Padre MacGuffie at St Marys-on-the Hill in Crater – I don't remember any church music. I have a New Testament given to me on my birthday in 1948 inscribed by Padre & Mrs MacG.

Much of my parent's life revolved around the happenings at the Union Club and what was going on in the harbour. Being one of the busiest ports in the world the volume of shipping passing through was enormous and different vessels could be seen daily from the Club verandah. The highlight for 1947 was Navy week which was held in October when the cruiser *HMS Norfolk* was in port.

Sitting on the outside verandah eating a plate of hot chips with tomato sauce while the parents were inside socialising was a highlight of a weekend. It was also from this viewpoint that I saw ladies arriving from the passengers ships dressed very strangely in the 'New Look'. This extravagant fashion was the creation of Dior and the very full, fairly long skirts with tiny waists looked so different from the clothes of war-time London.

It was at this time that my mother was also busy working for the Fairbridge Society, a name now synonymous with child migration to Australia and sadly child abuse too. Hundreds of children were being sent to Australia supposedly for a new life and as the ships passed through Aden my mother was involved in greeting and looking after the children for the short time that some of them were allowed ashore.

I have briefly mentioned Goldmohur Bathing Club, this place made life in Aden bearable over the next few years. Goldmohur was an anti-shark netted corner of the deserted beach below the lighthouse with a rickety diving board, a barnacle strewn raft, communal showers and dilapidated thatched-covered changing huts around a bar under the Gold Mohur trees, this seemingly unprepossessing place was the most magical and important place in the universe so I need to explain what it meant to me for the next five years that I was in and out of Aden.

Here we came to cool off in the late afternoons and to spend the day on Sundays. This was my father's best day at Goldmohur and started early. Mohamed Ali, our Yemeni cook would have the picnic basket ready by 6am, filled with fried egg sandwiches and flasks of tea and fresh lime juice. After driving through Steamer Point we eventually reached the traffic light, I think it was the only one in Aden at that time, on the narrow one-way viaduct that went down into Elephant Bay and then onto Goldmohur – from the viaduct to Goldmohur there was nothing but sand – no buildings, no people.

When we were newly arrived in the colony dire warnings were issued about the problems of the sun and sunstroke and to start with my mother wisely made me wear a cotton blouse over my swimsuit but even so after my very first day at Goldmohur my shoulders were covered in thick blisters, even through the material.

At the end of 1947 outside events were to impinge on the peaceful childhood life of school and leisure. The partition of Palestine in November caused riots between the Jewish community and the Arabs in Crater. As a child in wartime London I was accustomed to bombing and destruction so the noise of the mobs and the smoke from fires on that December morning did not frighten me but we had to evacuate our house in Crater which was close to Maidan Square and the scene of the riots. We could not leave Crater via the only road through the Main Pass so we travelled in a convoy of cars through a tunnel to Isthmus and on to Ma'alla where we stayed with Cliff and Nora Darton of Cory Bros. until it was safe to return home. I remember my Father saying that explosives were stored in the tunnel. Over the years I have mentioned this tunnel to other ex Aden residents but they said it was a figment of my childish imagination so I was delighted to find, 61 years later, through an internet web site that the tunnel does exist and that indeed it was used as an arsenal.

In 1948 my sister was born in the Civil Hospital, this must have been a long awaited child after the previous miscarriage(s) and here my mother had the help of Fatima, the very superior and handsome Somali ayah.

Because of the inclement climate the tours to Aden lasted only 18months followed by six months leave to 'recuperate', you can imagine the upheaval this caused with packing and unpacking the house, signing off and re-engaging the servants, changing schools and having to find somewhere to live for the time in England. In late summer 1949 our leave was due as well as that of other Civil Servants and for some reason no scheduled ships or aircraft could be found to take us all back to Blighty so the Government chartered a DC3 Dakota to make the long journey home.

On entering the aircraft we were confronted by a pile of life-rafts and jackets behind netting - just in case we came down over the sea, not an encouraging sight. The range of the aircraft, or lack of it meant that we had to make frequent stops for re-fuelling. First was in Luxor, another barren sandy waste, then an overnight stop at the

Heliopolis Palace Hotel in Cairo, a brief stop at Tripoli in Libya followed by an overnight stop in Malta. We all stayed at the Phoenicia Hotel, such luxury for a small child and I was impressed by the headboard of my bed which had switches in it for the bedside light and radio, truly a marvel. It is the bedroom at the Heliopolis Palace that comes to mind when I smell the perfume 'Blue Grass' as Mum used it and when I walked into her room I knew she was there.

The flight continued the next day with a stop at Marseilles which produced two memories, my mother's feet had swollen and she had to walk off the aircraft bare-footed, and my baby sister took a drink from a glass and bit a lump out of it. Onwards to Heathrow or London airport as it was then known. How different from when I was a frequent visitor in my working days. In 1949 it was newly opened and the terminal buildings were then just temporary 'prefab' cabins.

My journey now continued on a branch line as it was time for me to forget about Aden and to return to St Paul's Girls' School in Brook Green, Hammersmith. Because my grandmother knew the High Mistress, Miss Strudwick I did not have to take any entrance exam but my two years in the Convent School in Aden had made me lag behind my peers from Colet school days so I was put into a class below them, although Jessica, Ruth and Rosamund were still in my class, probably due to their ages. Miss Strudwick retired shortly after I started and was replaced by the formidable Miss Osborn, I don't think I ever saw her smile, she was so upright physically and in manner and unreachable too, unlike the later High Mistresses who came after I had left and who seem to have been more like senior girls.

For the brief time that my parents were on leave we stayed with Nanny and Grandad Thatcher in Pentland Street and then when they left I went to live with Grandma B in Putney. When their six months were up Daddy flew back to Aden and Mummy and my sister Mary sailed from Liverpool on 3 March 1950 to return Aden on the *S.S. Salween* of Henderson Lines. This was a very small vessel of 7000 tons and on this voyage carried only 48 passengers most of whom were going to Rangoon.

I continued at school and stayed for a while with the Jackson family in Cheam, Surrey who had a daughter Margaret, also at SPGS in a higher class. but I was not happy there so I moved to Putney and rather liked living with Grandma. She helped me with my homework, of which there was always far too much, and my end of term reports usually said 'could do better', or sometimes 'she has worked well this term'.

Saturdays were a treat. We took the bus to Oxford Street in London for shopping in Selfridges, Grandma had an account there so that is where she bought her clothes, we visited her friend in the book department and then had lunch upstairs in the restaurant. If we weren't 'going to town' then we would walk to Putney High Street and be enticed into Zeeta's restaurant, on the corner of the High Street and Upper Richmond Road, by the unusual -for those times- smell of fresh coffee wafting across the street. Grandma would then go to Boots the chemist where there was a small lending library on the mezzanine floor. For all her poetry books and classics in the bookshelf at her flat her taste in library books was very plebeian! We would come home with at least one book by Georgette Heyer and two or more brown covered Mills and Boon romances. The end papers of these books were covered in columns of pencilled initials from all the previous readers so that they could tell whether or not they had already taken out the book.

On other Saturdays I took myself off to a matinee at a cinema in Putney High Street, either the Regal or Palace. Sometimes I walked to Wandsworth to visit the other grandparents, it seems like a long walk in retrospect but I suppose not for young legs.

In June 1950 relief was at hand! I got back on track and returned to the main line station of Aden for my summer holidays flying by BOAC *Argonaut*. It was certainly a more comfortable journey than on a Dakota but inside the cabin you still felt shaken and stirred. The flights were always fun as each holiday I saw the same children, either my friends from Aden or other children going on to places in East Africa for their own holidays.

The family had moved to another house which was my home for the summer holidays. It was known as Lake House, the old Residency set into a hill at Tarshyne. I think Lake was a corruption of Loch who was the Resident in the 1870s. The buildings rambled along the hillside and were almost completely covered by bougainvilleas and

jasmine. The rooms had wooden lattice doors and windows, good for cooling the rooms but hopeless in a sandstorm. I can smell Imperial Leather soap when I think of this house as Mum had put the soaps and talcum powder in my bathroom for the hols.
Laura was on school holidays too and although still living in Crater we managed to continue where we had left off the previous year, exploring, swimming at Goldmohur, eating chips on the verandah at the Union Club and going to see all the latest films at the open air cinema in Steamer Point called the C.E.S.S.A.I., the Church of England Soldiers', Sailors' and Airmen's Institute. The soundtrack of the film had to compete with noises from the adjacent harbour and the local life going on outside. And when it rained - subject to the blue moon, well you just got wet and thanked heavens for the rain. It was here that I saw *National Velvet*, with Elizabeth Taylor and Mickey Rooney, seven times!

A notable event of this holiday was a flight in a small four seater aircraft to the island of Perim with my father. This is a tiny (5 sq.m) volcanic island in the Straits of Bab-El-Mandeb between the Red Sea and the Indian Ocean so you can appreciate it has strategic importance. There is no natural water and few inhabitants. I can only imagine that my father had to go there to look at the condition of the harbour or the lighthouse. It was an adventure for me and the first of what was to be many flights in small aircraft.

I had an epic journey in September back to England and school at the end of the holiday. I don’t know how I managed to manipulate my parents or indeed how they agreed, but I said I was tired of flying on the boring route straight from Aden to London and wanted to do something different like take the flying boat from Khartoum!! Remember I was only 13. Well I did, I flew from Aden to Khartoum via Asmara on 15 September, then a small bus took me from the airport to the Nile where I boarded almost the last service of flying boats on the Johannesburg to Southampton route. This service ended in November so I was very fortunate to experience this unique mode of travel. The flight had started on the Vaal Dam in Johannesburg and there were stops en route at Alexandria also on the Nile, Augusta in Sicily and then Southampton.

The aircraft was small, it only took 34 passengers in upstairs and downstairs cabins, I was seated downstairs and when take-off occurred the water rushed over and past the downstairs windows. Landing on the water was equally exhilarating. The journey ended with the boat train from Southampton to London and back to school.

I used to have a BOAC Junior Jet Club book which all colonial school children had in those days to record the many flights that were taken back and forth and in recent times (21stC) on social media there is much discussion from 'old' flyers' about their JJC books and how they are being resuscitated and used again to the amusement of contemporary British Airways pilots. My book has disappeared but I can imagine the astonishment if I found it and showed the flying boat entry to the pilot on my next overseas journey.

In 1951 Dad's second tour ended - you see how quickly the end of tour leaves come round, and they all came home on the *Llangibby Castle* of Union Castle Line. They rented a house No. 63 Mortlake Road, Kew, so that we could all be together and for it to be convenient for me to get to school by train. In August Grandad Thatcher died (Mum's father) followed six weeks later by Nanny Thatcher - it was a very sad time for all of us. As there was no-one living in the Pentland Street house, Aunt Dolly had moved in with Aunt Laura, they gave up the Mortlake Road property and moved back to Wandsworth. I think Mum and Dad must have been going through a bad patch as Dad returned to Aden alone.

As a good telephonist Mum was always able to find work, she had been at the Ritz and Stafford hotels and then the Institute of Personnel Management which was located just off Oxford Street. Wherever she worked she joined a theatre club with the other staff and I often went with her to shows. This was the time when it was the done thing to go the stage door after the show and get the celebrities' autographs, a quick flip through my autograph book for 1950/51/52 shows Anton Dolin (ballet dancer), Cherry Lind (singer), Christine Norden (actress), Lex Barker (Tarzan!), Alicia Markova (ballet dancer), Mary Martin (South Pacific musical and the epic hair washing scene), Derek Roy (Buttons in Cinderella) and Charlie Chaplin. On the page of Derek Roy's signature I have written ' Please may I have your autograph I'm cold - EAB'. I presume this was the

Christmas pantomime and I was tired of waiting at the stage door so got the man in charge of the door to take my autograph book inside.

The Festival of Britain took place on the South Bank of the River Thames during the summer of '51 and I visited it several times and went to a lecture in the new concert hall given by Thor Heyerdahl on his Kontiki expedition. The Festival site for that summer was an exciting place to be with the Skylon Tower and the Dome of Discovery. The whole area was to showcase Britain's recovery after the war.

My boring journey of school and homework continued, the only memorable stop being in February 1952 when King George VI died. On the day of his death assembly was called unexpectedly at school in the morning and Miss Osborn told us of this sad news. On the day of the funeral I went to Hyde Park Corner to see the cortege go past, I was squashed between hundreds of people and it was a sad occasion but I am glad I went and it was yet another memory-making event in my life.

When the 1952 summer holidays came round there was no way I was not going back to Aden and after much sulking and bad temper on my part it was agreed that I could go to be with Dad. I had after all worked jolly hard on my 'O' levels and managed to pass Latin, Maths, English, French, Geography, Physics and Chemistry. Mum made me a wardrobe of lovely clothes and I am sure she wished she had been coming with me.

The stop en route in Cairo was dramatic. As we landed the aircraft was surrounded by armed guards who then escorted us to and from the transit lounge - my summer holidays commenced on 26 July, the same day that King Farouk abdicated, the Egyptian Revolution had started on 23 July. Just another memorable event to put in my diary.

The six weeks of the holiday passed very quickly mainly spent - you guessed it - at Goldmohur with old and new friends. Laura was there too, also Anne, Gill and Jocelyn who later became a model in Australia - she had a super figure even then.

In 1952 the Brazilian Naval training ship 'Almirante Saldanha' called into Aden on its round the world voyage and hosted receptions for residents, this was a highlight of my holiday. I checked on the web for the correct spelling of this ship and found that the dates given for the Aden visit were 8th-11th September 1951, but this is incorrect as I have photos to prove it was 1952, it just shows you can't believe everything you read on the computer!

At fifteen it is perhaps not surprising that I was becoming aware of the opposite sex! I met at the beach two young Englishmen, they were 23, Paul worked for B.P. (British Petroleum) and Peter who was with A. Besse & Co, a large transcontinental trading firm. With the sad state of affairs in Aden in the 21stC it is hard to imagine that in the 1940s and '50s Aden was the second busiest trading and bunkering port in the world after London. Besse & Co traded in skins and coffee from the Yemen and had fingers in just about all the commercial enterprises in the colony as well as across the Red Sea in Ethiopia. The founder of the company, Antonin Besse was a philanthropist and in1950 he gave the University of Oxford £1,500,000 to found St. Anthony's College which retains a focus on Middle Eastern studies.

Because there were always two of them my father didn't seem to mind me going out with Peter and Paul, not just to Goldmohur but to the cinema and excursions to Sheikh Othman and Lahej. You will hear more of Paul and Peter later as this was not just a passing teenage fancy! In fact Peter wrote me long letters every week from when I returned to London in '52 right through '53.This was marvellous as it kept me in touch with Aden and my friends.

School and living in Pentland Street continued through the rest of '52 and '53.I was really enjoying St. Paul's, I had a good friend Sylvia, who is still my friend six decades later and I liked the freedom that being a senior entailed.

Let's pop off onto a siding for a while to talk about St. Paul's. I realise I was extremely fortunate in being able to go to St. Paul's Girls' School. It was a private school with expensive fees which were paid for by the Colonial Government as Daddy was a colonial officer and it was not deemed suitable for children like me to attend a local school for higher education. It isn't an old school, having been endowed by the Worshipful Company of Mercers and opened in 1904, the boy's school, also St Paul's was founded in 1509 by John Colet - hence the origin of the name of the junior part of SPGS that I attended. The class sizes were small and so tuition became very personal with an emphasis on academic excellence. There was a strong musical influence given that Gustav Holst (the St. Paul's Suite) and Herbert Howells had both been music masters here. My piano lessons had only lasted for a term when I persuaded my parents that they were a waste of money and instead took elocution with Miss Ellam - much more fun and no practice involved.

The Science block was a favourite place especially the Chemistry lab with the lovely Miss Hurley and Physics with Miss Craze who really did have a hint of craziness about her. In the summer sports were cricket and tennis, I wasn't much good at either, and in the winter netball and lacrosse. The latter was played rather than hockey as hockey apparently gave you a bad posture, I also failed at these games but I did enjoy bowling in cricket whilst Sylvia was batting.

Apart from the cost of the fees there was the cost of stationary and uniforms which had to be paid by parents. For each subject there was a different coloured exercise book and notebook of the best quality and these had to be purchased from the school stationary office, you couldn't get cheap substitutes from W.H. Smith.

Clothing was fairly flexible. There was a regulation overcoat which had to be worn going to and from school, a choice of two styles in navy blue, a belted trench coat and a more fashionable flared style worn with a navy felt hat with the school band. In summer the panama boater called a 'basher' (why?) had the same band. Indoors you could wear your own clothes or a gym slip with a blue and white striped blouse underneath. Games' wear was compulsory, in summer and for gym a ghastly beige linen tunic appropriately called a sack and for winter games you needed the gym slip and blouse. All these items as well as outdoor shoes, indoor shoes, games shoes and gym shoes had to be purchased from the school's uniform shop Daniel Neals in Kensington High Street.

If you did well at games or gym this was rewarded by the presentation of a white girdle which was worn on the sack or gym slip, a narrow one for the lower senior classes and a thicker one for the more senior girls. The everyone's amazement, mine included, I was given a narrow girdle!!!! I haven't told you previously but just before we left Aden in '49 I fell at school and broke my arm at the elbow, it was not set properly by Dr. Goodman with the result that my arm remains to this day slightly bent and I am unable to straighten it or hold anything heavy with it. Although I was useless at games I did try to do my best in gym but with a wonky arm I couldn't do handstands, vault over the horse or hang from ropes - but apparently I tried hard, hence the girdle. Bless Miss Haydock the games mistress, known as - you guessed - Miss Haddock.

The Coronation of Elizabeth II took place in June 1953, I had wanted to go to town to be part of the crowds but to get a decent viewing place I would have had to go the night before and camp out which wasn't acceptable and also Mum decided to buy a television so that we could watch the proceedings in comfort. The set with its bulbous screen was tiny by modern standards, only about 10 sq. ins. and in front of it on a cumbersome stand was placed a magnifying screen. It was almost impossible to see a good picture unless you sat right in front of the TV as from the side the picture was distorted. And so the TV entered our house forever, and many other houses too. In those early days the only thing that seemed to appear was the test card by which you adjusted the aerial and a goldfish in a bowl which filled the intervals between programmes.

The dreaded A level exams were approaching in '54 and the need to prepare for University, in those days there was no such thing as a gap year and certainly at St. Paul's there was never any question of what you were going to do when school ended - you went to University and had your name inscribed in gold lettering on panels above the High Mistress's office door.

I was studying Chemistry, Botany and Geography and was assured of a place at Imperial College, University of London to read Geology. With only three subjects the pace of life at school was quite relaxed, I could come and go as I pleased as long as classes were attended, experiments experimented and homework assignments handed in on time. The days of the coloured exercise and note books was long gone, now it was files and piles of paper. Sylvia had left school already so my friend was now Patricia who went on to become a Professor of Mathematics. I was invited to Patricia's 17th birthday party, she lived in a very luxurious block of flats near Hyde Park with her parents. Mum had made me a pale yellow linen summer dress with a tight sleeveless bodice and very full skirt worn over a frilly petticoat, I really did look lovely - yes I did. But when I reached the party I realised that Patricia had passed from being sweet seventeen into being a proper young lady. She was wearing a 'little black dress', very slim and simple which set off her ash blonde hair and with lovely pearl earrings and necklace, I felt very gauche to her sophistication. Wise words from Mum afterwards made me feel better - 'she was dressing too old for her age'. Patricia and I met for lunch fifty years later and she was still slim, blonde and sophisticated!

Whilst all this was transpiring Dad flew home on yet another leave and whatever their differences they must have patched them up as they planned to return to Aden together early in 1954. All this was too much for me so I decided that I just had to go back with them and continue my studies in Aden. My teachers prepared lengthy schedules of all the subjects still to be studied in the curriculum and Daddy promised to find a lab where I could do my chemistry experiments. Did I really think at the time that all this was going to happen? I must have, as going to University was my priority or was there just a part of me that was drawn to the thought Goldmohur, parties, no studying and the possibility of seeing Peter again.

On 26 February, aged 17, I embarked in London with mother, father and 6year old sister on *SS Kenya* on what was to be a voyage that determined my future in so many ways.

SS Kenya of British India Line. What a change from the *Empire Ken.* She was about 14,000 tons and had the capacity for 167 first class and 133 tourist class passengers on the East African route from London to Beira. On this voyage there were 162 first class, including we four Berrymans, and 77 tourist class, all but three being British citizens. The ports of call included Malta followed by Port Said (for two of the 'aliens') and then to Port Sudan for the Sudan, Aden where the Berrymans were the only passengers to disembark, Mombasa for Kenya, Dar-es-Salaam for Tanganyika and Beira for those going on to Northern and Southern Rhodesia. It is interesting to look at the occupations of the passengers bearing in mind that 99% had probably had their fares paid either by the Crown Agents or a commercial company and were going to work in a British Overseas territory. There were 58 housewives travelling unaccompanied with their children obviously going out to join their husbands, including one lady who gave her occupation as 'home duties'.

These passengers on the *S.S. Kenya* were going out to be part of the administration or to contribute in other capacities to the advancement of the overseas territories. The eclectic mixture of occupations found on the passenger list included:
Factory Manager/motor assessor/Civil Servant/accountant/Civil Engineer /farmer/nurse/secretary/engineer/planter/horticulturalist/ Co.Director/telecom engineer/motor mechanic/animal trainer/corn merchant/lecturer/police officer/ banker/ solicitor/ architect/ priest/kiosk attendant /professor /trainer/ clerk/ photographer fitter/ BBC announcer/medical officer/merchant/tailoress.

If you take these occupations as a whole I guess you have the requirements for any town. I did wonder about the lady kiosk attendant who went to Dar-es-Salaam, was she working in a cinema there, and the animal trainer who went to Kenya, was he going to a game farm? The BBC announcer disembarked in Port Said so maybe he was there for the BBC Overseas Service.

First class travel in those days would equate with a similar class of travel on the small up-market cruise ships of the 21stC. One 'dressed' for dinner every evening apart from the evening of shore visits, and the style of dress was determined by the weather. In the early days through the Straits of Gibraltar and on to Malta the men wore black dinner suits, after Malta when it became warmer white dinner jackets were de rigueur. If you weren't sure just when the changeover was to occur then you watched the officers and the furniture as not only did the officers change from winter uniform into summer whites as we neared Port Said but the chairs covers on the furniture were changed too from dark to summery chintz.

Days were spent playing deck games or in the small swimming pool and the evenings were for dancing. It is here that I introduce you to my first and for that reason very special adult, though innocent, love. You know about Peter but remember that we met when I was 15 and we had only corresponded since then.

Colin Duncan was a dashingly handsome young man of 24, he was from New Zealand but he had been working at Kew Gardens for over a year and was being seconded for two years to the Zeidab cotton plantations in the Sudan. I was almost the only young girl on board, a situation I became used to in Aden, so we spent all the days and evenings together. I have said 'almost' the only girl, there was another called Rosemary, who was a secretary going to Kenya and the same age as Colin, she set her sights on him but I soon saw her off! The last waltz of every evening was to the song 'Goodnight Irene', I made sure that I was in Colin's arms and no-one else.

Our first stop was in Malta where we were able to do some sightseeing and then we all, with Colin, had tea at the Phoenicia Hotel, quite unchanged since our visit in '49. On to Port Said, the bum boats were still there trading their wares, Mum purchased a camel stool, and we all went to shop in that well known emporium, Simon Artz. This Art Deco four storey building stood along the quayside with its name emblazoned in large letters on the roof line, it was quite unmissable and a magnet for all visitors and shoppers. Coming from England where rationing had not long ended it was a wonderland of everything you could possibly require from the mundane to the exotic. I visited Simon Artz again in the '80s and it was sadly dilapidated with hardly anything worth buying, with the Canal closed the only visitors then to Port Said were those taking Mediterranean cruises.

Travelling through the Suez Canal was an unforgettable experience, it seemed far too narrow for the size of the ship, but glide through we did with camels pacing us on the eastern side and trucks and cars on the west. It was one way traffic between Port Said and Suez so ships passed through in convoy, the transit taking I think about 15 hours.

All too soon the almost three week voyage was coming to an end and I paid a disconsolate farewell to Colin who had to leave the ship at Port Sudan for his journey into the interior. We each promised to write frequently, which we did and to try to meet soon somewhere, somehow, which we did - but that comes later.

Before the ship reaches Aden let's take a 'non sequitur' break and pop off into a siding and discuss clothes!

My mother Alice Berryman was a superb seamstress and tailoress, she was taught by her Granny who had been a Court dressmaker, her hand stitching was almost invisible and inside had to be as neat as outside. One year I turned up at Waterloo Station after a long journey back from Africa wearing a tartan wool suit that I had made and the first thing Mum did was to look inside the jacket and turn up the skirt hem, she was a perfectionist. I was always the best dressed child and then the best dressed teenager in Aden.

She made all my clothes and those of my sister too. The pink silk party dress when I was eight was succeeded by many more party dresses. In 1950 there was my first long dress in white silk with a blue satin sash, this was for the first ever Aden Dinner Reunion held in London at the Rembrandt Hotel, I was the only 'just' a teenager then. For some reason Mum didn’t make her own gown for this but she bought an absolutely hideous 'Carmen Miranda' like creation. She always maintained it was the height of fashion.

Gill and I had long blue broderie anglaise dresses for a party when we were thirteen in slightly different shades; there was a dress in white linen with flowers embroidered by Mum also when I was thirteen and then adult dresses for the later holidays in Aden. It is fortunate that a selection of beautiful materials was available in Bhicajee or Cowasjee Dinshaw, many of the silks and more exotic fabrics came from India and the East. For whatever function I was attending I only had to ask for a new outfit and for the 1952 holiday she made me a completely new wardrobe. One of the items was a two piece bathing costume to match a beach coat in a printed towelling - have you ever gone into the sea in a towelling costume? It becomes waterlogged with sad consequences! When I was going to get married in Aden Mum was really fired up with ideas for the wedding gown and trousseau but it was another 12 years before she actually made my wedding outfit, a blue lace dress over a silk shift.

My photo albums show the many gorgeous clothes that she made for me and it is to my eternal regret that I never told her just how much I loved and appreciated every single thing that she made for me. Instead I was always overjoyed when I had a ready-made outfit. There was the red cotton dress that came from a Sears Roebuck catalogue - Mum worked at the American Embassy in the early fifties and so could order from the USA via the Diplomatic Bag, the dress was very inferior cotton and didn’t last long. As an aside from clothes, when Mum was at the American Embassy she would bring home a large glass flagon with the syrup of Coca Cola, which was then diluted with soda water to make the Coca Cola as we know it - delicious. Then I bought myself, with pocket money, a blue and white striped dress in Richard Shops in Putney for the '52 holiday, I loved it but I can see from the photos that it was very shapeless. On my short trip to London in '55, you'll hear more of this later, I did make some good purchases. A lime green linen with a black patent belt, a pale pink and blue Linzi dress with an off the shoulder neckline and flounced skirt (always associated with Colin) and a Susan Small white silk cocktail dress which cost the unbelievable amount of 14 guineas. At least Mum approved of these purchases but it must have hurt her that I felt the need to buy when she could make. How cruel we can sometimes be without meaning it.

Back to the mainline station - our arrival in Aden, and we went to our new home which was one of the newly built houses in Khormaksar; two lines of houses surrounded by nothing and facing the sea – we were No.11, Downing Street. It was a large square white box, the rooms were high, large and airy. One problem was the water supply. Water was piped over ground from Sheikh Othman which meant when it reached the house it was hot, so in order to have a cool bath the water had to be run into the bath hours before it was required. This was our first house with a garage and during an early driving lesson I drove straight into the back of it.

Khormaksar was becoming built up. The salt pans were still in use, the airfield and related buildings were expanding as was the adjacent RAF base and there was a Causeway built linking Aden with Little Aden and the new BP oil refinery which opened in July 1954 shortly after we arrived. When the BP personnel were eventually housed we were invited to visit their club house; it was air conditioned and very modern compared with the Union Club and Goldmohur. The flare from the refinery became a landmark rather spoiling the until then untouched outline of the jagged rocks of Little Aden and from the beach at Goldmohur we could watch the oil tankers passing into the harbour, one of 80,000 tons stays in my memory as being the largest then seen in Aden! I suppose that nowadays the 250,000 ton tankers go to and fro' through Aden.

To start with studying was relegated to 'tomorrow' until one day my father issued an ultimatum, he was tired of my lifestyle, I couldn’t go on living on hand-outs so I either went back to England to re-sit the final year prior to University or got a job. I was horrified. I had been under the mistaken impression that I could continue my sybaritic way of life unchallenged and would get down to studying one day and after all my father could afford to keep me; this was a rude awakening for a seventeen year old.

I said I was staying so Daddy found me a temporary position as a clerk on £14 per month, in the Aden Municipality Office, filing and using a strange contraption for copying. Prior to photo copiers if you wanted a have lots of copies of letters you either put carbon paper between sheets on the typewriter or you cut a stencil. This entailed typing the stencil on the typewriter (I was an untrained two finger typist), if you made a mistake then the error was dabbed from a bottle of red correction fluid and typed over. My stencils always resembled a virulent attack of chicken pox. The finished stencil was then attached to the drum of the copying machine, flattened out and by turning a handle the copies then appeared. This boring exercise actually proved useful training for when I worked at Lusaka airport and had to type the passenger manifests before each flight departed. My only claim to fame in the Municipality Office was drawing a dhow on a stencil which was then used as the cover for minutes of meetings. This job was not for me, I lasted a month.

At the bar at Goldmohur one Sunday I was waiting for service - lime juice, nothing stronger, and the gentleman next to me, a friend of my father asked if I would like to work for him. He was General Manager of Aden Airways and the ticket office in the Crescent Hotel Annexe needed a junior booking clerk willing to learn on the job and I would also be sent overseas to train. I started immediately, £17 (EAS350) per month, and that was the beginning of 48 years in the travel industry before I at last went to University!

And so began what was a supremely happy and well-ordered part of my life, a social whirl interspersed with a new and fulfilling occupation. Whilst the older generation were sipping their pink gins at the Union Club in Steamer Point the young singles and couples from BP Bunkering, Luke Thomas, Besse & Co., Government offices and the American Consulate had a busy social scene centred on the Crescent Hotel and Goldmohur.

We hadn't been long in Aden when the Queen came to visit! She was on a tour of Commonwealth countries on the *Royal Yacht*

Britannia following her accession to the throne and whilst in the colony she laid the foundation stone of the new Queen Elizabeth II hospital, my 6 year old sister Mary and her friend Pamela had the honour of presenting her with a bouquet. The Queen was in a pretty green and white cotton dress with a white hat.

Dances to recorded music were held on Thursday evenings on the open roof terrace of the Crescent Hotel, it was a weekly 'must attend' social event and tables had to be reserved well in advance. The girls wore their prettiest dresses and the men looked dashing in 'Red Sea Kit'. In the hot months this consisted of white trousers, white short sleeved shirt with or without a bow tie and a black cummerbund. In the cooler months a black dinner suit could be worn or black trousers with a white 'sharkskin' jacket made by a tailor in the bazaar. Sunday evenings on the roof were devoted to classical music concerts again from records and this was a relaxing way to recover from the sun after a hectic day on the beach.

The day on Sunday was always spent at Goldmohur, it was the daytime social hub of the Colony. Gradually friends would arrive and we all had own favourite places to sit and would spend the day in and out of the water- playing own version of water polo if the tide was in or just cooling in the shallows if the tide was out. You had to be careful around the raft and diving board because if you were cut by the barnacles the wounds took ages to heal in the humid atmosphere. We could walk up to the lighthouse above the beach and gaze down onto a deserted Conquest Bay which was always known as a 'no swimming' area because of the heavy surf and threat of sharks. Elephant Bay was just along the beach from Goldmohur and because of how the rocky elephant's trunk was formed the water was always rough, with good waves, unlike Goldmohur where the water was always calm. I had been forbidden to bathe at Elephant Bay as there were no shark nets but I never confessed to my parents that on occasions some of us did go into the waves for fun.

A good Sunday at Goldmohur meant you returned home exhausted, sunburnt and sandy; ready for the Crescent Hotel concert in the evening.

There were other safe beaches for swimming – Cable and Wireless employees had their own pool in Telegraph Bay, the shark-proofing was done with concrete pillars, and the Port Trust had a small shark-netted beach at Ras Morbut but neither of these had the social cachet of Goldmohur. The emphasis was always on safe bathing – the wife of an RAF officer was taken by a shark whilst swimming in shallow water outside the nets at the RAF beach in Telegraph Bay.

I realise I have hardly mentioned the RAF. It is strange that the Forces and Civil ex-patriate communities led such separate lives. My only contact with the RAF came when I was asked in 1955 to do a live Desert Island Discs programme for their radio station. The excerpts of music I chose were very mundane and probably reflected more my father's taste as it was he who played the records at home. *Morning by Grieg, Birth of the Blues, American Patrol, Blue Moon, Victory at Sea, Lohengrin, Pathetique Sonata, Messiah.*

One Sunday morning a group of us decided to climb Sham-Sham from Crater and go down the other side into Goldmohur! There was a vague pathway from the Tanks to just below the summit where I turned round and went back the same way – I can't remember if anyone went down the other side – John, Paul, Maurice, Kay, Carmen – if you read this let me know if you made it.

Because I worked shifts for Aden Airways (8 till 1 or 12 to 5) I was able to gad around during the day especially with the BP Bunkering chaps when they visited the ships that were in port. This was a special treat, there was usually an on board shop and if I was lucky a superb lunch or dinner. Some ships were more in favour than others: I gave up on P & O and Union Castle as they had little to offer, but the Italian Line Lloyd Triestino and the French *Pasteur* were my favourites. Lloyd Triestino vessels were always coming and going, the *Africa* and *Europa* did the eastern and southern Africa run and the *Asia* & *Victoria* went to the east and Australia.

The Port of Aden is called one of the five best natural harbours in the world and in the days of the Suez Canal before it was closed in 1967 (it has since re-opened) it was strategically placed between east and west and apart from the ships that travelled via the Cape of Good Hope all shipping came through Aden, which was also a tax free port. Passengers streamed off the ships into the shops and gold and silver bazaars of Steamer Point. For us Aden residents we got to know all the shipping lines and ships. The alliteration names of P & O carried the £10 Poms to Australia in their white hulled ships - *Orion, Oriana, Orcades, Oronsay, Orsova* and the *Himalaya, Chusan, Arcadia, Iberia.* Union Castle had several vessels on the Round Africa service which called at Aden, including the *Braemar* and *Rhodesia Castles.* Add to these ships all the cargo vessels and oil tankers and it is easy to accept that the numbers of vessels calling at Aden in 1955 is given as 5239 which in that year made it the second busiest harbour in the world after New York.

Lying on the beach at Goldmohur and watching the ships pass into the harbour was rather like watching buses going by, they were so frequent and as far as I was concerned if it looked like an interesting ship, good for shops and food then I would contact one of the BP chaps and ask for a ride on their boat when they went out to organise the bunkering. On one such occasion I was wearing a brand new dress Mum had made, white linen with blue spotted collars and cuffs and as we neared the ship a fine spray of oil came forth and my lovely dress ended up spotted all over with oil.

When I wasn't at Goldmohur or otherwise enjoying myself I was working, it was all rather mundane to start with. My superiors were Betty Hudson for a short while, she was then followed by the elegant and glamorous Joan Goldsmith and then by Rita Witham. The office was on a corner of the Crescent Hotel Annexe and it was large and airy – not air-conditioned, and adjacent to the Italian hairdresser so we saw the latest in 'before and after' styles passing by. The uniform for ground staff was a white linen skirt and white blouse with epaulettes, I managed to avoid wearing the navy blue cap.

When she left to return to South Africa Joan passed on to me two of her pretty strapless cocktail dresses with matching stoles, they were quite sophisticated and again I loved wearing them as a change from my 'homemades'. Ungrateful teenager that I was.

The travel industry in current times is so different from when I started, now everything it automated, press a button and fares are calculated, flights booked, and Mr Google will tell you all you want to know and you don't even need a ticket to travel. I feel the travel clerks today are just computer operators not needing any specialised knowledge.

My introduction to airline work consisted of filing large quantities of amendments to B.O.A.C. manuals. These pages came in on the scheduled flights usually in thick bundles and as each new page was inserted the page it replaced was discarded and a note made on a covering sheet of the reference number of both the page inserted and discarded and I also had to count the ticket stocks at the start and end of each shift: large bundles of two and four coupon tickets and Miscellaneous Charges Orders which were kept in the safe. Eventually I was allowed to make bookings via the telephone to Space Control at the Crater Office and progressed to looking after clients who called by, usually to confirm or 'horrors' to amend, the itinerary of their onward journey. Today's travel clerks with their computerised booking systems have missed the joys of computing the fare for a journey 'by hand'. A B.O.A.C. manual gave fares for worldwide journeys with the mileage allowed for that fare so for non-straightforward itineraries the mileage for each section of the journey to be travelled – and that included the transit stops of the aircraft – had to be totalled and the appropriate fare, with percentage increases charged. The ticket for the remainder of the journey had then to be completely re-issued which could mean another four or five tickets to cover a long journey. There was no room for error, if you made a mistake by charging an incorrect additional amount or not charging at all then months later a invoice could come from the IATA Billing and Settlement Plan and of course your passenger had long gone. At the end of each month a report was made to IATA BSP of all the tickets used and payments received, this same system I believe continues to this day with airlines worldwide although it is settled daily and computerised.

With Aden as a transit stop between north, south, east and west, and the Crescent the only hotel, I was kept pretty busy adding up the miles – with no calculator. This method of calculating fares continued into the 1970s.

Very occasionally I was called to fill in at the last moment as a flight attendant and my first such flight stays in my memory. From the office I went straight to Khormaksar collecting a passport and toothbrush en route and was hustled onto a DC3 bound for Assab and Addis Ababa. The flight bag was thrust at me, the doors shut and with no training I had to make do as best I could, I even had to ask the Captain how to switch on the water heater to make tea. When we landed at Assab I handed over the flight bag with all the ship's papers and forgot to collect it before we took off so when we landed in Addis there was a terrible palaver. The stop in Addis was the first time I had stayed on my own in a huge hotel, it felt quite scary even for an international traveller like me. Then on my return to Khormaksar the following day when the aircraft door was opened, the lady in charge of cabin crew reprimanded me for having a dirty uniform as I was in my office 'whites' and had no flying 'khakis' Nevertheless I was occasionally asked to do other flights.

Later in 1955 the office moved from the hotel annexe into the main entrance of the hotel and I was then able to run the office on my shift on my own. It was a great place to be as I saw all the comings and goings of the hotel rather than just the hairdresser's clients!

To extend my knowledge of booking procedures Aden Airways sent me on a familiarisation course in February 1955 with visits to the B.O.A.C. and B.E.A. offices in Cairo, London and Khartoum. I had two weeks in London and worked both in the B.O.A.C. Regent Street ticket office and at the huge reservations hall near Heathrow which charted all the flight bookings for all the fights worldwide, the systems were all far removed from our small operation in Aden and looking back it is extraordinary to see how a worldwide airline ran itself in pre-computer days.

Decades later I was approached by Dacre Watson who was writing a history of Aden Airways, my memories appear in his splendidly illustrated book *Red Sea Caravan* published in 2008.

My journey was now on unreliable tracks and the destination ahead looked uncertain as I took on board love and romance.

After almost two years there were no more letters from Peter and with his posting to Besse & Co. in Assab he became engaged to a girl that he met there. Paul, Peter's and my friend from two years previously had married Kay and they were living in Aden, he was still with BP. I was part of the singles and young-marrieds set although I was the only young, single female. I spent a lot of time in the BP Mess mainly not to miss out on trips to the ships when they were bunkering, and with the diplomatic crowd there was always a party being arranged, dancing on the Crescent Hotel roof or an excursion planned to Sheikh Othman or beach and dune riding in Land Rovers.

On the February trip to London I had spent four days in Cairo at the beginning of the month and quite extraordinarily Colin drove all the way from Zeidab in the Sudan to see me. We were able to catch up on the year since we had parted at Port Sudan and to make plans for the future. The stay in Khartoum on the way back was only a day and a half but again Colin drove down to see me. We stayed at the Grand Hotel where there was a cocktail party on the first evening given by the local B.O.A.C office, we both attended and my new and pretty pink and blue Linzi dress had its first outing, together with a pair of pink shoes with a small heel which caused me to make an entrance down the garden steps - I tripped and fell - caught by dear Colin. We managed an excursion to the meeting point of the Blue and White Niles, not very noteworthy geographically but memory making for the two of us. This special time of what I consider my first adult romance had to end as I returned to Aden.

I never again saw Colin. I can only explain that what followed was due to absence not making the heart grow fonder but extinguishing a small flame. If we had not been separated by the Red Sea and had been able to reinforce our bonds with frequent meetings how different life might have been for both of us.

In the meantime Peter returned to Aden for a couple of weeks work at Head Office before going home on leave, he was now 'dis-engaged', we met, we both were lonely so a whirlwind romance ensued during which we became engaged, with my parents' permission - I think they were glad to have me off their hands. My mother threw herself into dressmaking for the forthcoming wedding and preparing a trousseau for when I returned to Assab with Peter. Laura came out for her final school holidays in the summer of '55 before starting a career in nursing, her family were still living in Crater and there she met up with Don, a radio engineer who worked for one of the commercial companies. He was twelve years older than us, a quiet, almost taciturn man but very good looking and he could be charming. Partying, dancing and socialising were just not his thing so as a result I saw little of Laura and she saw a lot of Don although we did go out occasionally together, Peter and me, Laura and Don.

I rather liked one of the stories going around Aden at the time. Apparently I had just met this man at Khormaksar airport and got engaged to him there and then - they didn't realise Peter and I had been friends and corresponded for two years. So when I did say farewell to him at the airport I had a diamond ring to announce my status and a gold watch.

It was 22 years before I saw Peter again.

. Laura's parents must have realised how madly in love she was with Don as they made her return to England early to get ready for her nursing training and as she was leaving she said 'look after Don for me'. And I did. We were both lonely, I liked his quietness and intensity and my parents thoroughly disapproved of him which of course made him even more attractive. I was forbidden to see him but we managed to meet and I had that gut wrenching, heart stopping feeling whenever we were apart. He left Aden in September, I followed and we got married in Scotland.......it was 45 years before I saw Laura again.

Farewell Aden

That is the land of lost content
I see it shining plain
The happy highways where I went
And cannot come again A.E. Housman

CHAPTER 4
Branch line to Scotland; main line station Northern Rhodesia.

'Marriage is an adventure, like going to war'.
Gilbert K. Chesterton

Scotland in winter is cold, especially in Elgin where Don and I were married with a couple of passers-by as witnesses. Married life continued in Edinburgh with the birth of a daughter Susan and for a few months the life of a suburban housewife with neighbourly friends and an elderly blue roan Cocker Spaniel called Flash who came from a dogs' home. Without parental guidance I seemed to manage the motherhood thing reasonably well. I even caught up with an old SPGS school friend Rosamund who was at University in Edinburgh. Don's work then took him north and we went to live in a cottage in Milltimber just outside Aberdeen.

Here there were no neighbours apart from an old lady in the house opposite so it was very lonely. This lady was a follower of Gaylord Hauser's way of eating and her bible was his book *'Look Younger, Live Longer'*. This was very avant garde in the '50s, a low sugar and low fat diet with little processed foods and she introduced me to natural yogurt which I thought was the strangest thing, it was a good few decades before yogurt became fashionable.

The village Post Office was nearby and I would push the pram there to collect the weekly child allowance.

In the winter of '56 Mum and Mary left Aden for the final time by air and came to spend some weeks with us in Milltimber before Daddy flew home too, they didn't last long because of the cold but whilst there Mum enjoyed the shops in Aberdeen and got stuck into her knitting, for herself a mustard yellow Aran cardigan from those days is still in the family and she made Susan a cosy blue knitted duffle coat with hood which made her look more like a boy than a girl as she was so chubby.

In a rather sad ending to my parent's time in Aden a hold in the ship bringing all their possessions home caught fire in the Red

Sea, and this was extinguished with sea water. All the water-logged goods were eventually off-loaded onto the cargo dockside at Southampton and the parents had to go to see what survived.

Mum always said if she hadn't been so greedy and bought so much the disaster might not have happened. Most of the china had been broken, dress and furnishing materials useless, books ruined, bone handles of cutlery discoloured from water or just separated from the knives and forks. It must have been a cruel homecoming for what was to be the start of another part of their lives.

During this winter Don was away at sea for much of the time, he was trying to sell echo-sounders to the Aberdeen fisherman as a way of improving their catches. It was the cold and the general bleakness of life in Scotland that turned our faces towards warmer climes and the final straw was when Flash was run over and killed one night. Don answered an advertisement in the paper for a radio officer with the Northern Rhodesian Police and almost at once he flew off. Susan and I went back to London to wait for all the documentation to be finalised for our journey to Africa.

In June '57 I received many letters from Don in Lusaka, where he was stationed which gave me an idea of my future home. He was concerned with me *'being firm'* when I spoke to Crown Agents about our passage out and *'not to be hasty'* - did he know me so well even I those early days! Much advice followed:

'you will love this place, it is wonderful, a thousand times better than Aden..'

'pack 4 crates and your personal cases and trunk..'

'clothes, linen crockery, Su's dolls and pram, you will require Cornish Ware vegetable tureens (why Cornish Ware??) *kitchen gear... all the glasses you can get'.*

'Su will need plenty of rompers and rather these than dresses, women are wearing summer dresses but you will require some cardigans and if you are shopping get yourself a good summer weight costume not tweed but something like my safari suit material, but make sure it is a good one'.

'bring material for curtains and cushions'.

'get your hair cut Aden style when you get to London'.

'St. Bruno tobacco is 1/7 an ounce compared with UK price of 4/5, I am spending very little money -£1 weekly should be enough for me'.

'I am still almost on the waggon , I am looking forward to home cooking though'.

'I'm glad you had your hair cut'.

'my pay works out at £88.5.3(per month*) less £4 for East African Widows and Orphans Fund. I shall have to repay the loan of £65 for a second-hand refrigerator this can't be much because it is over 3 years old'.*

'we should be able to manage quite comfortably if we stick to a cash basis and leave credit shopping severely alone'.

'spent most of the day flying in the Auster, I am thinking qualifying as a pilot with Government assistance'. (it didn't happen)

'if I may make a suggestion make yourself some cotton skirts with regard to shoes and sandals not the open type as they would make your feet dusty too quickly since there is an awful lot of sand and dust on the roads'.

'regarding a motor car ...it is possible to get an old runabout for about £100'.

'the house in the Police Camp is still on, it is quite large and has a nice lawn don't forget we shall have to provide carpets and rugs. The cushions by the way are the same used in Aden. Don't bring any curtain or cushion material as you have to pay duty on it'.

'I feel terribly homesick for you and Susan you know, I love you Ann - a million times over. I know what you mean about having nobody to talk to and relax with'.

The Crown Agents by the way were just that, agents for the government both in England and overseas and it is they who contracted civil servants for colonial territories, arranged sea and air passages for people and for freight and were generally the point of contact between the serving officer in the colonies and 'home'. Eventually the documents for our sea journey arrived and it was time to pack and say goodbyes.

Because I had been so spoilt in Aden with the beautiful clothes that Mum made me I really wanted to have a new wardrobe for my new life in Africa - the summery beach and party clothes of my teenage years did not seem appropriate to me as a married woman (albeit only just out of my teens). My mother was not well at this time so unable to make clothes so I had a go myself and made a couple of passable outfits including a rather good cheong-sam style dress in a turquoise Chinese embroidered silk, I was very proud of it and it came in useful for partying on the voyage south.

Susan and I departed from London docks on 5 July 1957 on the *Braemar Castle* of the Union Castle Lines. This vessel was 17,000 tons and had the capacity for 453 passengers in one class called Cabin Class, on this voyage we were 416, so not quite to capacity. The benefit of being one class was that the facilities of the ship were available to all but I must confess to be a first class passenger at heart. The Mail ships which sailed every Thursday from Southampton to Cape Town had both First and Second class, I was able to experience First later on in my journeys. All the Union Castle vessels had a distinctive livery of lavender coloured hull, white superstructure and a red funnel topped with a black band.

The itinerary for the *Braemar Castle* was London, Las Palmas, Ascension, St Helena, Cape Town (where Susan and I disembarked) Port Elizabeth, East London, Durban, Lourenco Marques, Beira, Dar es Salaam, Zanzibar, Tanga, Mombasa, Aden, Port Sudan, Suez, Port Said, Genoa, Marseilles, Gibraltar, London. At this time Union Castle had three vessels doing this Round Africa route with ports of call which catered for all the African colonies and territories. The passenger list for this voyage shows British Commonwealth citizens leaving the ship for Northern and Southern Rhodesia, Nyasaland, Tanganyika, Kenya and Uganda. There were four so-called alien passengers staying in South Africa, they were actually from Denmark and USA. The spread of occupations is very similar to those on the *SS Kenya* in 1954, all the sort of people you need to run and maintain a country together with housewives and children.

We had a 'bibby' cabin, if you have travelled on Union Castle you will know what I mean. Remember this was a one class ship but there were subtle differences in the three types of cabin. Inside cabins with no porthole, an outside cabin with private shower and toilet and the outside bibby with shared facilities. This was a small cabin with an upper and lower berth and then a short passageway which led to the porthole beneath which was the wash basin. The outside and two bibbys formed a group with the outside in the middle hugged by the passage of the bibby on each side and the main part of each bibby formed a small entrance to the three cabins.

A lot of partying went on in the evenings and I became part of a group of twentyish year olds and with some of the ship's officers. Susan was a good sleeper thank heavens so there was no worry about leaving her in the cabin in the evenings.

The only memorable ports of call were at Ascension Island and St. Helena. Ascension really is in the middle of nowhere in the South Atlantic midway between Brazil and Africa, it is volcanic with little vegetation. When we stopped there is was impossible to go ashore as the whole island was a prohibited area and the United Stated Air Force were building an airfield. The runway was once the longest in the world designed to accommodate the Space Shuttle and the European Space Agency now monitors rocket launches from here. The RAF returned later to Ascension and it provided a much needed refuelling stop during the Falklands War of the '80s. The island has become of strategic importance but in 1957 it was barren and there was no reason to even want to go ashore.

Seven hundred kilometres further south is the volcanic tropical island of St. Helena and I knew that it had been the place of exile of Napoleon and had a famous old tortoise called Jonathon. So

Susan and I had to take part in an excursion. It was a cold, wet and windy day but the bus left Jamestown and climbed steeply towards Longwood, the house where Napoleon had died and which was full of artefacts about his life. He died here and had been buried near the house, but the empty grave is there for you to see as his body was taken back to France. Jonathan the tortoise was wandering the grounds, aged about 120, he is still going strong into the 21stC. Although this had been a lovely day ashore the weather had been really bad and I succumbed to flu for the rest of the journey to Cape Town.

On arrival in Cape Town the representative for the Crown Agents came aboard to sort out everyone's onward transportation for Northern and Southern Rhodesia. The train journey to Lusaka, Northern Rhodesia took four days with a change of trains in Bulawayo from South African Railways to Rhodesia Railways. I was not well enough for the journey so we stayed in a hotel in George Street, Cape Town for three days until I was well enough and onward flights could be arranged.

On 27 July we flew from Cape Town to Johannesburg where we had an all day stop until the flight to Lusaka. In those days Jan Smuts airport, Johannesburg was just one large building housing arrivals and departures but there was a separate small lounge for families with comfy chairs and toilet facilities. Susan and I were the only occupiers so it was like having a private space for the day. I was able to take Susan in the canvas pushchair for a walk around the gardens in front of the terminal. If you know the terminal now it is fronted by multi storey buildings and car parks, in those days there was a beautiful, large rose garden, just the place to while away the hours with a year old child.

Onwards to Lusaka where we were met by Don and taken to our temporary accommodation, the police house was not ready for us so two weeks were spent in a flat near town. It was all so different from Aden, no sea, no mountains and very suburban.

Northern Rhodesia was part of a Federation with Southern Rhodesia and Nyasaland and was rich in copper and mainly self-supporting in agriculture. The population at this time was about 2 million Africans and 64,000 Europeans and 5,000 Indians. Lusaka, the capital is at an elevation of around 4,000ft and because of this height there is a less than tropical climate, it is more of three seasons with the cooler and dry season from May to August, hot and dry from September to November and wet from December to April so we had arrived in the cooler season.

Unlike Aden where, because of the harsh climate, the tour for overseas civil servants was eighteen months, here in NR the first tour of duty was for three years. We moved into the Police Camp a short distance from the centre of town and here I became a police wife and mother! It was very boring! I learnt to drive in a battered old Chevrolet but as we only had the one car I could only use it when Don was away.

He travelled all over the country sorting out radio communications and was usually away for at least two weeks at a time. He had a large single-decker bus fitted with radio equipment, sleeping and living accommodation and before each trip I would go to town to buy provisions for his trip, usually lots of tins particularly of baked beans. He used to like going far in Barotseland province where he would eventually come to the White Fathers' Mission, they welcomed him with the proverbial open arms as they were only allowed to drink alcohol if they were entertaining guests, and in that far off province there were few guests! On several occasions he had to go into the Kafue National Park and there he 'met' the two wild lions known as Big Boy and Little Boy. When he was away from his Land Rover they would arrive and sit on the bonnet of the vehicle as it was warm. In the photos they look even more regal than usual.

There was little for me to do at home and Susan was able to go to a crèche so I looked around for a job and was thrilled to be offered a place with Central African Airways at the airport, doing check-ins and generally looking after incoming and outgoing passengers. Occasionally this meant starting very early in the morning and I could only do these shifts when Don was at home. The airways bus would pick me up from the house and take me to the airport. I had been organising some work in the front garden which necessitated the digging of a large hole, it was the rainy season so was full of water and one morning the bus called for me around 4.30am for an early flight departure, it was dark and I walked straight into the hole. My uniform of khaki skirt and white shirt needed a swift change.

The skill with the copying machine that I had learned at Aden Municipality was put to good use as I had to type up the manifests onto a stencil as the passengers were checking in and then roll off the copies to go with the departing aircraft's papers.

CAA were using a variety of aircraft, Beavers and DC3s for their internal and bush flights and Viscounts and Vikings which also did the internal runs and also to Salisbury in Southern Rhodesia, Blantyre in Nyasaland and to Johannesburg. South African Airways Constellation came through each week en route from Johannesburg to London, one of the stewardesses, Rosemary soon married the NR Commissioner of Police. I went with Don on one of his flights in a Beaver to Mongu in Barotseland, we were due to have lunch with the District Officer there but when we got to his house found that he and his wife had gone to Lusaka, so we just walked in and the cook made us lunch.

The Lusaka Flying Club was adjacent to the airport and a good place to slip over for breakfast after an early start, one of the pilots, a New Zealander called Kiwi Furze always had poached eggs on toast and it fascinated me that he would put the whole unbroken egg yolk into this mouth. In my spare time from work I cadged the odd flying trip in a Tiger Moth aircraft, this was really exciting as the pilot sat in the back seat and the passenger in the front.

I had an interesting 21st birthday. I was working the late shift at the airport but had expected to be home in the early evening. It was raining more than cats and dogs. The Viscount VP-YNA was ready to taxi off for the last flight of the day to Salisbury when it glided in the rain straight into the muddy side of the runway with no hope of being extricated until morning. Having sorted out all the passengers with accommodation, the airport staff, the crew with the delightful Capt. Duncan Strange and I took the airways bus to the Blue Boar Inn outside Lusaka for a party - well it was my 21st. After so many years I can only assume that Don and Susan were safely at home.

It became obvious that working shifts was not compatible with having a child and a husband who was never at home so I regretfully left CAA and went to work for Rhodesia Chartered Agency in Woodgate House in town in Cairo Road. Wing Commander Everest was the Manager but he had no travel experience, Mr Alderson ran an insurance part of the agency, there was a receptionist cum junior travel clerk called June, and me.

The travel side was certainly less stressful than my work in Aden Airways as any difficult re-issue of tickets could be referred back to CAA. Over the years that I worked there I got to know many of the travellers who were working for commercial firms who came and went on a regular basis, for no reason two names appear, Mr MacGillivray from Blackwood Hodge and Mrs Ingles from the Red Cross. The most important part of our work was doing all the homeward bound and return leave bookings for all the colonial civil servants in NR. It could be flight bookings to UK or train to the Cape and onward ship bookings. So I got to know all the Lusaka based personnel who were forever in and out of the office particularly Don's colleagues in the Police Force. Most of the shipping bookings were with the Union Castle Line as it had the most frequency, a weekly service between Cape Town and Southampton. There were also the ships of the Shaw Savill Line, *Northern Star* and *Southern Cross* that travelled between Australia, New Zealand and Southampton via Cape Town, they were of the 20,000ton variety and carried over 1000 passengers in tourist class only.

For the more discerning traveller, who had a higher grade of pay and therefore a higher travel allowance there were the cargo ships of Ellerman & Bucknall, the City Lines, the *City of Port Elizabeth* for example was about 13,000tons and like all the City ships carried freight and cars and just 12 passengers. Of course all costs of travel, within the allowance for each pay grade, whether by air or train and ship were paid by the Crown Agents. If someone wanted to travel in a higher class, or go 'home' by a roundabout route then they could pay the difference themselves.

Throughout my career in the travel industry I have been fortunate to visit many parts of the world on what are euphemistically called educationals. The idea is for principals of hotels, tourist offices or tourist attractions to invite the agents who can sell these attractions to the public to see and experience them for themselves, then with this firsthand experience sell them on to their clients. This was the theory, in practice it later became an easy and tax free way of rewarding agency staff for work that was not necessarily related to that particular venue or attraction. The airlines were good at this, give airline 'A' lots of business to boring commercial destination 'B' and you might get a 'freebie' to exciting holiday destination 'C'.

In the late '50s this idea of educationals was still in its infancy but I was invited on two such 'jollys' or 'freebies' which provide a branch line in my journey to fascinating stations!

My first educational was more along the lines of being a thank you from the airline than trying to sell the product. With an agent from Lusaka and another small group from Salisbury we flew on 14 October 1958 in a strange aircraft, the Viking, to Durban. The seat configuration was like a bus with some seats in a line facing each other across the fuselage and the others in the standard two by two formation. I think the airline was Protea Airways but cannot find any confirmation of this, just the inside of the aircraft which is engraved on my mind. The reason for the flight was to spend one night on the *Boissevain*, a ship of Royal Interocean Lines. The R.I.L brochure says *Following the track of the ancient navigators, these new ships bring the world traveller to historically interesting islands of the Indian Ocean and the Gold Land - South and East Africa.*

This was a Dutch Line and their three ships *Boissevain, Ruys* and *Tegelberg* sailed between Japan, Hong Kong, Singapore, Mauritius, Durban, Cape Town and South America so there was no likelihood of my colonial clients in NR using these ships for their homeward bound leave and even if they had wanted to do the Durban to Cape Town section as part of their leave this would not have been possible as Union Castle also sailed this section so Government money had to go to UK companies, not Dutch. Anyway for whatever reason we were invited aboard and I had a memorable day and night aboard; dinner served that evening was a full Chinese meal of many courses, all accompanied by Sake - rice wine, and all delicious. Sadly I was very ill the next day and had a horrid flight back to Lusaka and since then have not been a fan of Chinese cooking. A letter to my mother on an R.I.L. Compliments slip dated 21 October says:

I went to Durban last week on an agents' free trip, spent Tuesday night in Salisbury, Wednesday night on the boat, Thursday in Salisbury again. A nice change except that I was very airsick flying back from Durban. Apparently Don and Sue had a marvellous time whilst I was away. Don has been away in Gwembe for three weeks - did you read about it in the papers. He brought back some souvenirs, throwing axes and spears! Hope you had a good birthday - I posted a parcel for you some time ago.

There is a photo of my table at the dinner accompanying this letter to which I have added *note the chopsticks.*

In the early '60s and onwards Central African Airways and later Air Rhodesia operated package holidays under the 'Flame Lily' banner and these proved immensely popular even to colonial civil servants as it meant they could take a reasonably priced break to local destinations during their long overseas tours. Livingstone and the Victoria Falls proved a very popular destination especially for those in Southern Rhodesia, it was a relatively easy drive by car for those of us in NR where a longer journey provided a lure to the fleshpots of Salisbury, the beaches of Beira and Durban or the prawns in the Polano Hotel in Lourenco Marques. The forerunner of these 'Flame Lily' holidays was *All-in Happy Holidays at the Paradise Island Resorts* run by Hunting Clan African Airways from Salisbury in the late '50s and which took me to Paradise on 25 October 1958. I flew with another Lusaka travel agent to Salisbury, Southern Rhodesia where we were joined by a small group of their agents and then on to the port of Vilanculos on the Mozambique mainland where we boarded a small yacht which took us on the 1¼ hour voyage to the island.

The enterprising Senor Joaquim Alves had the concession to run tourist resorts in the Mozambique mainland area of Inhassoro and the town of Vilanculos, and the Mozambique islands of Bazaruto, Magaruque and Santa Carolina (Paradise Island). All these areas were promoted for big-game or goggle fishing and some of the accommodation was basic but Senor Alves improved all the accommodation on Paradise Island. In his brochure for April 1958 he says: *new blocks of rooms have been built close to the restaurant and all the rooms and bungalows have been re-decorated and refurnished with new dressing tables, wardrobes, armchairs and rugs. You can lunch or dine on the terrace of the restaurant which opened last year and enjoy typical Portuguese dishes prepared in our new kitchens. Another acquisition is a launch, just arrived from London which will reduce the journey from Vilanculos to Paradise*

Island to 1¼hours has been built. A contemporary brochure shows a double storey, palm shaded block of rooms each with its own balcony facing the sea.

The blurb from the Hunting Clan brochure best describes the allure of Paradise Island:
Called the Pearl of the Indian Ocean, Santa Carolina is truly an enchanted isle, less than two miles in length and ½ mile wide, fringed with coconut palms and covered with tropical vegetation. The coral sands are dazzling white, and the crystal clear waters, protected by coral reefs are warm and shallow for children and non-swimmers. Conditions are ideal for goggle fishing and there are myriads of brightly coloured tropical fish to be seen around the coral reefs. Shoals of fish haunt the island's coves and equipped with a snorkel, goggles and harpoon it is hardly necessary to aim to make a catch. For children the island is a treasure trove of shells and fascinating sea creatures. Jaded businessmen have found Santa Carolina an ideal break from the rush of the big city - no radios, no newspapers, no telephones, no mailbags, just plenty of sun, plenty of clear blue water, plenty of goggle-fishing, sun-bathing and good Portuguese food and drink. As 21stC jargon would say - what's not to like!

A couple of photos in my album for that year show the island exactly as described in the brochure and Senor Alves made a wise investment in hosting our group of travel agents as we returned to work enthused about selling a new holiday destination to our clients. It was fairly accessible as there was a weekly flight of 2½ hour from Salisbury to Vilanculos and an all-in package holiday cost £40 for seven days for an adult and £20 for a child. At that time the flight from Lusaka to Salisbury was about 1½ hours and the cost for a return excursion was £14.4. These costs do not sound high compared with modern day prices but remember that Don as an Assistant Superintendent of Police was earning around £88 per month less deductions. We could never have afforded a holiday like this, our breaks were down to Livingstone and the Falls at regular intervals.

Let me just mention the Falls here. Now the areas surrounding them on both sides of the Zambezi are full of hotels, camp sites, safari lodges and shopping malls, then the Falls were surrounded by the bush on the NR side with the statue of David Livingstone gazing over 'the smoke that thunders' and overlooked only by the prestigious Victoria Falls Hotel on the southern side. Livingstone town had the railway station and a few shops as well as a passable museum of artefacts relating to David Livingstone; the road from the town to the Falls had Government houses on both sides, the ubiquitous red tin roofs and glorious gardens massed with bougainvilleas. You could walk right to the edge of the river and gaze down into the Boiling Pot and feel that the water rushing past could quite easily take you with it. Although we always stayed with friends in Livingstone the place to go for a special afternoon tea was the Victoria Falls Hotel. This old Colonial style hotel was the epitome of elegance, with gorgeous gardens leading straight into the rain forest to the Falls. On one of our trips we went by boat to Palm Island, upriver from Livingstone to see elephant who came right to the water's edge to drink, Susan was thrilled to see the ellies.

You have to pick the right time of the year to see the Falls at their best, in November and December the Zambezi river is low so the Falls almost dry up, conversely in March and April with the river in full flow the volume of water and subsequent spray make it almost impossible to see anything and October is very hot and dry - so take your pick! It's best to go in September as this is also the best game viewing month before the summer grasses start to grow.

I have been to the three largest waterfalls in the world, Iguazu, Niagara (more of them later) and Victoria, the latter is definitely the most spectacular, more than twice as high as Niagara, a third higher than Iguazu and it has the biggest curtain of falling water in the world.

I had mentioned Gwembe in the October letter to my mother. Gwembe District was in the Zambezi valley and home to the Tonga tribe whose main village was Chisamu. Building a wall to dam the Zambezi started here in the late '50s and by the end of 1958 the sluice gates were closed and by 1963 the maximum level of the dam was reached. The Dam is located approximately halfway down the Zambezi River and it is 2,650 miles from its source to the Indian Ocean.

But what of the Tonga who lived here? They had lived for centuries in the Gwembe Valley along the northern and southern banks of the Zambezi River and now this wide valley was to turn from river to reservoir. Whole villages were flooded, displacing 57,000 indigenous people. The communities resisted resettlement, but were defeated by colonial authorities in a short battle know as the Chisamu War. Villages were burned so the people could not return and they were relocated onto land which was insufficient to maintain their livelihoods.

"We shall die in our land we don't want to be moved."
- A note left by Tonga resistors in the days leading to the Chisamu War (1958)

The events were discussed in Westminster Parliament as a Gwembe District Incident and reported in Hansard on 26 June 1958:

Mr Stonehouse: *asked the Secretary of State for the Colonies what caused the disturbances in the Gwembe District of Northern Rhodesia when Africans attacked the District Commissioner, Mr. Allan Prior; to what extent the grievances were related to the compulsory migration of members of the Tonga tribe from the area to be flooded by the Kariba hydro-electric scheme; and what revised arrangements are being made to compensate and resettle on good land those concerned.*

Mr Profumo: *The incident arose from the unco-operative attitude of a headman and his followers towards proposals for their resettlement in preparation for the flooding of the area they now occupy later this year. The villagers demonstrated with violence against the arrest of their headman for contravention of a Native Authority Order under which he was required, but refused, to attend discussions about the proposed move. The headman and rioters have now given themselves up and the situation is quiet. Details of the move are still under discussion, but no change in the plan for compensation or the area for resettlement is contemplated.*

A further discussion of Gwembe District Disturbances was reported in Hansard on 4 November 1958:

Mr Sorenson: *asked the Secretary of State for the Colonies how many were killed and wounded in the Gwembe area of the Zambezi Valley in early September arising from the need of transferring tribesmen from that area; whether any further disturbances have taken place; and what action has been taken to ensure that the tribesmen in that area are fully acquainted with the reasons for the removal of population.*

Mr Lennox-Boyd: *The Governor has informed me that, when attempting to enforce an order for villagers to move from an area to be flooded to new settlement areas provided for them in the Gwembe District, officials of the Native Authority and of the Provincial Administration met with armed resistance. Determined charges were made by men armed with spears against the official party supported by police re-inforcements.*

In the resulting police action, I am very sorry to say that eight villagers were killed and 22 injured. There were no subsequent disturbances and the move has now been completed. Extensive efforts had been made to prepare the villagers for the need to move over two and a half years. The Governor has appointed a Commission to inquire into the circumstances, and it is still sitting. The Report will be published.

Mr Sorenson: *Was the resistance on the part of those who were to be transferred from the area? Were any killed or wounded on the side of the forces trying to effect the transference?*

Mr Lennox-Boyd: *It will be much better to wait until the Commission has reported.*

It appears from later discussions that compensation was to be paid by the Northern Rhodesia Government to the Gwembe Native Authority, a sum of £330,000 is mentioned amounting to approximately £5 compensation per head for gardens, £3.2s. 6d. for the loss of maize crop and £2 per head for the loss of huts. I can find no confirmation of the sums actually paid. Hansard, in case you are wondering, are official reports of all Parliamentary Debates . Whilst the problems were occurring at Chisamu village and in which Don seems to have been actively involved - uplifting axes and spears, a wildlife rescue operation was taking place to save as many wild animals as possible Huge areas of bush would be flooded and thousands of wild animals would lose their habitats. Between 1958 and 1964 Operation Noah moved over 6,000 animals; elephant, antelope, rhino, lion, leopard, zebra, warthog, birds and snakes mainly to the Matusadona National Park and around Lake Kariba. There is a monument to Operation Noah in Kariba, but none to the relocated Tonga people.

An important part of this period of my life in Northern Rhodesia is the friends that I made who have stayed friends over the succeeding decades. Wendy and her four children lived near our first flat and we regularly saw each other at the public swimming pool. Jann and her two children lived in Woodlands close to our second home, Lily was wife of the Assistant Commissioner of Police and took me under her wing and taught me much about cooking and gardening as she is still doing six decades later.

By 1959 problems must have started to appear in my marriage, I say 'must have', as I don't know. I think in the brain there is a box into which we put all our bad memories, and if we really want to this can be opened and the memories restored, but buried deep in the box are the really bad memories which our psyche prevents us from taking out as they would be too painful to revisit. I can only give you a few facts:

In the Police Camp house Don discharged his revolver in the sitting room whilst I was there, I do not know if the ammunition was live or blank.

I took a lift, with Susan, to Salisbury with the sales representative for Japan Airlines, we spent the night at a hotel at Mount Pleasant in Salisbury.

The stamps in my passport show Le Bourget airport in Paris on 31 October and 22 November and Salisbury on 23 November. I was friends with the Manager of UTA French Airlines in Lusaka, Ron Saunders and his wife Linda, so I must have been given either an agents' discounted or a free return ticket from Salisbury to London via Paris.

My sister Mary remembers that I arrived in Pentland Street, Wandsworth to leave Susan with my mother who told me to go back to NR immediately, but I obviously stayed until the end of November when I returned on my own. Mary was not pleased at having to walk Susan to nursery school every morning before she went on to school, Mary was 11years old at this time. She says she taught Susan her colours by the colours of the front doors that they passed on their walk.

I must have returned to the Police Camp house. Don's tour of duty was for three years so by early 1960 the journey continued as we left NR temporarily for a long leave in England. There was still the packing up of the house to do with crates to go into storage as we did not know where our next house would be, flights home arranged - by me, so not too difficult and then the task of finding somewhere to live in England for up to six months of leave and of course Susan would be coming back to live with us. The house in Pentland Street would have been too cramped for all of us besides which Don was a country not a town man. My father and mother were separated by this time.

As luck would have it my boss Wing Commander Everest had a sister who lived in Shrewsbury in Shropshire and she had a cottage in the country which she agreed to let to us for as long as necessary. The cottage was along a lane about a mile from the main road at Halfway House which was halfway between Shrewsbury and Welshpool. Even by African standards the cottage was very basic. There was an outside chemical loo and water had to be hand pumped from an outside pump. The bed had a feather mattress which had to be shaken each day to make it comfy. It is amazing what you can accept when you are young.

Don was happy as he could fish and meet the locals in the pub at Halfway House which was run by Mr and Mrs Clough. Their daughter Joan became a friend although I think she found my peripatetic way of life very strange.

I don't have many memories of this leave, but a few stand out. Picking some mushrooms for supper in the field opposite the cottage and when I went to cook them a myriad of worms emerged! There was a bookcase in the kitchen filled with Women's Weekly magazines in the blue and pink covers dating back to before and during the war; they made great reading. For some reason Don thought a dog might be just the thing for us, remember we were only here for a few months, and he came home with a delightful Border Collie - a real working sheepdog. Of course we spoilt him but what he really needed was training and it was sad that when we left the cottage he had to go back to his working life having experienced the comfy life of a family. One treat was driving into Shrewsbury for shopping, or just window shopping. Then it was easy to park in an area below the Kop which is now covered with multi-storeyed shopping malls.

When our leave ended in September we decided to return to Africa by ship and drive to Lusaka and to this end Don bought a new small white Ford Escort van - why a van heaven only knows. But political events in NR caused a change in plans and Don was recalled early from leave and had to fly back to Lusaka.

This was an uneasy time in Central Africa. Talks of independence for the three countries of the Federation had been ongoing for years and were now coming to a head. There was political upheaval too in NR with the ANC and UNIP between Kenneth Kaunda and Harry Nkumbula. In May1960 in Ndola there was an unauthorised public meeting and in the resulting disturbances a Mrs Burton and her two daughters were brutally murdered. Some of the suspects fled to the Katanga Province of the Belgian Congo. A trial of the perpetrators eventually took place in November, four of the witnesses lived in Katanga and could not attend.

I won't go into details about African countries' independence, cause and results, as it is far too complicated, but as it affects my journey just a few details are necessary. The Belgian Congo became the Republic of Congo in June 1960 and in July the province of Katanga under Patrice Lumumba proclaimed its own independence from the Republic, this was significant as Katanga and the NR

Copperbelt were near neighbours. The Republic did not want to lose the mineral resources of Katanga so troops were involved in keeping the peace - or not - and in August the United Nations sent its own peace-keeping force of mainly Swedish troops into Elizabethville, the Katangese capital. All this was happening on the borders of NR so you can imagine that the Northern Rhodesia Police were on high alert both for cross-border Katanga/Copperbelt disturbances and also for reaction to the forthcoming retrial in November concerning the Burton family murders.

So Don flew back to Lusaka and I was left in England with a car and a four year old daughter! Thank heavens for Union Castle. We sailed on 29 September 1960 in the *Edinburgh Castle* from Southampton to Cape Town. The ships on my journey were getting bigger, this one was28,000 tons and she carried 133 first class and 536 tourist class passengers, but hooray, Susan and I were in first class.

I was feeling daunted at the task of driving 2,000 miles to Lusaka with a small child (especially as I was pregnant!) so I advertised on the ship in both classes for a co-driver who had some mechanical experience. I had two responses from tourist class, an elderly gentleman and a younger one. I chose the younger one of course. He was only going to Bulawayo but that was good enough for me. In retrospect I feel that Don was being irresponsible for expecting me to undertake this journey and that I was foolish to do so but the wisdom of youth obviously overrode these concerns.

We landed in Cape Town on 13 October and the car journey took four days and three nights:

13 October Cape Town to Phillipolis	518 miles
14 October Phillipolis to Nylstrom now called Modimolle	561 miles
15 October Nylstrom to Bulawayo	429 miles
16 October Bulawayo/Salisbury/ Chirundu/Lusaka	522 miles

I cannot remember where we stayed overnight. In those days Phillipolis was on the main road north, now it is by-passed, so I guess there must have been a small hotel on the then main road. I pass through Modimolle fairly regularly now and the main street always looks familiar, it is also no longer on the main road north but again there was probably a hotel on the original main road. As for Bulawayo, I can see a small lodge outside the town with lots of vegetation and that is where I parted from my co-driver, whose name I have long forgotten.

The last day of the journey is more memorable. The back of the car was packed to the roof with suitcases and trunks (remember these were the days when you travelled on Union Castle with your baggage marked CABIN, BAGGAGE ROOM - accessible on voyage and HOLD, not wanted on voyage, and seated in the front seat was a four year old - no seat belts then.

Half way through the final 500 miles we came to the Zambezi Escarpment where the road descended very steeply from the plateau at 3,700ft down to 1,600ft into the Zambezi valley and then 1200ft at the bridge which crossed the Zambezi river at Chirundu, the border between Southern and Northern Rhodesia. It was that initial drop that caused a problem, all the cases in the back of the car decided to slide forward so I was trying to hold them back with one hand to prevent them from coming into the front seats and covering Susan, whilst negotiating a steep, narrow, twisting dirt road. The heat as we descended became intense, it was over 30° and the sound of the cicadas deafening. We made it safely to the Tsetse fly control station at the bottom of the escarpment where the car, with us inside, had to go through a disinfecting cabin. The final almost mishap was as we approached Lusaka, heaven knows how in a pre-mobile phone age, but Don was waiting for us by the side of a road and when I saw him the car went into a skid around the corner. He must have wondered how we had managed to drive 2000 miles unscathed. Especially when he discovered a dent in the roof of the car which I hadn't noticed and which must have been done when the car was lifted either into or out of the ship's hold - I think we received insurance for it.

And so began the final part of my journey in Northern Rhodesia with more branch lines and collisions along the way. This tour of duty was for 2½ years so leave would come round again in the spring of '63. We were no longer housed in the Police Camp but in a suburb of Lusaka called Woodlands, in Rochester Close. My soon to be good friends Jann and her children lived in neighbouring Winchester Close as well as the McIntosh family. It was very close to Woodlands Primary School that Susan and Carol (Jann's daughter)and Caroline (McIntosh) also attended. I was pregnant at this time and we had another daughter, Sarah Wendy on 30 May '61.

In early '62 I had a temporary job helping to collate the new voter's roll for elections which were to be held in October, it was boring work that I could do at home but it enabled me to send money to Mum so that she and my sister Mary could have a holiday in Majorca in August '62. I returned to work at Rhodesia Chartered Agency by mid '62 and Sarah went to Florrie Selwood's crêche during the day.

As a break-away from the ups and downs of my marriage let me share some lighter moments. I have always loved clothes as you know and so I did a lot of dressmaking on an old Singer treadle machine that I bought for £25. It was the time of Mary Quant and my wardrobe featured several dresses from her patterns and I made all the children's clothes too. Across Cairo road from RCA was a delightful dress shop called 'Milady' and here I bought two stunning dresses for evening wear for cocktail parties associated with work - Don wasn't the party type which was probably the problem. One was in pale pink brocade, strapless with a tulip shaped skirt and matching stole, the other a glorious cerise pink georgette, lined, with a frilled strapless top and a bubble shaped skirt. I wore the latter to a 'do' at the Woodpecker Inn in Woodlands and received many compliments. Truworths was also across the road and from there came a turquoise wool suit for a UK leave. At the end of Cairo road was a material shop called Modern Fabrics and I bought some black jersey and made a really nice cocktail dress for the boat trip home in '64. It did look very professionally made as I can see from the photo, a short sleeved lined, V necked bodice with two small ribbon bows, and a straight skirt falling from a high waistline. Another 'piece de resistance' was a Chanel type suit again made on the treadle machine, in a Black Watch wool tartan. It had a straight lined skirt and the edge to edge lined jacket featured two lines of navy braid along the front edges. When my mother met me on arrival in London when I was wearing it she couldn't believe that I had made it and minutely scrutinised the inside seams to check that all was finished off neatly.

This was also the time of beehive hairdos and I had grown my hair sufficiently to make a reasonable beehive which involved lots of back-combing and hair pins.

The 1963 leave came round and we four flew on British United direct from Lusaka to London in May. Sarah was just recovering from chicken-pox which we kept secret otherwise we would not have been allowed to travel. I had made the girls, then 7 and 2 similar outfits, red corduroy pinafore dresses and knitted a jumper and cardigan for both of them in pale turquoise. Through a police colleague of Don's whose family owned a house and a converted mill in Shropshire we would be spending our leave in Dolywern, near Glyn Ceiriog. On our drive from London to Shropshire on Friday 11 May we made a detour to call to see my father who was licensee at the New Inn, a pub in Manton near Marlborough, he lived there with his girlfriend Carol and Grandma B was also staying there on a holiday. We had lunch at the pub and Dad was able to see Susan again and meet Sarah for the first time - in their red and turquoise outfits.

We then continued onto Dolywern and the flat in the mill that we were to stay in adjacent to the main house all surrounded by beautiful gardens and fields on the banks of the River Ceiriog. On Monday 13 May I was called to take a phone call in the main house where my mother told me that Dad had died that day. It was a terrible shock having just seen him two days previously when he looked fine and he was only 53. He was diabetic and he drank a lot so that combination as well as running a pub must have been his downfall. Apparently he had a heart attack in the night. Grandma B was devastated as he had been her whole world and she returned to live alone in Putney in very sad circumstances. The local paper mentioned his passing under the heading' Licensee Dies'.
Licensee of the New Inn, Manton since December, Major Frederick Mark Berryman died at his home on Monday, aged 53. London-born Major Berryman moved to Manton from Dunbar Scotland, where he was a civil engineer. When he took the New Inn he joined the Marlborough and District LVA.

He was buried in the churchyard at Preshute near Manton, I had wanted to go to the funeral but Don said we couldn't make any more car journeys when we had only just made the journey north.

The mill and Glyn Ceiriog were beautiful places for a long leave, the children could play in the gardens and I was able to take long walks with the pushchair along the lanes surrounding the mill. Don seemed to get on well with a girl from the Isle of Wight who was a relation of the house owners and staying temporarily in the main house and I know they continued to write to each other after we had returned to Lusaka.

We must have had happy times as by the time we returned to Lusaka at the end of summer I was pregnant but these happy times were not to last and Sarah and I moved to a flat in Lusaka and Susan stayed with her father. The flat was unfurnished and I found great pleasure in buying just the bare minimum that I could afford. A cot for Sarah and a divan bed for me in the sitting room covered in a blue, grey and white stripe. A blue Parker Knoll type armchair, a really modern shaped coffee table and a splendid pale wood standard lamp with a flying saucer shaped shade in yellow material. This was the first time I had been on my own and could buy what I wanted, maybe having reached the age of 26 it was time to take responsibility for myself but sadly this affected my children.

As with our see-saw relationship I eventually went back to live with Don, and was in the Woodlands house in November '63 when two memorable events occurred. On 22 November President Kennedy was assassinated and that same weekend we experienced mild earthquakes in Lusaka which were caused by the land settling under the weight of water at Lake Kariba, 130 miles distant, which had reached its maximum capacity the previous year.

I'm afraid to say yet again there was trouble at home. In writing of all these comings and goings in my marriage I wonder why I just didn't up and leave for good at some stage and so save the trauma for all of us. Don brought home two black and white Cocker Spaniels called Jack and Jill supposedly to make me happy, rather like when he brought home the sheepdog in Shropshire, but this didn't make life any happier and for me the final straw was being forced, after an almighty row, to spend New Year's Eve '63/'64 outside in the car at five months pregnant. I know this doesn't make for happy reading, but I did say at the outset 'warts and almost all!'

Sarah and I moved out and went to stay with some dear people, Derek and Dorothy Wilson who had a small-holding on the Great East Road. Don would not allow Susan to come with me so she stayed with her father and became a weekly boarder at school. I continued to work for RCA in Lusaka with Sarah at the crêche during the day. It was so relaxing being on the farm in the evenings and at the weekends as the Wilsons made us feel at home with them. I had decided that in my current circumstances I could not look after another child and that when the baby was born it would be adopted immediately. Dorothy and Derek pressurised me into allowing them to adopt, they had a son and could have no more children, but I felt that it was not right for friends to adopt and might make for problems for all of us in the future. It was very hard on them as they had been so good to me but I felt it the best decision both for the baby and for me.

About three weeks before the baby was due in March '64 I moved back into Lusaka in order to be near the hospital and stayed with the McIntoshs. I carried on working until 18 March when another daughter was born and taken away from me immediately. I called her Sally-Ann and it was 33 years before I saw her again. I returned to work straight away and found a cottage at Kabulonga, outside Lusaka for Sarah and me. Very small with just one room and a kitchen and bathroom and a small garden and it is here that I have happy photos of Sarah celebrating her 3rd birthday with her friends including Neil McIntosh who had been born a couple of days after her. Whilst here I became ill for about a week, I think it was the mental strain of giving up the baby as well as physical and I couldn't leave my bed, aged three Sarah looked after me with snack meals, making tea and dishing out medicines. I have never forgotten her care at this time although she probably has no memory of it.

There were many problems in the country as the date of Independence in October '64 drew near. These were exacerbated by a lady called Alice Lenshina who founded her own Lumpa church which had strange beliefs and rejected any authority from the government, refused to pay taxes and established its own courts. Her church became popular taking people from the established Roman Catholic and Church of Scotland churches that were in the Northern Province of NR and eventually her church became involved in the politics of independence between the ANC and UNIP. Her followers were said to number 60,000 within Northern Rhodesia, Nyasaland, Tanganyika and the Belgian Congo. Villages were split as Lumpa leaders ordered their members to establish separate villages by moving out of villages where they lived alongside UNIP's members. The conflict between UNIP and the Lumpa Church reached a climax between July and October. On 24 July 1964 a gun battle broke out between UNIP and Lumpa Church members. The resulting riots were only quelled by the intervention of State troops, and the proclamation of a state of emergency by the new pre-independence Prime Minister, Kenneth Kaunda. Approximately 15,000 Lumpa Church members fled and took refuge in Congo; the Lumpa Church was banned on 3 August 1964 and Lenshina surrendered to police a few days later.

A member of the Provincial Administration, John Hannah wrote his personal account of the Lumpa uprising, part of which says:

*The Lumpa church members were mostly armed with sharp sticks, spears and pangas, whilst the Northern Rhodesia Regiment (NRR) were armed with automatic rifles. In spite of there having been a couple of casualties on the army side (mainly during their attempts to negotiate) there was no contest in the end. As many as a thousand Lumpas were killed. With independence approaching, the killings did not perhaps receive the kind of attention that they might have done in less tense circumstances. The government was more concerned with preparation for independence.*www.britishempire.co.uk/article/alicelenshinalumpa

Don was involved in this uprising as he took part in many flights of Police light aircraft dropping leaflets over the Chinsali area in the Northern Province, leaflets advising the Lumpa followers to down their arms and accept the rule of the country. It was the state of emergency which had been declared in July and the forthcoming

Independence that caused a major shift in the lives of Colonial officers, both police and civil. Many posts were to be Africanised upon Independence so officers were requesting transfers to other colonial territories, as was Don. He suggested we try again ' not again I hear you say', so in August Sarah and I left NR for the last time, leaving Susan to finish her term at boarding school and to fly home with Don after he had sorted out Alice Lenshina.

The night before we left, the McIntoshs gave a girls' party for me at their house as a result of which I was very hung-over during the four day rail journey to Cape Town. Sarah was kept amused by all her Lego pieces. My passport stamps say that we passed into Southern Rhodesia at Victoria Falls on 4 August, and entered South Africa at Mafeking on 6 August. The *Cape Town Castle* sailed a couple of days later. She was 27,000 tons and she carried 243 first class and 553 tourist class passengers and we were in First Class-of course.

As a female travelling on my own I was seated at the Captain's table for dinner with the senior officers and ship's doctor. The latter, whose name I won't give you, his initials were AR, made my homeward journey very special and we continued to see each other for a month after I arrived in London where Sarah and I were staying with Mum who now had a flat in Clapham Park Road. He lived with his parents who had a flat in Kensington High Street and a house in Brighton, we would go in his sports car for a very fast journey down to Brighton and back for the evening. He took me to see a performance in London of Marcel Marceau the French mime artist. All this came to an end when Don was due to arrive - it had been a fling on both our sides and given his profession it could go no further.

Whilst waiting to hear about the next posting we rented part of a farmhouse at Llynderw, in the country just outside Welshpool. It was jolly cold especially as we were here throughout the winter. Susan went to the small school just up the lane, Don did his fishing and was out and about most days. We visited our friend Joan at Halfway House. She now had twin girls Deborah and Diana a year older than Sarah. There was much snow this particular winter and we all felt the cold after African days. I had bought a new smart grey tweed coat at Harrods in London but it was unlined so totally unsuitable for a harsh winter. But we survived. At one stage I had seen some adoption papers in the kitchen which Don had to sign, for Rosemary Alexandra Haycock, so I now knew Sally-Ann's new name. The papers were never mentioned or discussed with me. You won't believe it but yet again, another dog appeared, this time a Springer Spaniel called Sandy.

In January '65 Winston Churchill died and I watched his funeral on the small television that we had in the kitchen. In due course Don's transfer arrived, to the Swaziland Police and we went ahead with getting all the necessary medical certificates from the hospital in Shrewsbury. On one such drive with the children into Shrewsbury I stopped to pick up a hitch-hiker (not the thing that you would do these days) and we got chatting and I explained that we were bound for Swaziland, thence followed a strange conversation about mountains and snow and I then realised he thought I had said Switzerland.

As it happened, and almost as Don was due to leave, his posting was changed to the Basutoland Mounted Police. Anyway he flew off and the rest of us plus dog returned to London to get our flights sorted out with the Crown Agents and to obtain all the necessary permits from the Department of Agriculture here and in South Africa for the importation of a dog. A specially sized aircraft kennel had to be bought, and he had to go into kennels until there was freight space for him to travel to Johannesburg. At last in May '65 we flew to Johannesburg where we were met by Don and travelled by car to Maseru. Two weeks later Sandy arrived and as we were waiting for him to be off-loaded from the aircraft at Jan Smuts we could hear him barking.

And so this part of my journey comes to an end, the tracks have given me a bumpy ride over the last eight years but they now forge ahead into the Mountain Kingdom.

CHAPTER 5
A steep gradient into the Mountain Kingdom

'A journey is like marriage. The certain way to be wrong is to think you control it'.

John Steinbeck

As we neared Basutoland the mountains came into view on the horizon, I thought they might have been capped with snow but it was still too early in the winter season. The drive from Johannesburg, 220 miles, had taken about four hours and much of the countryside was flat and dreary but within the Free State there was more agriculture and the start of the foothills. Here are some details about this fascinating and beautiful if stark country.

Basutoland was one of the three British High Commission Territories, the others were Swaziland and Bechualand. It is one of the few countries completely encircled by another - South Africa and is the only country in the world that lies entirely above 3,300 ft in elevation. It is the home of the Sotho people and in Queen Victoria's time the Paramount Chief had petitioned the Queen for protection from the Zulu Wars and Boer encroachment *Let me and my people live under the large folds of the flag of England before I am no more.* The Maluti Mountains are part of the Drakensberg range and a continuation of the Great Rift Valley. The highest mountain is Ntlenyana at 11,424ft above sea level and Maseru the capital is 5013ft above sea level. High in the Malutis are the sources of two great African rivers, the Tugela which flows eastwards for 312 miles until it reaches the sea north of Durban and the Orange which flows westwards for 1,367 miles reaching the Atlantic Ocean at Alexander Bay. The border between South Africa and Basutoland is the Caledon river. With the country being the source of so much water it is ironic that the lowlands of Basutoland are a very arid due to being eroded by immense dongas, deep gullies 30 to 50ft deep caused by bad management of the land in times past.

I have tried to get the exact figures to give you an idea of just how small was the European population of Basutoland when I arrived in '65; figures from the 1966 census show 1582 Europeans in the country of whom 1017 lived in Maseru and at the university at Roma.

We approached our house from town through a valley, just a mile or so from the main street, Kingsway, the house was in the Police Mobile Unit on the side of Badge Hill, so named as it sported a regimental badge picked out in white stones on the side of the hill. There were four fairly newly built Highway houses, all for police officers in a line with a rough track in front of them. No gardens had been made, there was just rough earth and stones. The houses had large airy rooms and big picture windows, lovely in the hot weather but freezing cold in the winter although there was an open fireplace in the sitting room. The McFalls lived next to us and at the end of the line the Willoughbys - Jackie and her sons Simon and Rupert are still friends.

I immediately felt happy in Maseru and in the PMU house and was determined to make it a home. We put a green fitted carpet in the sitting room - unheard of in a government house, and I made thickly lined curtains from a Sanderson's green floral chintz. It seemed very cosy and homely. Susan and Sarah had Simon and Rupert as playmates and as Jackie did not drive I would take her shopping in Bloemfontein, a drive of about 70 miles each way. Leaving Maseru involved signing out at the Basutoland customs post driving across the Caledon river bridge and then signing in at the South African border post, and of course doing the same thing in reverse on the homeward journey. It was a dirt road for about 5 miles before getting to the main tarred road from Ladybrand to Bloemfontein. The journey usually took about 75 minutes but I am ashamed to say I did do it in under an hour on some occasions. There were plenty of shops in the metropolis of Bloemfontein and a café called the Penny Whistle where we always stopped for a snack and later when the children were at boarding school in Bloemfontein they came there too. The two ladies who ran the café seemed to dislike any customers and were always sour-faced.

It was a pleasant life for a while, I played tennis on Wednesday and Saturday mornings, I was never very good at it but we played two foursomes at Maseru Club and I liked chatting with the other ladies. On Sunday mornings I took part in the Sunday Ride which apparently was a feature of the Maseru social calendar. We rode horses from the police stables at PMU, meeting at 7am and getting home about midday, usually between eight and ten riders including Cliff who was also Ex NRP and whom I had met in Lusaka when arranging his travel bookings. I hadn't ridden since the early days in Aden so I was given one of the quieter horses. We explored the open countryside away from Maseru, sometimes walking and trotting, sometimes cantering but the ground was so uneven, and when we turned for home and came within sight of PMU the horses 'sniffed home' and it was the fastest canter/gallop ever to get to the stables.

Further into my stay in Maseru I experienced very bad back-ache and the doctor advised me to give up riding, the pain continued so he said to give up tennis which I did. The pain was then alleviated but came back many years later.

Maseru Club was the centre of social life, it had a swimming pool, bowling greens, tennis courts, cricket pitch, a golf course and a bar. Films were shown here once a week and it was the home of Maseru Players, the local Am.Dram. society, but more of that later. As I was not working I had plenty of free time and I enjoyed walking around the golf course with Rosemary whilst she was practicing, it was good exercise too for Sandy the Springer Spaniel. I roamed all over Maseru with Sandy, he was a very handsome chap and the local people were fascinated by him never having seen a Springer before, they called him a lion and I had several offers for him to be mated with local dogs which I had to refuse!

Shopping facilities were restricted, Frasers was a small supermarket, Collier and Yeats sold some nice imported clothes, the local butcher sold fillet steak for 40p a pound, the pharmacy had the usual medicines and knick knacks for presents and there was a café cum vegetable shop which had the only source of fresh fruit and veg. On one of my first visits to buy vegetables I asked for a lettuce only to be told it was out of season and I should grow my own like Sandy Giles - he was the High Commissioner. Growing anything on our stony soil was virtually impossible, I had a go at broad beans as Don liked them but after much watering and feeding and just when they were ready to be picked a cloud of black beetles descended and ate the lot. After that I discovered that the only plants to survive at PMU were zinnias and African marigolds - I can't bear either of them now.

I did have the opportunity to earn a few pounds. Every week the British High Commission had to send by plane the diplomatic bag to the Embassy in Pretoria and someone, a British person, had to take it if no staff members were available. My passport stamp signed *'courier'* says that I did the journey on 2 and 16 July and 19 November 1965. It was no walk in the park or should I say easy ride. We travelled during the middle of the day in a small single engined aircraft when it was hot and it was therefore a very bumpy ride. But being chosen as a courier was eagerly awaited because of the bakery at Wanderboom (Pretoria) airport. Whoever was courier for the day was given a list of all the breads that were required so you left with a diplomatic bag strapped to your wrist and returned with many packets of deliciously smelling fresh loaves.

Susan was at Maseru Prep School, or MEMPS as it was known. Looking at a school sports day photo it appears there were about 50-60 children at the school. Sarah started there in January '66. For such a small school they had excellent teachers and they were given a good start in their education. The uniform was green and white checked cotton dress with a green cardigan and a green corduroy pinafore dress in the winter.

The Smarts, my neighbours from Lusaka who were on holiday in South Africa came to stay for a few days in August '65, we took them on a picnic up the mountain road toward Mt. Molimo Nthuse. This was the first of many such days out. The road was quite treacherous as it wound its way up the horseshoe bends toward the *God Help Me* pass at 7,500ft and the *Blue Mountain Pass* at 8,600ft. Just below the *God Help Me Pass* the river flowed close to the road and this made an ideal place for picnics and where the children could swim and climb the waterfalls.

In January '66 Susan started boarding school at St. Michael's in Bloemfontein, this was the oldest girls' school north of the Orange River and was founded in 1874 by the Mother Superior and nuns of the community of St. Michael and all Angels. When Susan and Sarah started school the nuns were very much in evidence but eventually they all retired and it became a public school in 1975, I understand it still has an excellent academic reputation.

The winds of change had started to blow into my life in 1966. Not again I hear you say! Friends told me that Don's car had been seen some evenings outside someone's flat, I was increasingly doing my own thing with my friends, excursions into Bloemfontein, visiting friends, becoming involved in amateur dramatics at the Club. In March Cliff said he was driving to the Copperbelt in Northern Rhodesia to see some old friends so I asked if Sarah and I could go with him as far as Lusaka where we would spend a week with the Smarts. It turned out to be an interesting two week holiday for both Sarah and I as we spent a few days at Victoria Falls and then on to the Great Zimbabwe Ruins which were amazing and I wish then that I had the interest that I have now in architecture and geology to enable me to appreciate all that I saw.

The granite walls were built between 11thC and 15thC and it is said they are the most impressive ancient structures in sub-Saharan Africa. There are turrets and massive walls as well as narrow passageways and the walls of the Great Enclosure are 16ft. thick at the base.

When we returned to Maseru Don inferred that Cliff and I were more than just friends which was not true but this did not help our already deteriorating relationship. In early September I had planned a dinner party for six friends, the first course was a prawn cocktail - that '60s 'must' for any dinner party! Don turned up late in the evening quite the worse for wear just as everyone was leaving. I was mortified and for me it was the final straw. Sarah and I left the house the next day and had a peripatetic existence for the next few weeks staying with friends, the Hancocks, the Shaws and at the Basuto Hat flat whilst decisions as to the future were made.

After ten years to what do I ascribe the end of our marriage? I don't think it was the age difference but certainly a difference in personalities. I was also a very different person at 29 from when I was 19. Maybe I had just grown up and needed more from my life, the fun days in Aden were long gone, the initial years of home and marriage building in Lusaka were gone, the children were no longer babies and therefore more independent and most importantly Don and I now wanted quite different things. He never was a party-goer or a people person, both of which are me, and Maseru in the '60s and 70s was geared to a hedonistic lifestyle, I suppose that in a way this *was* reminiscent of Aden in the '50s.

I found a partner in Cliff, and we had the same friends in Maseru. He was a very sociable and gregarious person and just right for me! Don had agreed to an uncontested divorce providing he kept custody of Susan and I went along with this, surely it was better for a child to be brought up with one parent rather than with two who were always fighting? Once the divorce arrangements were proceeding Sarah and I flew to England at the beginning October to be out of the way.

It was good to see Mum and Grandma B again and Mum made me a lovely wedding outfit. We went to John Lewis in Oxford Street, home to a vast selection of fabrics and bought some blue silk and matching ribbon lace. Mum made a blue silk shift with an overdress in a Mary Quant style with the ribbon lace. With off cuts from the lace I covered a helmet hat shape, it all turned out well!

We returned to Bloemfontein on 26 October where Cliff met us and took us to stay at Riverside Lodge for two weeks until our wedding could be arranged.

Riverside Lodge was always a special place for Maseru inhabitants. It was on the South African side of the Caledon River, just a mile from the Maseru border post. There were rondavels and a main building surrounding a swimming pool and all within mature trees, it was very peaceful and much used for Maseruites specially for Sunday lunches and expertly run by an old Basutoland family, the Poultneys.

Whilst I had been away Basutoland had become Lesotho! Independence Day was on 4 October '66 and the ceremony was presided over by Princess Marina, representing the Queen. So the police force was now the Lesotho Mounted Police.

Cliff and I were married on 12 November (Don and Ethel married in December) and we went for a short honeymoon to the Holiday Inn in central Johannesburg before returning to Maseru and our house in Maseru West. It was a small bungalow in a huge garden, the soil was obviously better than at PMU as there were roses, prickly pear, fruit trees and japonica. One morning I was looking out of the window and the wind was blowing the leaves in the nearby tree revealing a huge crop of cherries of which I had been totally unaware.

Living opposite were John and Astri who we had yet to meet. Astri tells the story of looking out of her window shortly after we had moved in and seeing Cliff hosing me down in the front garden. Not knowing the area we had gone for a walk down the hill and come to a fence by a large green field at the back of which was the river so we thought a stroll by the river would be perfect. We climbed over the fence and started across the green field which turned out to be sewage - hence the hosing down. We later became good friends with Astri and John and had some hilarious games of Scrabble. Although Astri's English was good (she is Norwegian) she didn't realize the meaning of some of the four letter words that she put on the board and even I, in my naivety was at a loss to understand some of them.

One evening we had been to see a scary film 'Wait Till Dark' with Audrey Hepburn as a blind lady, we invited Astri and John back for a late evening drink and managed to get home before them and hide behind the hedge to scare them when they arrived - it worked!

The house was a ten minute walk from the Hancocks with children the same age as Sarah. I would walk to Pat's house for the afternoon, the children would play, Pat would walk halfway back to my house and then I'd turn round and walk part of the way with her and then eventually come home. It was a peaceful walk through the lanes at the back of houses, with the beautiful views of the hills across the river in the Free State. We talked of retiring to live in England and opening a wool shop together where we would be grumpy old ladies and never sell any of our stock. The grumpiness may have come to pass but sadly not the wool shop. We did discover a real find in Bloemfontein which was a warehouse selling packs of wool for R10, so our needles were kept busy.

Come the end of July it was time for Cliff's home leave so we decided to make a real holiday of it. We flew to Athens and did all the tourist sites and enjoyed the Plaka for shopping and restaurants, Sarah obviously had had enough by day three as she said *not another church* after we had been on our feet all day, she was only six and it was jolly hot. This was the first of my many subsequent visits to Athens through work. In England I met my in-laws for the first time in Southport and we spent time with my mother in Clapham.

Astri and John were also on leave in Norway and had invited us to stay with them in Astri's home town Mosjoen in the middle of Norway. On 22 September we flew to Oslo where we spent three days. The first day was traumatic, we left the hotel in the morning for a walk, and walked for an hour or so by which time Sarah was tired and wanted her lunch and a rest, Cliff wanted to turn one way and I another - we had become completely lost so we called a taxi and asked him to take us to the hotel - name?? we couldn't remember except that it sounded like forbundshotel - which as it turned out was correct. We managed to see the Viking Museum and the amazing Holmenkollen ski jump and the sculpture park. Then we had an overnight journey on the train to Mosjoen, changing at Trondheim. Mosjoen was a small town on the fjord backed by mountains on one of which was a patch of snow which never disappears. We stayed with Astri's parents and had delicious meals, berry soup remains a favourite along with a pancake type dessert called lafsa. One day the parents took us out for a day's drive to Bodo on the Arctic Circle, it was a drive through very beautiful scenery but unfortunately as we did not speak each other's language it was a very silent day and we could not ask questions about what we were seeing.

We returned to Maseru at the beginning of October '67 and I started at the local travel agency Maluti Treks and Travel run by Mrs. Chaplin and her son Syd. The office was a small building opposite the Basuto Hat gift shop and the cricket ground of the Maseru Club. It was very unexacting work after my two previous positions with little of the Trek and more of the Travel, again for government officers going on home leave or holidays locally. Syd took care of the Trek side for clients from over the border or even further afield who wanted to get further into the mountains in Lesotho. Eventually for a short while we also took over the handling of the weekly flight to Johannesburg and Janette compiled the load sheets for the cargo and the passenger lists.

Because of the strategic position of the office it became a stopping off point for people passing by or shopping in the Basuto Hat and newcomers to Maseru would pop in to chat and find out what there was to see and do. November '67 saw a very 'with it' lady come in to check on the whereabouts of her freight consignment from England. Wearing a white hot pants all-in one suit and John Lennon specs she was the epitome of London chic; the last posting that Tess and Pete had was in Aden so we had plenty to talk about. Tess still manages to have that something special in her clothes.

It was whilst sorting out a freight consignment that I came across Peter from Aden again. I had written to a shipping company in Cape Town to organise space for a car to go to England and the confirmation letter was signed with Peter's surname and initials, so on the spur of the moment I phoned the office to enquire if indeed it was the same Peter, we had a brief chat but really there wasn't much to talk about, he was now married.

Time to have a break and visit the clothes shops on my journey! These nine years in Maseru were probably my most prolific with regard to dressmaking. It was a case of 'needs must'. I made all Sarah's clothes including her MEMPS uniforms, but when she went to St Michaels the uniform had to be bought. Bloemfontein didn't have much to offer in the way of up-to-date ladies fashions but Collier and Yeats in Maseru always had a limited range of expensive Pringle winter type clothes. Val would phone me and let me know what was coming in. I bought an orange wool skirt with a matching wool and cashmere jumper/top, and a sage green wool skirt with two matching tops, one plain jumper and one tunic style.

I made most of the rest of the dresses that I needed, I rarely wore trousers in those days and because our social life was quite hectic at one stage I had twelve long evening dresses, not all smart of course, but some casual. I was a great knitter - remember all those cheap wools that Pat and I bought in Bloemfontein. I took the monthly Stitchcraft magazine which provided lots of ideas and patterns, two memorable efforts were two dresses with knitted short-sleeved tops and crocheted skirts. One in a rust, the other had a pale blue top with blue, green and navy chevrons for the skirt. I also knitted a pair of orange woollen stockings - fortunately no photos survive of the latter. When in Norway I bought some patterns for the famous Norwegian fair-isle jumpers, and a Norwegian dictionary and subsequently made a jumper and cardigan for Cliff and myself.

Whilst talking about clothes I should mention my hairdresser in Bloemfontein, Martin, he was a whizz with the scissors and was always happy to try the latest styles. This was the time, '67, of hairpieces to add height to your hair and I had just such a piece which was pinned onto the crown of my head and then my own hair styled over and around it. He did make an error one time with colour. I went to have highlights re-done, that was when you had a bathing hat with holes in it put on your head and then a junior in the salon took a crochet hook and tweezed strands of hair through the holes, these strands were then bleached. On this memorable occasion the stupid girl had actually pulled through all my hair so I ended up white blonde all over instead of with blonde highlights. It looked ghastly and I was on stage that weekend too. I tried using a hair dye at home but it had no effect and the bleached hair just had to grow out.

My grandmother died in October '68 aged 86, she had had a sad life since my father died in '63, circumstances meant that she had to leave her nice flat in Upper Richmond Road and move to a room nearby in St. Margaret's Crescent in Putney, her letters show how unhappy she was and maybe I should have done more to help her, hindsight is a wonderful thing.

Unfortunately she never got on with my mother otherwise I am sure Mum would have helped her, as it was it was Mum who had to see her when she died and to arrange her funeral, her ashes were scattered on my father's grave. I look back at her life and see an emancipated young woman who had a career in teaching, who married a reasonably well-off older man. They had a beautiful home, a beloved only son, her own school, and holidays in Europe. Sadly her husband's investments which were meant to look after her in her old age were diminished with the nationalization of the railways so from being a wealthy widow she then had to earn her own living. There is a message here for us all to prepare for our own future wisely.

The years from '68 to the political upheaval beginning in '70 continued on a straight and carefree track exploring more stations en route.

August '68 saw us visiting the Smarts in Swaziland and then all of us going across the border at Nomohasha into Mocambique. The journey is memorable because of the game that we all played in the car during the long drives. Not at all 'pc' now (please forgive me) as it involved using the word 'munt' which is a derogatory named for an African. It meant substituting ment in a word for munt; judgemunt - the judge, pavemunt - the streetwalker, parliamunt - the politician, catchmunt - the baseball player; the list became endless and provoked much merriment (merrimunt - the comic) which the three children, Sarah, Carol and Russell didn't quite understand. We stayed in a very run-down property, I hesitate to call it a hotel at Punta-da-Oura but it was right on the beach and the bar introduced us to katembe, a drink of red wine and coca cola.

During this time I occasionally saw Susan at the swimming pool at the club and we took her out for the odd day out from St. Michael's, in particular a good day remembered was to Kimberley to explore the diamond diggings at the Big Hole.

On a journey there are always restaurants, sadly none existed in those days in Maseru until the Holiday Inn was built but nevertheless entertaining was expected. Dinner and cocktail parties were a necessary part of our social life. The Embassies gave cocktail parties, National days had to be celebrated and Christmas meant that the higher-ups in government gave cocktail parties too and it was de rigueur to put the gold embossed invitations on the mantelpiece, if you had one, or the sideboard or bookcase for everyone to see. When you visited your friends you could take a sneaky peak to see if they had received an invitation that you hadn't or even better, vice versa.

Safari dinners were very popular especially when we lived in Maseru West and our friends were within walking or short driving distance. Starters would be taken in house one, main course in house two, dessert in house three and finally coffee and liqueurs in house four. We usually ended up spending a long time in house four!

One memorable party was a fancy dress do where we had to come as film titles. The Hancocks, Roachs and ourselves went as 'Carry on Fighting' which seemed appropriate for the times, we had military style clothes including medals and Sam Browne belts, caps and toy weapons, the photos show that the cap badges were shamrocks, I have no idea why. Amongst others at the party were 'Goldfinger', 'Mary Poppins', 'Pink Panther', 'Lawrence of Arabia' and 'Waterloo' - presumably the song title.

Another fancy dress party was a 'Roman Orgy', everyone dressed in sheets with laurel wreaths on their heads, rather boring compared with the film titles.

Dinner parties at home were quite formal and there was an unwritten code of trying to outdo your friends and neighbours in the style and elaborateness of the courses. What could originally be a three course dinner of starter, mains and dessert might then morph into a five course meal with the addition of a savoury and cheese course too. I have memories of nightmares the night before a dinner dreaming that I had forgotten to shop or that there had been a disaster in the kitchen. Fortunately I did not have to worry about the non appearance of my husband.

There was a kitchen at Maseru Club which occasionally served only very basic food so Pat H and I decided to start the 40 Club, whereby once a month she and I, and other ladies would take it in turns to would prepare a three course menu for forty discerning diners. Our first effort had steak and kidney pies for the main course, an individual pie for each table which necessitated twelve pies. However as we were taking the pies out of the oven the last pie fell on the floor and the pastry broke into pieces, we hastily put it back together and served it up. Our piéce de résistance though was the dessert trolley which apart from the trifles and chocolate sponges featured my cream caramel, a recurring dish through many future family occasions!

My go-to cook books of the time were those of Lynn Bedford Hall, *'Food with Flair'*, *'More Food with Flair'* and *'More Food with More Flair'*, I liked her style of writing.

Liver pâte: There are 2 ways of making pâte, the proper way, when you use fresh liver and grind it and so on and the quick way when you cheat and hope no-one will know the difference. They will of course but this one is very nice nevertheless and useful in emergencies.....

Chicken mousse with almonds: All cold buffets should include one or two meece as a contrast in colour and texture......

<u>Peach Cream Flambe</u>:An awfully useful pud to know about because although it looks rather fancy the number of ingredients is minimal and you can run it up in no time. Actually it takes 2 mins to assemble - but what is 2 mins between a cook and her reputation?

When the Holiday Inn opened we were able to go out for a restaurant meal to the music of the resident band, Los Indonesios, and on one occasion they had to play 'Raindrops keep falling on my head' as the new roof was leaking badly on the diners. It wasn't the done thing to entertain at the hotel, it had to be home cooking!

My sister Mary came to visit in August '69, it was my birthday present for her 21st birthday earlier in the year, she was supposed to stay for six weeks and eventually stayed for six months until she had to leave because of the unstable situation in Maseru. We were still living in the small house, 118 Maseru West, so it was convenient for her to get around and she became part of the younger unmarried set in Maseru and thus the six weeks went by and the holiday continued. Through a friend that she made, Sandy from Evesham who was visiting her fiancé in Maseru she eventually met her husband to-be, Michael. When the State of Emergency was declared in January '70 the British High Commission said that Mary must leave.

The first general election after independence was held at the end of January '70, there were two political parties involved, the Basotho National Party (BNP) and the Basotho Congress Party (BCP), when it looked as though the BNP would be defeated the Prime Minster declared a state of emergency, suspended the constitution and arrested the opposition leaders. The King was placed under house arrest and took asylum in the Netherlands but he returned to Lesotho in December.

From our house in Maseru West we could hear the gunfire coming from the town and even closer from near the PM's house. Cliff showed us how to find the safest place to hide, away from windows and doors and within the inside corridor. It was a scary time not knowing exactly what was going on, some fires were started in town and there was looting. As this fighting was going on the police families were rounded up and we were taken to the police commissioner's house by the dam at PMU. Here we all spent a couple of nights bedded down on the floor.

This was when Mary was told to leave, obviously the British High Commission was responsible for British personnel in the Colonial service but did not want to be responsible for holiday makers.

At this time the Don, Ethel and Susan left Lesotho for Kenya and as they were no longer living in PMU we were able to return to PMU as it was deemed safer to live there than in Maseru West. We moved into the Highway House at the end of the line of four, the house that had been the Willoughbys. The political situation calmed down for the time being and we were allowed to take our next home leave and were away for six weeks mid April to the end of May, it must have been school holidays as Sarah accompanied us. It was another epic journey. Friends from Maseru, the Wainers, had been posted to Kenya so the three of us stopped there for three days. We had a day out to Lake Nakuru to see the flamingos. Lake Nakuru is in the Rift Valley and the alkalinity of the water and the green algae draws the birds in their thousands. I understand there are not so many birds now but then the lake was pink with the birds until they decided to fly off and then the sky turned pink - an amazing sight.

We visited my old school friend Sylvia, she and her husband lived in Kenya, he was also in the colonial service and I hadn't seen her for many years, lunch was at the Muthaiga club, well known from its 'Happy Valley' days.

Onto to Greece for two days where we took a one day cruise to the three islands of Poros, Hydra and Aegina. All the islands are very different. Poros is small with narrow streets, Hydra a mass of tiered white houses and expensive small yachts in the harbour and Aegina has its Temple, an archaeological site. My photos remind me that we did a lot of walking and I hope that Sarah remembers some of the places that we saw. It is said that a child's mind is most receptive up to seven years, we certainly did our best to introduce new places and ideas to our young daughter.

The next stop on our journey was Istanbul, for four days. Apart from the usual sights in central Istanbul of the Aya Sofia and the Blue Mosque we visited Tokapi Palace. A day was spent taking the normal passenger ferry along the Bosphorus to the Roman Fortress at Rumeli. This was a spectacular sight of walls and towers on the hillside above the Bosphorus, it was then not a much visited tourist attraction but to me it was a special place. There was one downside to this day out. On the ferry Sarah needed to go to the loo which turned out to be a hold in the floor, she was not impressed!

We saw the 'other' Cleopatra's Needle in Istanbul, much cleaner and the hieroglyphics still sharply incised compared with the Needle on the Embankment in London. The last evening was spent at the Kervansaray Restaurant for dinner and belly dancing, Cliff looks rather shocked to be clasped by a scantily clad dancer, Sarah looks on bemused. A month in England seeing all the family and then it was back to Africa. Whilst in Southport we discussed buying a house as an investment and found a chalet bungalow in nearby Formby, in Deansgate Lane, it cost about £5600 and we arranged for it to be rented out. Apart from Sarah and I spending a couple of weeks in the bungalow in December '70 when I bought some furniture, curtains and carpets for the property we never lived in it but it proved a wise investment as when it was sold later at a profit these funds enabled us to buy our first house in Johannesburg.

In November '70 the South African Police in Ladybrand, the nearest South African town to Maseru, invited the Lesotho Mounted Police to their annual Police Ball. We ladies decided to make it memorable by wearing some startling fashions. I made a dress in a green and pink fabric which had a fish tail at the back lined in pink silk but the front was cut high above the knee. Patricia's dress was split down the sides and loosely laced together, Barbara's had a low décolleté and Joan's had a low back. The pre-ball photo shows us looking very smug. I think we were completely outclassed by the Ladybrand ladies who were attired in silks and satins with much jewellery and feathers.

My sister's meeting with Sandy in Maseru and then being introduced to Michael in Evesham led to their marriage. In December '70 Sarah and I flew to England for a short break to attend the January '71 wedding. This was sufficient time for Mum to make Sarah's bridesmaid outfit. A long red corduroy coat with a fur collar, together with beige fur muff and headdress. This was the era of midi fashions, and I bought an emerald green lower-calf length coat over a pale turquoise midi dress and a grey fur hat. I also bought the latest in fashionable boots, in beige linen lacing up the front. Patricia R had bought similar boots and had gone into midi dresses too so we introduced the latest fashions into Maseru.

We returned to Maseru and escalating tensions within the country, Cliff and the other police officers were busy with unrest in the town and chasing miscreants up and down the mountains further afield. There is more that I could write about this time, how South Africa was involved, but I think this will one day be written about in more official terms. Suffice to say that we ladies in PMU learnt how to shoot! Patricia R whose husband Fred was the police commissioner and whose house was below us by the dam, myself and another two ladies were taken to Munda Wanga gardens, just outside PMU and shown how to load and use a revolver and how to prime and throw a grenade. Back in the house I slept with a grenade under my pillow and a revolver on the bedside table.

I was no longer working for Maluti Treks, the manager of Lesotho Airways had asked if I would like to work for him in the airport office for just three mornings a week for roughly the same pay that I was receiving at Maluti Treks. This seemed a good idea and I said I would work on Tuesdays, Wednesdays and Fridays - I couldn't do Thursday as this was the day I had my hair done. Flights to and from Johannesburg had been increased so there was lots of activity and I got to know many of the Government officials who were coming and going between UN offices worldwide. I particularly enjoyed seeing Rev. Desmond Tutu who was such a jolly, friendly person as I am sure he still is - as an Archbishop. The only downside was the dreaded re-issuing of tickets such as those I had to do in Aden.

Another dog came into my life at this time - not an Alsatian or guard dog as you might expect given the uncertain times, but an adorable Springer Spaniel we called Rufus. Cliff had arranged it whilst I was away at the wedding via an advert that he saw in *Farmer's Weekly*. I had to go to Bloemfontein railway station to collect the puppy. I went with Pat H and from the train came the porter with a small wooden slatted crate which had come overnight from Addo in the Eastern Cape. Inside was this fat brown and white bundle with a spotted nose and huge paws, a chuck of bread and a tin of water, empty. He was a great joy to us all. On our walks he received the same offers of marriage as had Sandy!

Sarah's 10th birthday was in May and the problem for parties at this time of the year was always what to do with a group of children in the winter. Cliff hired a small van, put a large label on the front saying *Sarah's Safari* and we took ten children for a picnic up the Mountain Road. We cooked over a fire and the children had all the countryside to explore together with Rufus who of course could not keep out of the freezing cold river. Since then Sarah has had many safaris on her birthdays.

As the journey proceeds to the ongoing political events of '72 a brief stop will look at that other important pastime of all colonials - amateur dramatics. On my first visit to Maseru club I had seen *The Captain's Table* and had been impressed with the professionalism of the production. Maseru Players usually put on three plays annually plus an Old Time Music Hall near Christmas.

Cliff and I became involved both on and off stage. Six weeks of rehearsals were followed by performances on Friday and Saturday evenings with the addition of Thursday evening if the performance was thought to be sufficiently popular. The Music Halls followed the standard lines of all Victorian Music Halls with a Chairman of Ceremonies who gave forth innuendoes and witty comments. The Chairman was Fred R and then his place was taken by Cliff, immaculately clad in full Victorian evening dress. The programme consisted of various sketches, mostly humorous even lewd, always a scantily clad chorus and ended with a one act Victorian melodrama. One that I took part in was called *Temptation Sordid or Virtue Rewarded.* The audience who sat at round tables and were served drinks and snacks were encouraged by the Chairman to boo and cheer throughout the performance. Patricia R and I took part in several of the music hall melodramas, for some reason I always played the good girl dressed in white and she played the bad one dressed in red. We kept a bottle of Here XVII (a South African fizz) behind the stage and fortified ourselves as we came and went.

I played Miranda the mermaid in *Mad about Men.* This involved a day trip to Johannesburg to the theatrical costumiers to hire a flowing blonde wig and a mermaid's tail. The tail was very effective but once on it meant that I had to be carried if I needed to move. At one point in the play I had to say 'I hear the sound of a conch shell', the chap in charge of sound effects got his tapes muddled and instead of our version of a conch shell we had the National Anthem. Cliff and I acted in *Murder in Company* and I produced and acted in *Home is the Hunted.* There were other productions but I have forgotten them.

1972 turned out to be a busy year, Sarah started boarding at St. Michael's in Bloemfontein in January, this meant that I had many opportunities for going into Bloemfontein for shopping and catching up with her in school. Early in the year Cliff's mother came to visit for a short holiday and we took her to visit the Chans at the Chinese Embassy and for the inevitable picnic up the mountain road.

Even though outwardly our social life continued as before political events were accelerating, there was still much unrest in the country, even in Maseru and there were mutterings as to how involved the police had been in both sides of the political divide. With such an uneasiness lurking and not knowing what the future might bring we, along with others in the PMU decided to pack into a trunk our treasures - books, silver, special knick-knacks etc which were taken into store in Ladybrand.

Easter Sunday saw us sitting in the garden with friends including Fred and Patricia R having a lunchtime braai. Remember that Fred was Commissioner of Police and lived in the house below us. During lunch young Rufus began digging a hole under the fence and we laughingly remarked that he was trying to escape.

The next day Fred was told to leave the country so he and Patricia immediately crossed the border to Riverside Lodge where they stayed until their homeward passage by ship could be arranged. That same day Cliff and I went to their house and took out everything that we could and gradually ferried their possessions across to them at Riverside. Changes then occurred within the police force and PMU and Cliff was asked to leave PMU and become Director of the Prison Service. This meant that we had to leave our house at PMU and we moved to a large house in Maseru West which had formerly been occupied by Yvonne and Tony, another police (also ex NRP) couple.

I need to tell you about Yvonne. She was French and had been in the Resistance during the war, she had been captured and escaped and had many stories to tell. She was invited to meetings to talk about her exploits but always read from notes. When asked why she did this she said that it was important for her to tell her story exactly as it was when she wrote it immediately after her experiences otherwise if she had talked without her contemporaneous notes she might have unwittingly embellished her story.

It was good to be back in Maseru West again within walking distance of friends. I haven't previously mentioned our maid Alina who had been with us since I married Cliff, she too was glad to be back in town as being in the police camp had meant that she was far from her friends and her shops.

Our next home leave came round again at the end of May, this time Sarah stayed at boarding school whilst Cliff and I left for an interesting holiday en route to England where Sarah would fly home on her own to join us. We flew to Athens for a couple of beach days before joining the Epirotiki Lines ship *Orion* for a seven day cruise around the Greek islands. One day we spent on the beach at Glyfada, this was the nearest beach to the centre of Athens and easily accessible by the local bus, lovely white sands and very few people. At one stage there was a sound I can only describe as heavy, I know sound can be loud but this was definitely a feeling of heaviness rather than loudness, the beach seemed to shudder and the sound/feeling approached and then seemingly within touching distance Concorde went over our heads on one of its test flights. All we could see was the underside of the aircraft as it passed apparently slowly on its way - I was so fortunate years later to fly to the USA on Concorde.

This was to be the first of several such cruises that I made through work. I have to mention clothes again as Patricia R gave me two beautiful outfits that her sister had passed on to her. A black lace skirt, black silk pleated sleeveless top and a most gorgeous black lace jacket which was covered in black silk flowers which shimmered and fluttered as I walked. The other was a red silk pleated cocktail dress. I had made other dresses for the cruise, mostly in crimplene for ease of wash and wear.

The seven days offered the very best way of seeing the Greek islands and I never tired of repeating the same itinerary with groups in the future. The first stop was at Santorini, that iconic island that everyone knows from its bright whitewashed houses perched on the side of this volcanic island. In those days the only way from the harbour to the top of the island was by donkey up a zig-zag path, the journey taking about fifteen minutes. Going up was easy as a rider but going down felt more precipitous as you tried to sit upright as the donkey went fast downhill. Nowadays there is a cable car that does the same journey in just a couple of minutes.

Next stop was Mykonos - no nude bathing for us, just a wander around the main part of the harbour with excellent restaurants, even then it was becoming touristy with lots of shops selling tatty souvenirs. A pelican called Petros was a feature of the harbour, he wandered at will amongst the shops and cafes and was made a mascot for the island. I understand he died in 1985 aged 30 but he has been replaced by other pelicans. Walking away from the harbour we followed a path on the edge of the water around a promontory to Little Venice, a quiet area of cafes and restaurants built right on the edge of the sea with their balconies overhanging the water. Just minutes from the main harbour this was a area of peace with few tourists.

Whilst the ship was docked at Mykonos we took a small boat for a visit to nearby Delos, one of the most important historical and archaeological sites in Greece. Here is the spectacular terrace of Lions, seven remaining stone sculptures of mythical beasts made more impressive by the avenue that they create.

On to the coast of Turkey and the port of Kusadasi which is used by cruise ships for people to take a tour to Ephesus but we decided to explore the small town which then had few facilities for tourists. A short walk along a nearby narrow causeway took us to an almost deserted island with a ruined Byzantine Castle. There was no-one else there except us and a hippie that we saw sleeping under some trees. It was impossible to imagine that the next time I saw this place it was accessed by buses and restaurants lined the island's water's edge.

The final port of call before returning to Athens was Istanbul. As we had been here before we knew what to expect. We had a shopping spree in the bazaar. I bought a brown suede long coat and a pale blue leather jacket and Cliff a leather jacket too and we went to see the new bridge which was being built to span the Bosphorus and so join Europe to Asia. On to Athens, a flight to Rome for a couple of nights and then a flight to Basle to embark on a cruise down the Rhine. We had a whole day to spend in Basle so after wandering around decided to go to the zoo where it was possible to sit down and relax without having to spend any money in what was a very expensive country. We found seats at the top of an auditorium above a pool where apparently there was to be eventually a display from seals and penguins. We whiled away the hours waiting for the show as we had such a good view of the pool. The show began, the rest of the audience stood up, and we couldn't see a thing. Thankfully we left and embarked on *M.V. Helvetia* for the cruise to Rotterdam. The scenery en route was stunning particularly Heidelberg and the Lorelei Rock but I have two rather silly memories. Firstly I had never come across a duvet before and was not sure how to cope with it - where was the sheet. Secondly we came to a lock on the river and Cliff and I were on deck watching the lock fill with water when I had an OMG moment, I had forgotten to close the cabin windows!

The month spent in Southport and London was busy as we met up with Patricia R and Fred and their families and had a riotous supper at Flanagans in Baker Street which went on until very late, the Flanagan's menu was in the Old Music Hall poster style and printed on a large board, as we left the restaurant Fred put the board under his jacket.

We then planned with Patricia and Fred and his family a day out in Paris so off we set by train from London - no Eurostar in those days. At Dover Fred's Mum said she had forgotten her passport so there was a delay whilst somehow she obtained a travel document. Off we went on the hovercraft to Boulogne where we were told not to bother to go onto Paris as it was Bastille Day and all the shops would be shut - we had quite forgotten the date. Nevertheless we had a marvellous day around Boulogne market and in and out of bars and restaurants. Our only purchases were several boxes of liqueur chocolates and a couple of bottle of wine, all of which were consumed on the Dover to London train. Also I had just that week started to wear contact lens and one decided to disappear as we arrived in Boulogne, I thought it was lost forever but as is the way with contact lens it eventually reappeared in my eye!

Leave over and back to Maseru where in December my mother came out for a four week visit and we took her on a tour to visit friends away from Maseru. A few entries from her diary give a flavour of her holiday:

12 December. Ann drove me around town, bought an evening dress at Collier and Yeats, present from Cliff, another dress in the sale £2. Went round Basuto Hat, lovely things.

13 December. Up early to fetch Sarah from school, Pat H came, did some shopping, picked Sarah up went over her school, very modern. Had lunch, very nice restaurant, kebabs and rice. Drove back home at 4.30pm went to Neil's house for a swim, absolutely super house and garden and pool, has Alsatian, sheepdog and Siamese kitten. Came home changed Neil took us to Holiday Inn for dinner, Cliff, Ann, Neil played roulette, made for the machines, won few bob and came back and sat on patio and had a few drinks.

14 December. Went to Robertsons for drinks. Beautiful house and furniture, came back for dinner party at Ann's. Super food, Avocado mousse, chicken in barbecue sauce, peach mousse (ah ha one of Lynn Bedford Hall's meece) *strawberries and ginger tart. Super evening.*

17 December. left 6.30am, marvellous drive, breakfast at Graaf Reinet reached Mossel Bay 1pm.Children went to beach, braai in garden, super weather, great fun.

18 December. Ann and I went to shops and bought some presents, light lunch, onto beach for swim. Ian got boat out and they went fishing, late dinner very good, they bought back some large fish, bonito, cooked them in newspaper over the fire.

19 December. Went to Ostrich farm, went into caves had a meal in restaurant came home and early night.

22 December. Messed about and packed. Rained. left at 2.15pm, arrived motel 6.30pm. Good Motel Bethesda between Graaf Reinet and Middelburg. very nice flat, 2 large double rooms and bath and loo, peacocks and fantail pigeons, rose garden, had good dinner and in bed 9.30 did not sleep very well.

23 December. Breakfast at Colesburg, ice creams at Edenburg home at 1pm. 1500 miles in the week, 607 miles to Mossel Bay from Maseru. Took Rufus for a walk over the golf course, had a drink in the club house and met the Walters who are coming for Christmas dinner.

24 December. Cliff off to play golf with the Fairbairns 9am, beautiful am, lovely breeze, lunch at club. Came home had a rest, changed for dinner at club, 14 on our table, left at midnight. all came back to Ann's for coffee and mince pies, Mabel and Roger from TY were there Got pretty wild so I went to bed about 2.30am. Sarah and I did Christmas presents in the afternoon.

25 December. Cliff brought in tea at 8am. Mary rang from England 8.30am, lovely to hear her voice. Opened presents I had some lovely things, bracelet from Sarah, my evening dress from Cliff, Lesotho dress length of Khotso print, E. Arden makeup, notelets, all from Ann. Went to Mr. Clifford's for drinks and mince pies at 11am, back at 12. Super Christmas dinner, went for a swim at Neil's, quiet evening on verandah until Chris and Anthony arrived (Fairbairns). Sarah played her tape recorder back to us. Boys and Walters left at 10pm.......finally in bed 10.30 pm. Hectic day, tomorrow to look forward to.

28December. Wrote some cards, went into town with Ann to do her weekly shopping, bought some t shirts for Bruce, very cheap, 30c each. Had a lazy afternoon - Ann took Rufus for a swim. Went to Fairbairns for dinner. Discussed New Year's Eve Ball, all going as Charge of The Light Brigade. Mr. and Mrs. Pike were there and the boys brought some girls, left at midnight very tired.

30 December. Took picnic to the mountain stream, 42 miles away up very rough roads. Beautiful spot - lovely wild flowers and everything looked lush/ Cows fat and shiny. The water was very cold but went in after much persuasion.

31 December. Washed my hair early and Ann set it for me.....we left with Linda and David at 11.30 for TY for lunch, arrived at 12.10. Saw Mrs C, looking very ill. Invited to Paul's wedding next Saturday, met his fiancée, very young. Blue Mountain Inn very nice- lovely pool and gardens. Bought some pottery(this would be from the excellent Kolonyama Pottery). *Super lunch, 10 of us at table after lunch the rest played badminton and swam in the pool. Home early to rest before going to the dance. Wore my green dress. Went to Maurice and Audrey for drinks at 7.30 onto the club about 9pm. Hall very nice. Jolly evening. Ann took me home at 3am, they went back to Pike's to swim and got home 4.30a.m.*

1 January '73. All woke very late then went to Neil's to swim, crowd there including Myra's sister and parents. Poured with rain, terrific thunderstorms so all had to go inside and listened to records and had coffee, then on to Fairbairns, played badminton and I left there at 6pm with Sarah when they started playing poker. Sarah and I played scrabble and draughts, we went to bed 9.30pm Ann and Cliff home soon after 10pm. Pat H rang - had a burglary. Temp only 72.

3 January. Went down to bank then to café for fruit and vegetables and Collier and Yeats. Picked up Cliff and Sarah at Hancocks for lunch. Drove to Ladybrand and went for a swim at Leliehoek - super place - very cheap, then to cinema at drive-in. Had supper in car. 'Gumshoe' with Albert Finney and Billie Whitelaw, not very good. Back across border at 10.30p.m.. Edwina stayed the night.(Edwina is Sarah's friend)

4 January. Telegram from Mary wanting to know when I was due home. Called at florist to buy plant for Yvonne Dare- picked up Linda Fairbairn and drove to Kolonyama, Dares have a beautiful house, children swam nearly all day, went over the pottery before lunch and bought some things, very nice lunch and then drove to the weaving place not far away....drove Linda back and left for home. Very hot, Had a drink with Linda whilst Sarah and Edwina played badminton, Cliff playing tennis with Audrey - they won. Paul C married in Maseru at 4p.m. to Patricia C. Reception on Sat. at TY, we are invited but not going. Called at Pat's to take Edwina home and stayed for a beer. Curry puffs for supper, Cliff and Sarah played chess for a while. Thunder and lightning still no rain.

5 January. Very hot and humid - stayed in nearly all day and read. Cliff played tennis and won. All went to Pat's for dinner, super meal, onion soup, prawns and rice, meringues and peaches and coffee. Sat on verandah until midnight.

6 January. Ann off to airport for an hour's work when she came back we went to Riverside Lodge for a swim and drink. Invited to dinner dance at the club, Pikes, Fairbairns & BEA pilot friend of Maurice. Super evening, very nice meal and home at 1.15a.m.

7 January. Did some packing.

I make no apologies for including so many of my mother's holiday diary entries as she provides an insight into what life was like in Maseru in those days, the timetable, the visits and dinners, the friends, all carried on just as she said both before and after her holiday. I am not sure how we coped with all those parties and late nights but we did.

In January, not long after Mum returned to London my sister Mary, her husband Michael and small son Bruce arrived for a short holiday. Mary and Michael flew to Semonkong and took Basuto ponies to ride to the Maletsunyane Falls. It is one of the highest waterfalls in Africa at 192m. Our maid Alina looked after Bruce for the day, she called him young master, a grand title for an 18 month old boy!

July '73 saw one of the Music Halls that I have already mentioned and the year slipped away towards a grand camping adventure for New Year's Eve. Together with the Hancocks and the Woods we were a party of six adults and seven young children plus of course Rufus the Springer. We had three tents, numerous items of camping equipment and a gas ring for cooking. Pat H and I made a large pot of stew which Rufus partially knocked over but we piled the stew back into the pot and no-one was the worse for wear - or even knew about it. Since it was a similar occurrence to what had happened with the 40 club dinner I think we must have been jinxed.

The journey in the Mountain Kingdom was slowly coming to an end. Changes were taking place within the Government which suggested that officers from overseas were no longer necessary to run the police or prisons departments or that it was a question of off with the old guard and on with the new. Patricia and Fred R. had made a new life for themselves in Johannesburg after spending only a short time in England so it seemed that this might be the way for us to go. In the meantime we were approached by a lady who lived in Maseru and who wanted to build a luxury hotel in TY and asked if we would be prepared to run it. It seemed a daunting task as neither Cliff nor I had any experience whatsoever but we thought with some training it might be possible and it was a way for us to stay in Lesotho, which we loved. However the Government had other ideas and would not renew our resident's permits after our colonial service ended. For a final option to stay cocooned within the colonial framework it was suggested to Cliff that he apply for a vacant position with the police department in the Turks and Caicos Islands. We found them on the atlas and they looked remote in the Caribbean, further investigation meant that Sarah would have to go to boarding school in England and all provisions came by boat or air from Miami. It seemed a step too far and too great a change in a way of life. Now of course the Turks and Caicos are a renowned high class tourist resort, white sandy beaches and azure blue sea and luxury hotels, its sounds idyllic for a holiday but I think we made the correct decision.

Before leaving my job with Lesotho Airways I took advantage of cheap fares so in July '74 Sarah and I flew to Calpe in Spain, via Madrid to stay with Susan for ten days who was living there with her partner Terry before going on to England for the rest of the time. We caught up with the Hancocks who were also on holiday, touring in a camper van and they spent some time in Evesham. We had a memorable day out in Stratford upon Avon. As we arrived at Anne Hathaway's cottage and parked the car, a tourist bus was seen approaching, so we dashed into the cottage and probably had the fastest ever run through the house to get out before the busload arrived. The children remember it to this day - the rush, not necessarily the history of Anne Hathaway.

We returned to Maseru - Sarah back to school in Bloemfontein and Cliff and I reluctantly to pack up to leave after nine years in this special country. Our farewell party was given by the Maseru Players and took place under the stage at the Club and our farewell gift was a dinner service of Kolonyama pottery - lovely to have but so heavy to pack and to use.

'Tomorrow to fresh Woods, and Pastures new'
John Milton

CHAPTER 6
Heading to the Highveld....and other foreign parts

' The truth is you don't know what is going to happen tomorrow, life is a crazy ride, and nothing is guaranteed'. Eminem

Before we left on our onward journey in August '74 some planning had to take place. Sarah was at boarding school until the end of the school year in December and we then had to think about where she would continue her education in Johannesburg. Up to now all school fees had been paid by the Crown Agents, as was standard practice for children of overseas colonial civil servants. In fact Crown Agents had a good deal with us as if Sarah had gone to a boarding school in the UK the fees would have been more expensive and they would have had to pay for her flights to Africa for each holiday. Following on from my own example with fees for St Paul's and my holiday flights to Aden.

We had looked at Greenside school in Johannesburg but it was obvious that Sarah should stay at St Michael's and fortunately Cliff was able to afford the fees and I think the overnight train journeys to and from school provided great entertainment for Sarah and her friends.

Of major importance was work for Cliff and through contacts he was offered the post of a salesman for a company selling wooden pallets, not a very fulfilling position compared with being Director of Prisons, but a job is a job and it filled a gap between leaving Lesotho and getting established in Johannesburg. His office was in Germiston, just outside Johannesburg so we rented a two storey flat at Lake Club in Germiston, it was not an ideal place for Rufus as there was no garden which meant he had to be taken for walks several times a day. I started work for a travel agency in Germiston and very boring it was too, I think I lasted for three months before joining Avex Air at Rand airport also in Germiston to look after their charter division.

Apart from the hours, 5.30a.m. to 12.30p.m. or 12noon to 6.30p.m. it was really interesting work, taking the bookings for charter flights, all on small mainly single engined and twin Cessnas to many small airstrips in southern Africa. Calculating the cost of the flight was very simple. There was a large wall map of southern Africa, a pin and piece of measured string at Johannesburg and so you used the string to measure in a straight line where the client needed to go and costed it per mile per type of aircraft. All of the pilots were part-time so then it was a question of finding a pilot who was registered for whichever aircraft you were using, telling the hangar which aircraft were needed the next day and phoning the catering lady to order packed breakfasts or lunches. There could therefore be many comings and goings during the day with flights going to disparate parts of the country connected for example with commerce or the mining industry. The type of aircraft used had to be compatible with the length of the runway and able to cope with the weather forecasted.

Avex also flew crop spraying aircraft which were used all over the country and the manager had a Pitts Special aircraft of his own for acrobatics. In the two years that I was at Avex there were two fatal accidents, Linda, a young pilot flying alone in a charter aircraft crashed and a crop sprayer, Peter, also crashed the same year - his girl friend had just arrived from England and I had to go to her flat to give her the terrible news.

Although we had only been away from Lesotho since August by the end of December the call to return for a visit was very strong and so the three of us returned for another camping trip with the Hancocks up the mountain road where unlike the previous year the weather was awful, it rained continuously, I think Rufus was the only happy creature there. We went unannounced to the lunch party held by the Dares at Kolonyama on New Year's Day, in retrospect I think this was not the right thing to have done. We had said our farewells and everyone there had got on with their lives and weren't really interested in what we had been doing in Johannesburg.

1975 brought another wedding in the family, no not mine again, Susan and Terry married in England at Wandsworth Town Hall, my sister Mary and her son Bruce were there and they visited Mum later in the day.

Selling wooden pallets was not the fulfilling work that Cliff needed so he began looking for something else and was fortuitously made head of security at Wits University which was situated in Braamfontein, almost in the city centre. This meant leaving the flat in Germiston and finding somewhere to live in Johannesburg. We sold the house in Formby for nearly twice its original cost and were able to purchase a small house in Parkhurst, a suburb just four miles from Wits.

All the houses in Parkhurst were small! Unlike the other northern suburbs with their large plots of land and equally large executive style houses those in Parkhurst were originally simple tin-roofed houses built on 200sq.m of land. The houses date from 1919 when a farm in the Braamfontein area was designated for use as a new suburb of Johannesburg. The design of all the houses was the same although looking at the same houses in current times most have had a make-over with extensions and re-modelling. A feature of the interior of the main two front rooms were the pressed steel ceilings which had a border of flowers and designs around the edge and also around the ceiling lights.

Our house was No.79 Sixth Street, on the main road through from Parktown to Greenside, it was surrounded by a high wall with 79 painted in huge letters on the roadside of the wall. A small garden had been well designed in the front, at the rear was a lawn and hedge and a collection of reeds and bulrushes. Shops were nearby in Fourth Avenue, there was a greengrocer, shoe mender and a small café and supermarket, a liquor store and a shop for baby clothes. Today Fourth Avenue is full of trendy shops and restaurants and on the site of the shoe mender is a café called 'Cobblers'. We were close to the stream at Victory Park which was an ideal place to walk the water loving Springer Spaniel.

I continued to work for Avex Air although it meant getting up at 4.30a.m. when I was on the early shift but for Cliff it was only a short trip to the University.

We had a house warming party in August '75 and the photos show all the friends who would become part of our social scene in Johannesburg. The Roachs were back in SA and lived fairly near in Parkwood, the Woods, Sheila and Tony, Bernard and Em, Blanche, the Fingers and the Hancocks who were visiting from Lesotho. I am not going to go through all the parties that took place as they followed along the same lines each time with the same people and alternating at the same venues.

After a year at Wits Cliff was due for leave so we had a few days in Calpe, with Susan and Terry, Susan was pregnant and Simon was born in September then on to Evesham to stay with Mum and then Southport. We had nowhere to stay in Southport so we hired a VW camper van which was parked at Cliff's sister's house for us to sleep in, it was far too uncomfortable for my bad back so I was given a mattress in the house. I am not sure how we afforded this holiday since we would have had to pay our own air fares!

Back in Johannesburg we had two visits from friends, in August Jim and Jean Melvin, old friends from Lusaka days came for two weeks followed by Chris Willoughby our neighbour from Maseru who was now a Queen's Messenger. This meant that he had to carry the Diplomatic Bag between the UK and overseas countries, just as I had done as a courier between Maseru and Pretoria. But he had far more interesting tales to tell especially of his journeys to places like Siberia and Russia. He gave me a yellow luggage label stating 'On Her Majesty's Service', of course I never used it and eventually passed it on to his son Simon. One of the benefits of living in Johannesburg was that it was a stopping off point for our friends going from one country to another and enabled us to keep in touch with them.

In November '76 we decided that a swimming pool was needed in our tiny back garden and within two weeks the lawn had gone to be replaced by a reasonable sized pool with a fountain - I wanted the sound of water in the pool to compensate for being so far from the sound of the sea. To keep down the costs Cliff said he would dispose of the spare soil - quite a considerable pile! He hired a lorry from the University and some helpers and took the soil to Zoo Lake where some grounds were being developed, our ex garden soil made a nice slope in that part of Zoo Lake. We nearly had a fatality in the pool in early '79 when my sister Mary came for a holiday with Ross aged 2½, he was sitting on the edge of the pool, at the deepish end when he fell in backwards, fortunately Cliff managed to scoop him out. It was on this holiday too that Mary, and I walked to Fourth Avenue, Parkhurst to do some shopping and Ross sat down in middle of the main road and had a wailing fit! Mary just walked away and left him till he calmed down, in the meantime one of the local African ladies was so horrified she picked him up, obviously not appreciative of our way of coping with tantrums!

The pool was a great success and the site of many noisy lunchtime going into evening parties which then ended with us hiring a film and a projector and squeezing into our small sitting room to watch, usually a scary, film. Often as the first reel started there was a shout 'seen it'! The film was helped along by sustenance from a quick visit to the American doughnut shop at Hyde Park.

I made a quick visit to England in February '77 to celebrate my fortieth birthday, it was hard to reconcile the fact that I was now a grandmother before I became forty but as my mother said, she was a great grandmother before she was seventy. So four generations of us were together, Mum, me, Susan and Simon

The Roachs, our friends from Maseru and who lived in Parkwood now decided in July to return to live in England. They had a big sale at the house which turned into more of a party than a sale and then a sad farewell braai at the Tuckers farm. Cliff and I went to Cape Town to make sure they boarded the Windsor Castle for their homeward voyage and incidentally the final voyage of that ship. We had a few days touring the Western Cape with them, visiting the wine farms at Franschoek and one day Patricia and I had a morning in Cape Town for shopping. We passed by the offices of a shipping company and the name rang a bell with me, so I said to Patricia leave me here there is someone I want to see and I will meet you later and in I dashed, she subsequently thought I might have gone for good! Anyway I found Peter's office and we talked for a while catching up on the past twenty two years. Later that day I met Peter and his wife for a drink but as she did not know Aden we had nothing in common - apart from Peter, and the evening fizzled out, I didn't see or hear from Peter again and he died some years later in South Africa.

Patricia and Fred subsequently became the licensees of the Town Arms in Wallingford, not for too long though as the spell of Africa eventually brought them back to Johannesburg.

Sarah's matric dance at St. Michael's that year had a Greek theme and I offered to make the dessert which meant that I had the epic task of making baklava for 200! Having made the individual pieces they then had to be stored in the freezer and then transported to Bloemfontein, all went well but I haven't made baklava since.

Cliff's sister Clemence came on holiday in January '78 and we took her on a grand tour of the tourist sites. The Eastern Transvaal has always been an attraction for holiday makers with the mountains of the Highveld falling down into the Lowveld at the Blyde River Canyon. There was a panoramic view of the Lowveld from God's Window looking down 900m into the forests below. The Mac Mac Falls were spectacular, as it was the rainy season they were in full flow, and we bathed in the pools below the Falls. We stayed at Mount Sheba Hotel which also should have had stunning views but the whole time we were there the surroundings were covered in mist. I think Clemence must have been tired of hearing us say 'oh such a pity you cannot see the lovely view from here' etc. We visited Pilgrim's Rest, now a national monument, it was here that gold was found in 1873, and this small town has been kept largely unspoilt to give a flavour of what mining life was like in the early days of the gold rush.

A visit then to Pretoria to see the Union Buildings, seat of the South African government. The building was a splendid creation by Sir Herbert Baker in 1913 and has many echoes of the work that he did with Lutyens in New Delhi. Whilst in South Africa Baker also designed some of the grander sandstone houses in Johannesburg. Because the Union Buildings were constructed on a disused quarry the gardens are terraced downwards in what were the quarry sides and this makes a perfect setting for the buildings themselves.

To end Clemence's holiday we were fortunate, through our social contacts, to take her down a gold mine at Elsburg. I can't tell you how deep we went, certainly not as far as the deepest mine in Boksburg at 11,000ft. but it was deep enough to feel very hot and almost compressed by the rocks above. Photos show us clad in gumboots, white overalls, waterproof jackets and hard hats. Having an image of the dirt and blackness of a coal mine I was astounded that inside this gold mine everything was so clean and orderly.

By now I was getting tired of the early morning starts and decided to leave Avex Air and find work somewhere nearer to home. Whilst at

Rand airport I had met Monty Fuhr, the owner of Tuli Safari Lodge in Botswana and who flew in his own aircraft to and from the Lodge. Monty had purchased the land in 1964 and was creating a luxury lodge for families to have a wild-life experience. He had an office in the centre of Johannesburg, on the ground floor of a block opposite the Carlton Centre and it is here that I went to become the mornings only receptionist. Frankly there was very little to do other than answer the odd phone call and pass on messages from the Lodge to Monty in Johannesburg regarding provisions that were needed at the Lodge. The odd tourist came in to find out about driving to Tuli - about six hours from Johannesburg, or chartering an aircraft.

For me the best thing was being in the centre of town where I had friends who also worked there and who could visit for a coffee. Sheila DB skated at the ice rink in the Carlton Centre and Blanche worked opposite too. I took the bus to work in the morning and before opening the office went to the bakery in the basement of the Carlton Centre where there were always fresh Danish pastries. Monty was quite flexible regarding my working hours and this became useful.

Across the road in Commissioner Street were the offices of British Airways, and one of the Sales Reps, Mike Hogan, that I had known from his visits to Maluti Treks called into the Tuli office on occasions when he was in Johannesburg, and he asked if I would like to go to Swaziland for a couple of weeks to help sort out the Swazi Air reservations office, I am not sure how BA and Swazi Air were connected but anyway it seemed like fun at the time so in April '78 I took a couple of weeks off from the Tuli office and flew to Matsapa in Swaziland and stayed at the George Hotel inManzini. It wasn't so good being in the hotel on my own especially as I didn't know anyone so I soon sorted out the reservations system at Swazi Air and was home at the end of the two weeks.

Having been in South Africa for twelve years I still hadn't experienced the 'wild' side of the country until Em S. suggested we make up a small party to do a walking safari in the Umfolozi Game Park in Natal. The Umfolozi is the oldest nature reserve in Africa and has all of the Big Five, elephant, rhino, lion, buffalo and leopard, and it has the largest population of white rhino in the world.

The Five Day safari was planned for November, and taking part would be Cliff, Sarah (school half-term) and myself , Em and her husband Bernard and friend Liz and of course a Ranger to lead us. Base Camp where we started was a mixture of rondavels and wooden huts but after that we had overnights in simple two-man tents. We each carried a day pack with water and lunch, everything else was transported for us, unseen, by porters. Walking each day was at a leisurely pace as the Ranger would stop to talk about beetles and leaves and animals along the way. We saw many white rhino, and paw prints of leopard and lion, and at night the sound of a lion is very chilling. On the first morning we were asked not to talk whilst we were walking so that we could be aware of what was around us, also advised that whilst rhino have bad eyesight they can smell humans and can run fast so in the event of coming across a rhino we should be prepared to climb up the nearest tree, in fact to mark our nearest tree all the time whilst walking - all very well but all the trees were thorn trees. The Ranger carried a gun 'just in case' we were approached by leopard or lion. Apart from the beauty of the bush two memorable experiences linger; crossing on foot the very wide and shallow Umfolozi river and actually lying down and cooling off in it fully clothed during the heat of the day (crocodiles??) and all of us squashing into one tent for supper one evening during a ferocious thunderstorm. This brief taste of a safari gave Sarah the experience to take with her to Canada.
Sarah was accepted by the Rotary Club of Bloemfontein to be part of their exchange programme which took place each year when students of above average in terms of academic ability, with pleasant and outgoing personalities were sent to other countries in the role of ambassadors. She was sent to the Rotary Club of Langley, south of Vancouver where she spent 1979 staying with Rotarians and attending the local school.

Time now to talk about the Zulu War, Isandlwana and Rorke's Drift. Cliff has made an in-depth study of these last two battles and can give an hour by hour account of what happened and who was involved. We have always commemorated the anniversary of one or the other battle on the 22nd or 23rd of January, the battles took place in 1879. In January 1979 we went to Natal to be at the sites of the battles for the 100th anniversary. It was a very strange day on the 22nd at Isandlwana. We had expected there to be many sightseers and dignitaries but no-one was there but us until eventually a minibus arrived bearing some obviously military men who laid a wreath at the main grave which bore a commemorative plaque. All over the battle site were cairns of white stones covering where men had fallen and Cliff explained the progress of the battle. We then walked to the ford on the Buffalo River known as Fugitive's Drift as it was here that Lieutenants Coghill and Melville were killed trying to take the Queen's Colour of the 1st Battalion of the 24th Regiment to safety. The flag was eventually found in the river in February '79 and what survives of it is in Brecon Cathedral, South Wales, where I have seen its bedraggled remains.

On to Rorke's Drift where Cliff showed how the defence of the garrison had progressed. When we visited it was still relatively unspoilt with just a small museum in what had been the hospital which was so heavily defended.

It was two years since I had been to England so having Sarah in Canada was a good excuse to combine a visit to see her with an stay in England to catch up with all the family so in five weeks away from the end of July I made my first crossing of the Atlantic and saw old friends here and there.

Sylvia and Dermott were on leave from Kenya and I spent a day with them in Bristol where we visited Dermott's brother who was an expert in pewter. His workshop was in an intriguing part of Bristol called Christmas Steps. The very narrow streets lined with small shops and workshops are part medieval Bristol and so different from the modern high rises and the port area.

Off to Southport to see the Hurst family and then to Evesham. Susan, Terry and Simon (who then were living in Nailsea) came to stay in Evesham so we had a lovely family get together further enhanced by friends from Maseru, the Fairbairns coming for a Sunday lunch. In London I spent the day with the Smarts, on holiday from Swaziland.

I realise how fortunate I was to be able to travel frequently which enabled me to keep in touch with my family and friends from earlier days and places.

Sarah's host family in Langley, Rick and Wendy Buck, gave me a wonderful insight into Vancouver and its environs, the city itself is skyscrapers but surrounded by beautiful countryside and special features. Grouse Mountain is a backdrop to the city and in winter is snow covered and used for skiing but a cable car to the top in summer gave a superb view over the city and towards the Rockies. Together with Sarah we had a day out up the Fraser River, a twisting and turning road on the edge of the gorge. The sign in my photo says :

FRASER CANYON

This awesome gorge has always been an obstacle to transportation. Indians used ladders and road builders hung shelves to skirt the cliffs. Canoes rarely dared its whirlpools; only one sternwheeler traversed it successfully. Railroads and highways challenged it with tunnels and bridges, but today man and nature still battle here for supremacy.

At Hell's Gate, where the water is compressed into a narrowing of the river we took at short ride across in a suspended gondola; the river was not so full at that time of the year but I believe at the end of winter the torrents really rage! We picnicked in a forest not far from the road, there were comfortable wooden tables and benches and rather alarming signs saying *Beware of the Bears.*

Stanley Park is a green oasis almost in the city centre and apart from the trees and plants it was the totem poles that were the most memorable. These intricately carved and painted objects stand about 25ft. tall, I can't remember how many there were in the park and I know that in recent times some have been moved, but I can see in my photo at least four totem poles.

About 40 miles south of Vancouver are the Shannon Falls and Howe Sound at Squamish. I have never been to New Zealand but the juxtaposition of water, snow capped mountains and forests ishow I imagine NZ from photos I have seen of that country. The Shannon Falls drop 100 ft, not in one curtain but a series of steps almost like a bridal veil. This same day we continued south across the Canada/US border into Washington State and to Mount Baker. At over 10,000ft. and partially snow-covered it was a formidable mass and is one of the snowiest places in the world (Wikipedia) which must account for the amount of snow still visible in the height of summer.

A final visit was to Gastown, an old part of Vancouver which has thankfully been preserved with narrow streets and old buildings of superb Victorian architecture. Rather similar to Bristol where the old is preserved amongst the new.

On the return journey to Johannesburg I stopped in Toronto to visit Cliff's relations at St Catherine's, Ontario and to meet old Johannesburg friends the O'Hagans, who took me to Niagara Falls. They are half the height of Victoria Falls and surrounded by skyscrapers and all the trappings of urban life. They had no magic for me. There is something so much more appealing about a rural rather than an urban waterfall! Victoria Falls, Shannon Falls, Maletsunyane Falls (and Iguazu which I haven't yet taken you to) have a romance and a mystery surrounding them, I could sit beside them or gaze at them and become lost in the essence of their power, water and spray, at Niagara I just got wet!

I have got ahead of myself in telling you about Canada as at the beginning of '79 I had a career move and joined Thomas Cook and this was how I was able to travel to Canada, on an agent's discounted air ticket - 25% of the normal cost. I joined the Wholesale Department which had various sides to it including being the General Sales Agents for various hotel chains. My position was in the group tours department, putting together worldwide tours to be sold through magazines or in our own in-house brochure. We did not deal with the public, only with agents who booked our tours for their clients. Going to work for a company as large as Thomas Cook was very different from the small companies where I had been previously. We wore a uniform and there was a TC way of doing everything! In this pre-computer age all was done manually in both senses of the word, with hands and manuals!

I have already introduced you to the B.O.A.C manuals from my Aden Airways days, but Thomas Cook was manual driven. The red and blue ABC volumes were issued monthly and contained timetables of all flights everywhere in the world and without them it was impossible to operate in the travel world. I had used them in Aden but there the flight details we required were very limited, in

Johannesburg I was dealing with flights for groups all over the world. Then there were manuals for hotels worldwide with descriptions and prices, useful for planning an overseas tour although we had to deal with TC offices in various countries to make the hotel and ground arrangements and yes there was a manual of all the approved ground handlers worldwide, mostly TC but some others affiliated with the company.

There were two 'bibles' in the office, the Thomas Cook European Rail Timetable and the Thomas Cook Worldwide Rail Timetable. All railway journeys were recorded in full as well as maps of the centre of major towns. There were two older gentleman in the department who had spent their entire working lives with TC either in England or South Africa and they had an encyclopaedic knowledge of these Timetables, when they worked in London twenty or thirty years previously they were mainly dealing with clients travelling everywhere by train. These Timetables of about 500 pages each had been published monthly from 1870 and I understand publication ceased in 2013, the printed word being overtaking by online sites and as well as being unable to cope with changes in train times due to rail strikes and 'leaves on the line'. Although I was introduced to the Timetables by the two venerable gentleman who made sure I understood their complexities I did not have the need forrail journeys for my group tours.

However I did have occasion to use the South American Timetable. Although in the wholesale department we did not deal with individual clients two of the wealthy patrons from the travel shop downstairs were referred to me in order to give them a quiet and personal service and plan their journey across South America - by rail. It was a continent of which I then knew nothing but after some homework I was able to assist and they went on an extended journey through Brazil, Argentina, Chile and Peru. All must have gone to plan as on their return they came to the office to give me a present of a leather travel wallet.

Together with the Marketing Department we were planning tours to be promoted the following year in magazines and also preparing the Thomas Cook brochure of tours from South Africa. There was 'The Land of the Midnight Sun' to Norway Denmark and Sweden, 'Hong Kong and Bangkok', 'The Far East' including Japan,

Taiwan Hong Kong and Singapore, 'Andes and Amazon' including Brazil, Peru, and Bolivia and 'India and Nepal'. There were short tours to Greece and Italy for the magazine readers, all other European requests could be accommodated via tours from the UK Thomas Cook brochures. Apart from Norway and parts of Europe I had no personal knowledge of the other countries so had to do much creative writing when preparing the 'blurb' for the tours.

So I planned the itinerary, booked the flights, contacted the ground handler for the transfers, local touring and hotel arrangements and prepared the costing based on an estimate of how many people we hoped would book the tour. With various foreign currencies involved these had to be bought forward so that any fluctuations would not adversely affect the prices. A tour leader always accompanied the tours, either from the magazine or from amongst the staff. In December there was a seven day tour to Rio de Janeiro and I was asked to be the tour leader, it took place over Christmas but Cliff was well looked after with parties and Sarah was in Evesham for the festive period on her way home from Canada to Johannesburg.

We were only a small group of ten plus me and a week was just the right amount of time to see the sights in Rio. Rio is often compared with Vancouver as one of the most scenic cities, and Rio certainly has the edge for beaches with Copacabana and Ipanema but I prefer the backdrop of snow covered mountains in Vancouver. Nevertheless the Statue of Christ the Redeemer and the Sugar Loaf mountain provide focal points for tourist photos. On the day we went to the Christ statue it was above the clouds so the views were mostly obscured, we took the cable car to Sugar Loaf, hardly a mountain, but it does provide fantastic views along the coastline. A memorable day was spent going by schooner to the island of Jaguanum, south of Rio. We swam from the schooner in the beautiful clear, warm waters and then swam to the island for lunch.

Back in Johannesburg Cliff, with friends, was busy converting the maid's room into a pied á terre for our soon to be university student daughter. It turned out well, an ensuite study bedroom right by the swimming pool and with access to the road without coming through the main house. The photos show the very '70s style of curtains, cushions and bedcover. It was all ready for when Sarah returned in January '80 just in time to start the academic year at Wits University.

My mother came for a short holiday in January, her last visit was in January '73 to Maseru so this was her first to Johannesburg but this time she left no diary entries to record her activities and I have the usual photos of lunch time braais and evening parties with friends.

Cliff , Sarah and I decided to explore more of South Africa during the Easter break and we travelled with the Smiths to Plettenberg Bay via Graaf Reinet. This town is in the middle of the semi-arid Karoo desert in the eastern Cape Province and it is one of the oldest towns in South Africa. Many of the buildings are in the iconic Cape Dutch style and one of these is the Drostdy Hotel where we spent the night.

Our flat overlooked the beach at Plett, beautiful white sand with hardly a person to be seen and well known for its emblem, the pansy shell. These shells really do look like pansies, and we were able to find some as we strolled along the sands. At this time Plettenberg Bay was completely unspoilt, just the one hotel called Beacon Island, and at the end of the bay the peninsula Robberg was pristine without buildings. Seeing this place many years later it was sad to see the encroachment of civilisation along the beach, on Robberg and in the town.

A short drive from Plett is the small secluded bay of Noetzie and we stopped here to see the 'Castles'. An extraordinary collection of what are in reality private homes which were constructed during the 20thC from the local stones. Why do they all look like castles?

The oldest castle, at the end of the beach, was built as a holiday house by Herbert Stephen Henderson, who lived in what was then Southern Rhodesia. He started building it in 1930 out of the local natural stone. The story goes that he had no intention of building a "castle", but simply used the stone for practical reasons, when Rex Metelerkamp, a member of a well-known local family, who was watching the building, jokingly said "All you need to do is to add a few turrets and you'll have a castle". And he did! That set the trend, and Pezula, up on the hill, was completed in the late 1930's, and became known simply as "The Castle" , in 1942 his son Ian built

Montrose in the 1970's and the Lindsays built "Perekuil ", now known as Lindsay Castle, in the 1960's.

http://noetziecastles.co.za/history

This area of the Eastern Cape known as the Garden Route has its own beauty, the coastal area is backed by the Tsitsikamma mountains which run from west to east along the coast and in the forests are the ancient yellowwood and iron wood trees. Yellowwood has been used to make some distinctive items of furniture, as the furniture ages so the colour of the wood turns from yellow to a mellow orange. Another town near Plett that we visited is Knysna a small town on the edge of a lagoon which is protected by two headlands which almost join to encircle the lagoon, these are the Knysna Heads. There is a well-known story about George Rex who died in Knysna in 1839. It was suggested that he was the illegitimate son of George III and his mistress Hannah Lightfoot and that he had been banished to the Cape, given large areas of land, and forbidden to marry. It was he who founded Knysna and played a key role in its development. Modern DNA technology has disproved his royal lineage and he was descended from a Rix family in Norfolk, England.

Further journeys in South Africa continued in July when Rick, Sarah's Rotarian host from Langley came to visit for a short holiday. With Blanche (she always seemed to be with us) and Sarah who was on University hols we went back to the Eastern Transvaal and this time, being the winter and rain free the views were what we had hoped to show Clemence when she had been here during the rainy season of mists and clouds. We stayed again at Mount Sheba Hotel and took Rick to see the breathtaking views of the Blyde River Canyon. A photo shows us on the edge of the Canyon looking over to the rock formations known as the Three Rondavels.

The Three Rondavels are spectacular peaks which look exactly like rondavels – round and fat, rising to a peaked top, but much, much higher than any traditional dwelling. In fact, when you stand on the viewpoint, 1 380m above sea level with the Blyde River Canyon below, you'll still be looking up at those three distinctive peaks which tower 700m above the surrounding countryside.

http://www.southafrica.net/za/en/articles/entry/article-southafrica.net-the-three-rondavels

Writing about all these journeys that we took around South Africa I realise how fortunate I was to see so much of the country, some residents hardly set foot out of their own Province except to take an annual trek to the sea for their December holidays. And I wonder how many colonials, after their tours of duty in Basutoland, Bechualand or Swaziland actually took time to explore South Africa. The current marketing slogan for South Africa 'The World in One Country' says it all.

Finally for 1980 my passport stamps show that I spent four days in Lisbon at the beginning of December but I have no recall of this and no photos. Over the years I did become as familiar with Lisbon as I was with Athens and I guess this must have been a work related visit to look at hotels for a proposed tour.

1981 turned out to be a year of travels and upheavals. I had to go to Athens for a week at the end of February to sort out some hotels and touring arrangements for prospective groups. I met for the first time Lena who was a ground handler and she became my Athens friend. She met me at the airport with her car piled high with pillows, blankets and clothing. There had been a terrific earthquake in Athens two days previously causing widespread panic and as there was a fear of an aftershock Athenians were sleeping in their cars. The earthquake was 6.6 on the Richter scale and centred only 44 miles west of Athens; added to this it was snowing! As this was my third visit to Athens I had already done the tourist things so the days concentrated on seeing hotels and features for tours. I stayed in the St George Hotel on Lycabettus hill in the area known as Kolonaki with its small shops, galleries and museums. For me it was in a far better situation that the more well known properties in the Plaka and Constitution Square. Being on the hill you could look out across the centre of Athens to the stunning view of the Acropolis. In the summer it would be cooler and hopefully above the traffic fumes of central Athens.

Back in Johannesburg we decided to sell the house in Parkhurst and move to a larger house in Berea, why we would leave the house with a pool where we had been happy I have no idea, maybe the pull of a large house more suited to socialising was the answer? Who knows. As it happened we had to move into temporary accommodation in a flat in Senate House in Wits for six weeks whilst the house renovations were completed. At the same time Susan and Terry with Simon 5yrs and Robin 1½ decided to leave England and re-locate to South Africa so they squashed into the flat with us for a few days whilst they recovered from the flight and planned their onward move to Natal. At least Cliff and Sarah were on the spot for work and classes and I could still get the bus to work.

Work finished in May and we moved into 27 York Street, Berea, on the corner of Lily Avenue. - yet another station along the line. Berea was one of the older suburbs, proclaimed in 1893, and the houses built around the first two decades of the 20thC. Our house was given a date of 1919, I am not sure by whom. Prior to the renovations it was a fairly simple looking house but with a pillared porch, verandah extension and a high surrounding wall it became quite pretentious. The rooms were large and ceilings high and it generally had a grander feel than the Parkhurst house. In May we had a house warming party 'The Theme of the Era - 1919' and photos show a mixture of garments interpreting this theme from late Edwardian through to twenties 'flappers' with Tony DB dressed as a miner, appropriate for remembering Johannesburg's origins; Sheila DB always glamorous; Trish H a flapper in white tassels; Peter H another miner; Paddy P an Edwardian gent; Blanche another flapper - they are all dead now. Cliff in a red smoking jacket, me in a brown negligee heaven knows why; Jenny as a Can-Can girl, Sarah not sure what she came as; Em S a gold and green flapper; Chippy in his Cambridge Blue blazer with Julie in a yellow flapper dress and headband; Rina in a '20s bathing outfit and so on.

Sarah celebrated her 20th birthday in May and had now moved out and was sharing a flat with friends so we took as a lodger Rina from TC.

Who can forget the day of Princess Diana's wedding, 21 July 1981? I took a day's holiday from work and spent the day in Bryanston at Sheila DB's house together with all our lady friends.

We made a party of the day as we watched the TV transmissions from London. Diana's dress was gorgeous even if it did swamp her tiny frame but we loved all the pomp and ceremony and seeing who we recognised in the congregation in St Paul's Cathedral.

I was coming home on the bus from work in September when it started to snow!!!By the time I had arrived at the house the snow was 5 ins. deep and everywhere looked extraordinary, the photos actually look like stage sets and have that eerie light that you associate with the onset of a snowstorm.

This year was becoming one for journeys to Greece, after the February visit there were two more short trips involving looking after groups, one for twelve days at the end of June which included a four day cruise of the Greek Islands and for a week at the end of August which included a seven day cruise of the islands. Now you can understand why I was getting to know Athens and some of the islands so well.

Cliff and I had a three week holiday from mid October, back to Athens for a couple of nights and then a seven day cruise on *MTS Atlas* of Epirotiki Lines. Because of all the business that I had been giving this company I was able to get free cruises whenever I wanted them - within reason.

On this particular cruise we stopped at Rhodes for a full day and explored the Old Town where I bought a gold bracelet, and then to the beach at Lindos. The next stop was Haifa where we had a full day for exploring Jerusalem, visiting the Wailing Wall and walking the Via Dolorosa and sitting by the Olive Tree in Bethlehem. I did this same cruise some years later when the walk through Jerusalem was very tense behind a guide who was well armed. I had particularly wanted to do this cruise as it stopped in Port Said and I wanted to see the changes from my 1954 visit on the *Kenya.* The iconic building of Simon Artz was still there by the harbour offices so we went ashore to see what we could buy. Remembering from my previous visit that Simon Artz had seemed like Harrods of the East this time it was more down market bazaar. Gone were the exotic and mundane replaced by pathetic souvenirs for the tourists. It was very sad.

Next stop was Kusadasi in Turkey, still as relatively tourist free as in our previous visit, my 'if only' moment came about when browsing the shops. In an antique cum junk shop was a very pretty cup and saucer, I am certain it was a Clarice Cliff crocus design, it may have been fake but for the few cents that it was priced at I should have bought it - 'if only'.

We then flew on to UK and a gathering of the Hurst clan in Southport. They were nearly all there, Cliff's mother, his sisters and their other halves, and all their children, looking at the photos thirty six years later is to be reminded of those who have since died, and to appreciate how all the children have become adults with families of their own, and I am pleased that in spite of subsequent events Clemence's children and grandchildren are still part of Sarah's life.

November saw me flying to Malawi for two days. We had a problem at work with getting Indian visas for a group and as the nearest Indian representative was in Malawi I was summoned to go and see what I could do. I flew into Blantyre and then took a car to the capital Lilongwe and met the Indian chap in charge of visas. I remember him as being very unhelpful but in the end we did get the visas for the group. This tour of India and Nepal was a new one that I had put together with the help of the Thomas Cook offices in India and as one of the places that I really wanted to see was the Taj Mahal I lived in hope of being able to take one of the tours. The other place on my bucket list was Macchu Pichu in Peru so I was quite interested in how popular the Andes and Amazon tours became!

The year ended with a party on New Year's Eve, themed 'The Circus'. I suppose that we had so many parties in our social circle that in order to have some interest beyond eating and drinking there was the competitive interest of fancy dress. Cliff went as the bearded lady and looked fearsome in my long blue dress and a blonde wig with his own beard, Rina and I were clowns and quite unrecognisable under our makeup and false red noses. Perhaps it is fancy dress that makes us less inhibited as the photos show that it was a wild party.

The battle of Isandlwana was commemorated on 22 January with a dinner party in the house, no fancy dress this time, it was a strictly black tie event. Somehow we arranged seating for 42, with four large tables between the dining room and sitting room. A large Union Jack flew over the fireplace and Cliff's bone china small statue of the 24th Regiment's drummer boy oversaw the proceedings. Cliff gave an account of that day in 1879 and although the menu has long gone I remember it as a good evening amongst so many friends. Followed by the inevitable lunch time braai - back at ours- on the next day. The Little Drummer Boy mentioned above was made by the porcelain sculptor Michael Sutty (1936-2003)and is perfect in every detail of uniform and accoutrements, Cliff donated it some years ago to the Regimental Museum in Brecon, South Wales.

Now it is boring time again, telling you of further journeys. One of the insurance companies in Johannesburg, clients of Thomas Cook, ran an incentive programme for their sales personnel called the180 Club, and the prize for the winners was a tour to exotic places, the best of everything had to be included, the best hotels, gifts in rooms, high class touring to out of the way places and so on. The number of winners in this incentive programme was about thirty so together with partners the group numbered sixty. A TC staff member always had to accompany the group to ensure that all went to plan so at the end of April Cliff and I went with the group for a fifteen days tour to include Hong Kong and Bangkok. Cliff was able to come as we needed two tour leaders for such a large group and no one from TC was available. It was such a perfect introduction to the East for me and I am grateful to Thomas Cook for giving me the opportunity to experience both destinations as it became useful years later when I was planning more incentive tours to Hong Kong and Thailand.

The most hair-raising experience came before you even landed in Hong Kong, as the aircraft descended into Kai Tak airport it passed over blocks of flats at the height of their washing lines, how did we miss gathering washing along the way? Then the aircraft lands and only just manages to stop before the end of the runway disappears into the China Sea. Sadly, or not, this adventure is no longer possible as a new airport was opened in 1998 about twenty miles from the city centre.

'With a perilous runway that juts out into the sea, and a descent through skyscrapers and craggy mountains, Kai Tak airport in Hong Kong was seen as the ultimate test of a pilot's skills. The airport-

which was shut down in 1998- was the site of botched landings that included planes crashing into the water and pilots aborting landings when conditions were poor'. http://www.dailymail.co.uk

We stayed in the five star Hyatt Hotel on Hong Kong Island which was an excellent base for seeing the Island and then crossing on the Star Ferry to Kowloon. The photos show that we did all the touristy visits expected of us; Tiger Balm Gardens, dinner on the Jumbo Floating Restaurant, shopping in Stanley Market, a cruise around Aberdeen working harbour - very smelly- and a particularly good day out to Cheng Chau island. This was about six miles by ferry from Hong Kong and although it had the usual harbour and markets it had a much quieter atmosphere than the frenetic pace of the Mainland and Hong Kong Island. Whilst here we were aware of what was going on in the Falkland Islands but perhaps there was less impact than if we had been in England at the time and watching the conflict gradually unfold on television.

There had been much for me to buy at Stanley Market, some beautifully embroidered table linen and two bags USD5 each, rather like chain mail, for evening dressy wear. Several of the 'incentive' wives were buying these too as they seemed to be fashionable. On the next 180 Club tour - more of that later - one of these ladies came to me and said I had made her buy rubbish bags in Stanley market and they had fallen apart. Well I bought two of these bags and they are still going strong after thirty five years. I found that on these sort of incentive tours where everything of the highest standard is paid for by the commercial company there is always someone, usually a wife, who complains.

I had some free time and wanted to buy a 21st birthday present for Sarah so visited a recommended jeweller to look for a pearl necklace. This was an experience, whereas in England or indeed South Africa you would go into the shop, be shown several necklaces within your price range and then chose one, here it was a lengthy process. How long would you like the necklace to be, which size and colour of pearl, graduated or all the same size and finally what sort of clasp - diamonds, pearls, sapphires? Eventually after much deliberation and cups of tea I bought or should I say compiled two necklaces, one for Sarah and one for me. Somehow all this was fitted into five days in Hong Kong and then we were off to Thailand.

Our hotel was the Siam Intercontinental in Bangkok, thankfully not a high rise but a pagoda style low rise surrounded by acres of gardens with a swimming pool, tennis courts, peacocks - it was thought to be 'the epitome of beauty and graciousness of all hotels' and this right in the centre of the madness of Bangkok. How sad that all this was demolished in 2002 to make way for yet another shopping centre.

However our room, as were all the others, was luxurious and filled with arrangements of orchids, so exotic to us but as common here as zinnias or pansies in South Africa. We were only here for four days so there was much to see in a short time. A day out at the Rose Garden Thai village about thirty miles from Bangkok in Nakorn Pathom. It was a scenically pretty area and we saw traditional Thai dancing, and elephants being trained to perform - Thai elephants are so much smaller than their African counterparts. I think it was a rather contrived day specially prepared for tourists, not my cup of tea but the group seemed to enjoy it - no moans anyway.

The morning at the Floating Market of Damoen Saduak was more my style. There was a coach journey of about 40 miles to start with before we reached the village where we embarked on the long-tailed boats each seating ten persons, down the winding canals, through villages and waterside gardens. You really see the village life on the water's edge. At the market were boats selling food, fruit and vegetables and on shore were stalls selling cheap counterfeit watches and handbags of well known brands as well as local handicrafts. It was busy and touristy but still had an authentic atmosphere.

One of the best ways of seeing Bangkok and avoiding the horrendous road traffic is by water and the group had lunch and an afternoon cruise on a rice barge on the Chao Phyra River, the day ending with dinner at a seafood restaurant where there was the dubious pleasure of selecting your own live lobster.

During a free morning when the group were temple visiting Cliff and I were invited by our ground handlers, representatives of Thomas Cook in Thailand, to visit the Oriental Hotel in Bangkok, obviously with the eye to future business from South Africa. This was such an opportunity as the Oriental was not a place you could just walk into and order a coffee! Apart from the sumptuous surroundings and luxuriously furnished suites some named after famous authors I was impressed by the mountainous arrangements of orchids and the beautifully carved cedar wood chandeliers and lampshades.

After four days in Bangkok it was off to Pattaya for the final four days of beachside relaxation. But before this occurred I should explain part of a tour leader's work. The group had to place their suitcases outside their bedrooms by 11pm, the baggage, probably three or four cases for each of thirty rooms was then taken by the porters to the basement. Complaints arose of course - in the morning where am I going to pack my nightie and toilet bag? - I had heard it all before. In the meantime the ground handler had contacted the next hotel to ascertain bedroom numbers so that the baggage could be placed in the rooms to await the occupants' arrival - we don't want to have to wait for our cases do we? After midnight my job was to go down into the basement and locate all the cases, remove old labels and attach new labels with the room number for the next hotel. This took at least two hours.

At 8a.m. in the morning we set off by coach for the 90 mile journey to Pattaya and the Royal Cliff Beach Hotel. At this time the hotel was quite isolated on a promontory but only a short distance from the town of Pattaya which then had an unenviable reputation for drugs, drink and sex! We did make an trip into the town to 'Alcazar' for an evening's cabaret and entertainment by the gorgeous 'girls'. They were all extremely glamorous, with eye-catching brief costumes and they were all transvestites.

We took a lunchtime cruise to Koh Lam, known as the Coral Island, with an excellent Indian style lunch and then time on the clean sandy beaches of the island. The farewell gala dinner - a must for every incentive tour, was set up on the patio by the swimming pool to the accompaniment of a local band. It went well to start with but then the rain came and that was the end of the evening, and the tour as we departed the next day for the homeward journey via Hong Kong. I loved the sea and beaches at Pattaya and was then not to know that I would be returning again and again in the future.

We had to celebrate Sarah's 21st on 30 May and with Fred and Patricia R we decided to have a joint party at our house for their middle daughter Jenny who was 21 on 4 April. It was a gathering of the great and the good which started on the actual birthday with a lunchtime braai at the farm just outside Johannesburg where Teresa R lived. Susan and Terry with Simon and Robin as well as Tess (she of the John Lennon specs in Aden) and Peter D came up from Durban for the celebrations. With six Roaches and sundry other friends it was a large lunchtime do. The actual party took place on 4June and it was such a happy and joyous occasion. Perhaps my comments on the pages in the photo album for the party can give you a flavour of how the evening passed.

The Cake. Suitably inscribed with their names and with 2 keys of the door, 21 candles and flower decorations. Flowers on the table in burgundy and pink. Napkins in burgundy, pink and beige.
The Birthday Girls. Jenny and Sarah standing each side of the cake.
A drink before the rush - in the kitchen. Patricia, Ann, Fred and Cliff toasting each other.
A Speech. Cliff delivering the eulogy!
A Toast. Some of the guests caught raising their glasses. Blanche, Sheila, Helen, Mr Tucker, Em, Tess.
The Reply. Jenny and Sarah holding pieces of paper and looking puzzled.
The Reaction. Cliff and Jenny kissing. Ann wiping away the tears. Susan looking smashing in a very revealing black outfit. Cliff helping himself to Chateau Cardboard- actually Autumn Harvest.
Dinner. Lots of people queuing around the buffet table, names already mentioned as well as Tony, Graham C, Roland, Peter H, Rina, Anne C, Dr and Mrs Hayes, Helen L, Anne and Rim, and many more of Sarah's and Jenny's friends.

Menu

4th April *30th May*

Mousselines Jennifer
Venison Rue de York
Chicken á la Sarah
Pommes Patricia
Salade Ann
Crème Caramel Clifford
Salad Fruites Frederick

Fromage Varies *Here XVII*
Pain aux fines herbes *Vin du Sud Afrique*

Gateau Vingt et Un

Maseru Prep School & Headmistress - a few years on. Mrs Hayes surrounded by eight former pupils including two Roaches, two Hancocks, Sarah and Justine.
The Tall Stories. Cliff, Fred and Peter D, gesticulating in the manner of 'the fish was this big'.
The Jokes. Dr Hayes standing in the middle of the room surrounded by everyone sitting on floor and chairs not looking terribly amused
Near the end of the evening. Only a few guests remain, sitting on the carpet with shoes off, dirty wine glasses everywhere.
Morning after the night before - why the hilarity? We three, the Deans and their two boys, Patricia and Fred, Susan, Terry, Simon and Robin, all in the kitchen and all in great spirits!

In retrospect it was probably the last large party we had in the house, I'm not sure how many attended but it must have been over forty. Cliff and I were due for a three week holiday at the end of September so using my Agent's discounted air tickets and the contacts that I had made in South America we set off on an exploration. We repeated the Rio de Janeiro sites that I had already seen, Corcovado, Sugar Loaf, and the Tijuaca Falls and sampled the national dish Feijoada which was a lunchtime special at the Copacabana Palace Hotel. This dish is similar to the South African Potjie being a stew of many different kinds of meat with the addition of black beans.

We flew on to Iguazu on the Argentina side of the Falls. I have mentioned these Falls previously contrasting them with Victoria and Niagara Falls, And whilst Victoria Falls are still the most impressive and awe inspiring it cannot be denied that those at Iguazu are beautiful. Not as tall as Victoria Falls they are much wider - about 1.7 miles and they comprise several curtains of water not one large curtain as in Victoria Falls when it is in full flow. Apparently Eleanor Roosevelt reportedly said, on seeing Iguazu for the first time 'poor Niagara'! The Falls run between Argentina and Brazil and nearby we saw the closing stages of the completion of the dam for the Itaipu Hydroelectric scheme on the Parana river between Brazil and Paraguay. The enormous scale of the dam could only be seen when it was under construction with all its concrete structures still laid bare like the skeleton of a gigantic beast; the dam was finally completed and opened in 1984.

On we flew to Manaus in Brazil, what stays in my memory is the flight over the Amazonian forests where the complete view from horizon to horizon in all directions was of forests and where it was possible to see the curvature of the earth. I know that now these forests have suffered terrible deforestation through logging and mining activities so we were privileged to see this area in an almost pristine state. The Tropical Hotel was not far from the airport on the banks of the Rio Negro and surrounded by rain forest, it was huge, with long wings radiating out from the central block and I think our suite was at the furthest distance - but as it was free there were no complaints!

Manaus was a busy vibrant town with amazing architecture. The prosperity of the town was based on the demand for rubber which came from the trees in the Amazon forest and the market for this rubber expanded during the last part of the 19^{th}C. The market place had been designed by Eiffel and the stained glass windows brought from Paris in the early 1900s. My photos show gentlemen's residences in the grand baroque style and the piéce de resistance was surely the Renaissance style Opera House, opened in 1896, which would not look out of place in an Italian setting. Most of the materials for the Opera House were imported - glass chandeliers from Italy, tiles from Alsace, furniture from France and the floors were an art form in yellowwood and a darker wood. I heard that Sarah Bernhardt performed here but have no confirmation of this.

It is interesting that many of the pavements in Manaus featured the wave patterns known as 'Meeting of the Waters' created in black and white stones, these same pavements are found on the beachside promenades in Rio de Janeiro and also in Portimao in the Algarve, all original or current Portuguese territories. On a day cruise from Manaus on the Amazon we came to the actual meeting of the waters where the dark waters of the Rio Negro meet the paler waters of the upper Amazon known as Rio Solimoes, combining to form the mighty Amazon. The differences are due to differing density, temperature and speed and the two rivers flow side by side for about 4 miles before the waters eventually combine. There is no diving off the side of the boat for a swim here as this river is home to piranhas!

The harbour at Manaus was full of vessels of all sizes including large freighters loading and off-loading at the docks, nothing remarkable in this for a port except that Manaus is 1000 miles from the sea at the Atlantic Ocean. We were invited to visit the Army Zoo outside Manaus, I am not a fan of zoos as I prefer to see wild animals in their natural habitats, and sure enough seeing a jaguar and a large black cat - a panther? in cages was very sad, there were lots of colourful birds, parrots and macaws too.

The onward flight from Manaus to Iquitos in Peru was by a small aircraft making two stops en route, Tefe and Tabatinga where an assortment of colourfully dressed locals embarked together with their chickens and a myriad of bags. I was particularly interested to see Tabatinga and to photograph the corrugated iron sheds of its 'International' airport. To a non travel person of my era or indeed any current travel person it is difficult to explain, but I will have ago. I have told you about having to compute air fares in those early days according not only to the mileage of the itinerary of the passenger but also according to where the aircraft stopped en route between points A and B, and that all fares between direct points had a MPM or maximum permitted mileage that could be flown. If the itinerary exceeded the MPM then a surcharge of 5,10,15 or 25% was charged. But an anomaly occurs where you can sometimes get round the MPM by using another destination with a higher MPM that the passenger is not actually going to so if you make a routing using the actual itinerary and insert fictitious sectors to this place with the higher MPM you can make the fare come within the MPM. I hope I haven't lost you! Tabatinga was one of those places, I can't now remember the mileage that was allocated to this airport of tin roofs and chickens in the middle of nowhere but for any South American fares and indeed some to the USA and even Round the World journeys, good old TOT, the airline code for Tabatinga, featured in the fare computations. Its other claim to fame is the town where the Amazon passes from Peru into Brazil.

Iquitos like Manaus was founded on the rubber boom of the late 19thC and it is said to be the world's largest city that cannot be reached by road - only by air or river. The harbour, over 2000 miles from the Atlantic was busy with smaller ocean going vessels than in Manaus. From here we went by coach and then small boat deep into the rain forest for a stay at the Amazon Village Lodge. Accommodation was in very basic thatched roofed huts with an open thatched central space for eating and meeting. We spent four days here taking excursions by small boats along the river to see the local villages and how the villagers lived. Travelling along the river the exercise was to see glimpses of the colourful birdlife as this was macaw and parrot territory, I surpassed myself by spotting far ahead on a tree on the river bank a large bright blue bird which had the guide flummoxed for a name, when we got closer it was a plastic bag, pollution reaching so far up the Amazon too.

The next flight took us to Lima, the capital of Peru with its beautiful Spanish Colonial architecture, I particularly like the wooden balconies on the upper floors along narrow residential streets. It is said you can tell a tourist in Lima as he always carries an umbrella expecting rain! The weather is such that it is generally cloudy and even foggy on many days due to the cool waters of the Humbolt current in the Pacific Ocean. An interesting visit was to the archaeological site of the cemetery at Puruchuco, constructed by the Incas in the 15thC. This was my first introduction to the massive scale of constructions of the Incas, huge symmetrical blocks of finely finished stone fashioned into walls and ramps.

Onwards across the snow capped Andes to Cusco, gateway to one of my 'must see' places, Macchu Picchu. But Cusco did not disappoint, it is a picturesque town of red tiled roofs, Spanish

Colonial architecture and elaborate churches. The altitude here is 11,000ft so tourists are advised to take it easy for a day or so, no long walks or too much exertion but coming from Johannesburg at 5700ft we did not seem to be troubled by the altitude. I expect that now there are many large modern hotels in Cusco but we stayed in the delightful Alhambra, an inn on a side street with wooden shutters and delicate wrought iron grilles over the windows. The local women wore the national dress, a bowler hat, striped woollen skirt and knitted shawls, babies were carried on mum's back in the African style. The main square, Plaza de Armas is dominated by the 16thC Jesuit church, over the top colonial baroque in style on the exterior and opulent in gold and statuary inside.

Close to Cusco is the site of Sacsayhuaman (pronounced sexy woman!), a series of walls and terraces constructed from unbelievably large blocks of stone. My introduction to Inca building technique's had been in Puruchuco but those at Sacsayhuaman far surpassed them. The official wording best describes what is in my photos.

The largest stone blocks at Sacsayhuaman (some of which are over 28ft high), are regularly estimated to weigh over 120 tons, while more enthusiastic estimates place the largest stones at 300 tons, 361 tons, 440 tons. So precise was the masonry that one block on the outer walls, for example, has faces cut to fit perfectly with 12 other blocks. Other blocks were cut with as many as 36 sides. All the blocks were fitted together so precisely that a thickness gauge could not be inserted between them.
http://www.ancient-wisdom.com/perusacsahuaman.htm

Even the high walls along the narrow streets in the town feature large blocks of finely finished stone. There is no resemblance here to the limestone rubble walls of old houses in the Cotswolds, but more of a step in line with the fine ashlar constructions of the University of Oxford buildings.
The journey by train to Macchu Picchu winds along the Urubamba River Valley thence by a small coach, to cope with the hairpin bends, up the mountainside to reach this once lost city which is at 8000ft, at a lower elevation than Cusco which makes it less breathless for

walking. The site, the views, were all I expected and more so. As it is such an important place, one of the new seven wonders of the world, some of its history is worth recording.

Machu Picchu is an Incan citadel set high in the Andes Mountains in Peru, above the Urubamba River valley. Built in the 15th century and later abandoned, it's renowned for its sophisticated dry-stone walls that fuse huge blocks without the use of mortar, intriguing buildings that play on astronomical alignments and panoramic views. Its exact former use remains a mystery. In *1911 American historian and explorer Hiram Bingham travelled the region looking for the old Inca capital and was shown to Machu Picchu by a local farmer. Bingham brought Machu Picchu to international attention and organized another expedition in 1912 to undertake major clearing and excavation. He returned in 1914 and 1915 to continue with excavations.*

You stand on the steeply terraced hillside of the mountain Macchu Picchu, looking down into the Urubamba Valley and across to the lower conical mountain of Wayna Picchu which is at the bend of the river. On the terraces are series of stone walled structures using the huge blocks of stone seen in previous Inca sites all closely fitted together without mortar, there are roofless buildings with gabled ends, solid walled square buildings with rectangular openings for windows and doors which draw you forward to gaze through them at the incomparable views. We were fortunate to be there with so few other tourists and just the odd llama grazing the terraces. I had yet to visit my other 'must see' place, the Taj Mahal built in the 17thC, but in retrospect the strength and grandeur of Macchu Picchu far outweighed the glamour of the Taj. Since we visited, a hotel has been built here and to stay and see the sunrise or sunset over the ruins would be magical. Back to Cusco for a night before the journey onwards to Bolivia.

It was a long day's train journey from Cusco to Puno on the shores of Lake Titicaca. The train gathered the usual collection of passengers and livestock en route and the first stop at Sicuani provided a visit to the market and a chance to become acclimatised to the increasing elevation of nearly 12,000ft. Travelling further into the Andes the next lengthy stop was La Raya at 14,000ft home to llama, alpaca and vicuna. The market for the wools from these animals is important to the area and the animals are not farmed in the sense of being enclosed in fields but they are more 'free range' over the Andean plains. Lama and alpacas are now kept in England so we are familiar with them but the shy and beautiful vicuna said to be 'of bewitching eyes and a golden cloak' only exist in altitudes above 13,100ft. The animal is sheared every two years yielding only .5kg of wool, cost for 100grams is about USD1000!

After a night in Puno we embarked on a small boat to cross the lake. Titicaca is the world's highest navigable lake, at 12,500ft we were making a slight descent as we crossed from Peru to a stop at Sun Island, in the Bolivian part of the lake to see more Inca ruins before reaching the Bolivian mainland at Copacabana and an onward journey by car in the early evening to La Paz. The first glimpse of the city is as spectacular as it is unexpected. Driving up a steep road at the top of which you look down into a hollow amongst the mountains and there is La Paz at 12,000ft, almost hidden except for the twinkling evening lights.

With only two days in Bolivia we managed to see the centre of the city with its Spanish Baroque government buildings and the market with rows of stalls of the ubiquitous colourful striped blankets and other stalls with unmentionable and disgusting looking animal parts for native medicines. I bought two oil paintings from the street artist, of stylised ladies in their traditional dress of bright colours of red, blue and green, they continue to brighten our home. Moon Valley just outside La Paz was a strange place of eroded clay and sandstone rock making an area of tall stalagmites in various colours from beige to red due to the mineral content of the rock, that it would be impossible to walk through. I believe there are circular walking tracks through this lunar landscape but we had no time for that type of adventure.

Our final day in South America took us to Chacaltaya, then the highest ski resort in the world at 17,000ft. The journey by car (with driver) up hair pin bends was an adventure and the views downwards from the road showed small lakes interspersed in the valleys where the water was a perfect emerald green and turquoise blue. On arriving at the ski resort, actually a couple of wooden chalets, we stepped out onto the snow and were greeted by a guide who was preparing cacao tea for us on a small fire, this concoction being said to help with the effects of high altitude. However, we could only manage a few steps before becoming breathless. The summit above was 17,785ft, higher than Mt Everest Base Camp. Chacaltaya and the surrounding mountains were snow covered and magnificent and in front of us just two skiers coming down from the summit to the lodge. What is so sad is that this ski resort is no more as there is no snow. The glacier and snow which covered Chacaltaya gradually receded until by 2006 it had entirely disappeared.

Climate change has shrunk Andean glaciers between 30 and 50 percent since the 1970s and could melt many of them away altogether in coming years, according to a study in the journal The Cryosphere. Reuters, Jan. 24th, 2013

Travelling is about seeing new places and people and having new experiences and this journey was certainly one of contrasts, I look in my1982 album and the last Bolivian photo is of the two figures skiing down Chacaltaya, turn the page and see... Mickey Mouse! We flew to Miami and took a local bus to Disneyworld. I particularly wanted to see the newly opened Epcot Centre, the Experimental Prototype Community of Tomorrow, from all the pre-opening advertising material it seemed that this would be the place to promote in our Thomas Cook tours to America. There were pavilions showcasing foreign countries and a cinema with a 360°screen and surround sound, it was all very exciting in spite of the queues for all the attractions. And of course being in Disneyworld we had to meet Mickey and Minnie and see the Fairytale Castle.

The following year 1983, brought more travel overseas and also momentous changes in my life. Easter saw us joining the Vaalies trek to the coast to spend time with Su (as she now liked to be called) Terry and the boys in Hillcrest, Natal. Every Easter and Christmas too it seemed that the entire population of the Transvaal took to the road to the coast, many times we had joined this procession of cars, either from Maseru or from Johannesburg and there was always the excitement of who could first see the sea, although on this occasion we did not get as far as the sea. Hillcrest in those days was a pretty village on the hills before the road rushed down to the coast. Su and Terry had a lovely house and garden with a large pool so there was no need to join the crowds on the beaches. Tess and Peter, our old Maseru friends joined us for the day as they too now lived in Natal.

After Easter came Sarah's graduation from Wits University with a BA, the first of several degrees that she eventually obtained and then because of various happenings in Johannesburg she and I had a short holiday to England to stay with my sister Mary in Evesham.

Remember the 180 Club tour to Hong Kong? I now planned and joined them for their May tour to Greece and Istanbul. Because it was a larger group than previously I took two more Thomas Cookies as tour leaders, Renee and Connie - still my dear friends. We sailed on Epirotiki Lines *MTS Jupiter* for the seven day cruise that I have already told you about - Mykonos, Istanbul, Kusadasi etc with the final four days at the beautiful Astir Palace Hotel at Vougliameni. Kusadasi was still relatively unspoilt and the rustic hotel near the harbour 'Keravanseray' had an art gallery showing paintings by a Turkish watercolourist. After buying the two oil paintings in La Paz I decided that pictures would be a good memento of my travels, hopefully I would always have wall space but maybe shelf and cupboard space might be limited for knick knacks, so I bought a watercolour of Turkish women cotton picking, and there was no sign of the erstwhile Clarice Cliff from my previous visit!

The Astir complex of hotels at Vouglameni is worth mentioning in more detail as I stayed there several times. On this occasion we were in the original hotel block on a hillside overlooking the beaches of Vougliameni, which is about 10 miles from central Athens but a world away from the hustle and bustle and pollution of the city. Another hotel in the group was built right at the water's edge, the storeys of the building were stepped back and each suite had its own balcony. The edge of the sea had been sensitively paved with steps and diving boards so you could dive or jump straight into the deep waters, it was heavenly. The third hotel which was eventually built, called Nafsika was a de luxe boutique type property and although I did not take groups there we could use it for special functions.

September saw me off to Portugal for three days to look at hotels for a prospective group, briefly in Lisbon and then to Praia da Rocha in the Algarve. Those times in the Algarve were before the era of mass tourism and high rise hotels, Praia da Rocha in particular had one large hotel, the Jupiter, and then just pristine beaches with the amazing rock formations. Thirty four years later the whole area is covered with multi storey apartment buildings and hotels and as a visitor you could be in any over-populated summer holiday resort - Benidorm, Paphos, Brighton, Blackpool, they are all the same.

During this year I had been planning a journey to India and Nepal, the tours that we were selling to the public were going well and I still had the Taj Mahal on my 'must see' list and I wanted to see the places associated with the history of the Indian Mutiny of 1857. The Thomas Cook offices in India were handling all the ground arrangements for our tours and I knew that if I asked I would be able to get reduced or even complimentary rates for whatever travel I decided to do in India. Cliff was not interested in coming with me so I asked Patricia R, she had been born in India and was thrilled at the thought of a holiday at reasonable cost and also being able to see her daughter Jennifer who was backpacking and 'doing India'! Graham H, a TC colleague who also had an interest in the history of the Indian Mutiny said he would accompany us but at the last minute he could not travel due to work, so it was just us girls to conquer India. We had been putting some money away into a special bank account and in conjunction with TC India planned an exciting itinerary including far more than was offered on our standard TC 'India and Nepal' tour. We each bought a cabin sized bag for our three week holiday as we did not want to trust our possessions to the vagaries of Indian airports and baggage handlers. As the weather was going to be warm to hot summer clothes would suffice.

You will have to bear with me for a while as I travel through India and Nepal, it was such a wonderful journey with many memories made and each photograph in three albums brings the experiences so vividly back to life. We flew from Johannesburg to Bombay via Lusaka on Zambia Airways which alone was an experience hopefully not to be repeated, I don't want to be non pc but the cabin crew were dreadful, and the toilets unimaginably awful, the only upside was when the captain came on to make his announcements and we realised he was an ex South African Airways pilot. Jennifer met us at Bombay airport and at the hotel we were garlanded with flowers and had the customary tika painted on our foreheads. There are images a plenty from Bombay which is not your usual tourist destination but a city certainly worth a visit of a couple of days if only to give an instant flavour of the real India.

The dhobi lines stretch for acres, large industrial sized washing tubs and lines upon lines of every Bombay citizens' laundry. The coconut seller with his cart piled high with green coconuts - out comes a sharp knife, off goes the top of the coconut and you drink the milk from it through a straw. This is a fairly safe way of imbibing a liquid as the water is not safe unless boiled and the bottled drinks are very sweet. We 'did' the temples, and saw the Gateway to India, rather grandly described as a 'bold basalt arch of colonial triumph'. This was close to the Taj Palace Hotel where the local TC lady gave us a superb Thali lunch. This is a buffet of many small dishes set onto a large brass tray and you just help yourself.

Talking of lunch, the most notable event of the Bombay day is the arrival of the tiffin carriers at Victoria Terminus. The station itself is worthy of a few words as it is a magnificent edifice, built in what has been called the Bombay Gothic style and opened in 1887 to celebrate Queen Victoria's Golden Jubilee. It far out does London's St Pancras station, there are spires, turrets, domes and gables, and sculptures of animals and flowers. It is now a UNESCO World Heritage Site and every day 1,250 trains come into the station with about 3 million passengers a day. Early each morning the workers leave their homes to travel to Bombay by train, at home the wives prepare lunch-tiffin for their husbands and put it into a round double container and take it to their local railway station. At Victoria Terminus the carriers have large hand carts taking about one hundred containers (I counted these from my photo) they collect the lunches from the trains and somehow they know where each lunch is destined, around midday a procession of handcarts proceeds from the station throughout the business district.

A rather gruesome sight just outside central Bombay which could well be left off the tourist itinerary was a visit to the 'Towers of Silence'. This structure, fortunately tall, has dead bodies placed on it for the vultures to dispose of; this is part of Zoroastrian culture.
An onwards flight to Delhi. As we were standing in line preparing to disembark an Indian gentleman tapped me on the shoulder and said to Patricia and me 'ladies of your age should be at home minding the children', there is not much you can say that is polite in reply to that is there?

We were in Delhi to start a luxurious seven day adventure through Rajasthan on the 'Palace on Wheels'. At Delhi station we were met by handsome moustachioed and turbaned men who escorted us to our carriage where we met the lady who would be sharing the carriage with us. The train, for that is what the Palace was, consisted of six carriages that had belonged to the Maharajahs from the late 19thC onwards. Each carriage was quite different in the opulence of its furnishings and accoutrements. Our carriage was the only one with a verandah at one end where we had breakfast each morning. There were four compartments of which we occupied only three, there was also a bathroom and a kitchen where the magnificent moustachioed bearer prepared breakfast for us. There was a separate dining and bar car for evening dinners but as each carriage was individual there was no communicating corridor. When it was time for drinkies and/or dinner the train stopped wherever it happened to be, we all got down onto the line and walked back to the dining car.

The compartments were quite small with one or two beds, a cupboard and table, the beds were oriented from front to back of the train not across the train as one would imagine and this made for a strange movement when lying down and the train was moving. Patricia's daughter Jennifer had come on the train in Delhi but later that morning when the train slowed down in the middle of nowhere she just got off and walked on her own to …where… we were quite worried about her.

On the first morning Patricia knocked on my door and said open the curtains and look outside. The view is ingrained on my memory, green fields stretching as far as you could see but full of ladies working in those fields in the most vivid coloured saris of shocking pink, reds, emerald green, electric blue and gold. This is an impression that one gains throughout India that in spite of their hardships and poverty there is an explosion of colour everywhere. The days followed much the same pattern, travelling overnight then breakfast on the verandah to watch the passing scenery or if the train slowed down to pass through a station then there would be hangers-on to the train to see what we were doing. During the day we stopped for excursions, more details shortly, and then in the evening it was a question of changing for dinner, as dinners were very formal, waiting for the train to stop and walking back to the dining car for a refreshing G and T.

The daily stops were at Jaipur, Jaisalmer, Udaipur, Jodphur, Agra, Fatephur Sikri and Bharatpur. As the train arrived at each of these stations there was a welcoming party sometimes of painted elephants, camels or local musicians. All these stops are special, and deserve a mention.

Jaipur is called the Pink City due to the colour of the sandstone of its major buildings. The Palace of Winds is a five storey building of elaborately carved windows and alcoves through which the ladies of the royal household could keep purdah but still see Jaipur life. Opposite is the Royal Observatory, nothing like the Observatory at Greenwich. This is a collection of large geometric type sculptures dating from the early 18thC which were used for measuring the heavens. It looks extraordinarily modern in concept and such a contrast to the adjacent pink palace. Lunch was at the Rambagh Palace, another hotel made from a maharajah's home, splendidly grand and in later years I stayed there too.

From the Royal Observatory you could see a fort on a hillside outside Jaipur, and it was here we went to see the beautiful Amber Fort, travelling part of the way by car and then up the steep hill by elephant - a most uncomfortable mode of travel - and not helped by trying to restrain the 'driver' and his use of an elephant prodder. We had folk dances at Naharangarh Fort and Patricia posed in a suitably reclining position in the princesses' octagonal bedroom in the Fort.

The next stop on the journey was Udaipur and here the train was due to stay overnight, knowing this I had made other plans for Patricia and me. Jennifer miraculously turned up as the train arrived and took us to see her room in the city, her gap year was certainly an exciting one! After the ceremonial arrival featuring horses and

dancers we left the rest of the train's passengers and went by taxi to Lake Pichola and then by boat across the lake to the hotel.
You will remember the palace in the middle of Lake Pichola from the 1983 James Bond film *Octopussy*, this was yet another maharajah's home transformed into the Lake Palace Hotel. Built in the 18thC of white marble it seems to emerge from the waters in the middle of the lake, a really beautiful setting - on this journey I find it hard not to use the terms beautiful, magical, splendid as they apply to so much of what we saw and don't even begin to describe the Lake Palace Hotel, said to be the most romantic hotel in India, I would say 'in the world'. We were the only guests and wandered through the magnificent rooms, gazed across the lake through lacy sculptured arches and reclined on sofas in rooms covered in mosaics. As if this wasn't enough for one day we had been invited to dinner, courtesy of TC, to yet another palace on the shores of the lake, the Shiv Niwas Palace. This was built in the 20thC for royal guests and is a vast edifice rising in parts to five storeys from the edge of the lake more in the style of the Taj Bombay hotel and sumptuously furnished. It was after dinner here that we had one of those never to be forgotten moments. We walked down to the lake's edge, it was late and dark, there wasn't a soul around, by a tree was a bell by which we had to summon the boat from across the lake to collect us, as we sat and waited an owl above us in the tree started to call - it was magical, I am there now as I write these words.

I have a letter that I wrote to Graham H, who should have accompanied us, which he kindly returned to me, it gives my contemporary thoughts on the journey.

Saturday 8th. 4pm. on Lake Palace Hotel, Udaipur notepaper.
en route from Udaipur to Jaisalmer.
Each day seems to get better on this train if that is possible. Jaipur was the pink city of forts and palaces, Udaipur of lakes and marble palaces. We found a haven called Shiv Niwas which has been turned into an <u>*exclusive*</u> *hotel only 14 suites, each grander than the other with views which cannot be surpassed anywhere, wherever you look beautiful hills and the lake and other palaces framed by arches like on this notepaper but all delicately inlaid with coloured glass and silver. We had dinner in this palace and then visited it again in the*

morning - only one guest there - an author. Then it was goodbye to Jenny, Patricia's daughter, and off on the train again, some of our companions are friendly , some are not. There is an English photographer on an assignment for the Palace on Wheels and a mad middle aged Australian couple.
A

In the morning we re-joined the train heading for the next station, Jaisalmer, the golden city. More forts, extraordinary buildings in yellow sandstone with lacy balconies jutting over the narrow roads reminiscent of the wooden balconies of medieval houses in 16thC London. We had a memorable tea party here, not your usual venue for tea and cucumber sandwiches with linen napkins, this time we travelled by camel up and over the dunes into the Thar desert which surrounds the city. Waiting were the bearers from the train with tea laid out on the sands to the accompaniment of six men playing traditional instruments, to everyone's delight Patricia took her turn dancing to the music. Another thought from Jaisalmer, why did so many of the children have blonde hair and startling grey green eyes, I mentioned this to our guide who said it was the result of Alexander the Great and his men who passed by many years ago! It could I suppose be true.

Onwards to Jodhpur, known as the Blue City because of its painted houses and the Mehrangarh Fort which is placed on a hill top with walls reaching to 36m high in places, it is very impressive. We were privileged to be taken to lunch at the Umaid Bhawan Palace, then and now home to a maharajah. It only dates from the 1920s but built in marble with teak interiors has echoes of the European Art Deco design of the period. In one photo Patricia stands beneath a stuffed tiger placed high on the wall above her.

The next leg of the train journey heads towards everyone's dream, seeing the Taj Mahal at Agra. But first there was an early morning stop at the Bharatpur bird sanctuary where we had a short tour by small boat and then on to the abandoned city of Fatepur Sikri. It is called the Mughal's finest folly. All the usual adjectives apply, huge, grand, magnificent architecture and so on. Shoes had to be taken off when entering the gates and thin slippers supplied, memo to future travellers take your own socks or slippers as the marble and stones of the surfaces become extremely hot and difficult to walk on.

Built in the mid 16^{th}C as the new capital of the Mughals it was abandoned not long after due to lack of water.

And so to Agra and the Taj Mahal. It is beautiful, the mosaics inside and out were stunning but very dirty and in need of a good clean. It is heavily invaded by tourists and so almost impossible to get a photo of the view of the Taj from the beginning of the water feature (where Princess Diana sat alone); but I managed it, with Patricia standing to one side and the monument reflected in the water - stunning! As I said previously Macchu Pichu and its surroundings made more of an emotional impact on me.

One more overnight before we arrived back in Delhi and farewell to the Palace on Wheels before continuing our Indian journey with a flight to Lucknow to explore the city of the 1857 Siege. The captions to my contemporary photos explain its beauty - *a long view over gardens and trees to 'the golden domes' of M.M Kaye's novels*. She wrote several novels about India and really captured the flavour of the 19^{th}C. Lucknow station - all domes and turrets, what is it with Indian railway stations that they have to be so grand? A street view of ramshackle shops, bicycles and many many people and two facades of the most extraordinary buildings of Lucknow. Ours was definitely a businessmen's hotel, I think we were the only tourists in the whole of Lucknow and certainly the only two European women. Let me give you another letter that I wrote to Graham H as it gives my thoughts at that time.

Friday 14th October. on notepaper of Clarks Avadh Hotel, Lucknow.
I wanted to send you a postcard from Lucknow - but no postcards available. This is a city of surprises, we came as a pilgrimage to the Residency scene of the siege and start of the Indian Mutiny in 1857 and Lucknow turns out to have so much to offer - an incredible array of stately buildings Oriental and European in influence, mostly forgotten and crumbling, there is no tourist influence here at all. Only the Residency is preserved as a national monument, as it was at the Relief in November '57, the grounds are neatly manicured grass, Patricia and I were completely overcome our first morning, saw everything through a mist of tears, the graveyard was full of ghosts and in the underground chamber where the women and children and wounded lived and died for140 days, you could almost hear their voices. Even more extraordinary we returned in the evening when

the whole area was tastefully floodlit, just the two of us with all those memories of the past. As you walk through the grounds through the trees and bushes the buildings appear to be lit and inhabited and waiting for guests to arrive. It occurred to me whilst we were walking around in the dark, alone, that we were a mugger's dream - but India appears to be safe for women on their own, even Jenny, Patricia's daughter says this. We returned to the Residency again in the morning - I wanted to put flowers on Sir Henry Lawrence's grave but could not find any - have you read accounts of the Siege? I know the details fairly well but after this visit will be an even more avid reader of this period,...

What I hadn't said in my letter as Graham might have thought we were mad was a feeling we had as we sat of the steps of the Residency that evening and gazed across the lawns to the ruins of the Banqueting House, still with walls standing and internal staircases, in form it was not unlike the Banqueting House in London. Prior to the siege it had been used for entertaining but during the siege it was the hospital. As we sat on the steps we could see a haze of lights within the Banqueting House and a murmur of people issuing from the building. Ghosts? Yes I think they were, ghosts who had returned to remind us of happier times in that building, even my photo of the Banqueting House at night has a ghostly aura. The Union Jack and the Indian flag flew side by side over the ruins of the Residency.

There are several heartbreaking memorials to both Indian and British soldiers and women and children in the graveyard and a tablet to honour a special man who survived the Mutiny.

In Honour of One
Whose name should Never be Forgotten
THOMAS HENRY KAVANAGH V.C.
Who
On the Night of the 9th November 1857
With the Devotion of an Ancient Roman
Taking His Life in His Hand
Went Forth From The Beleaguered Residency
And Passing Through a City Thronged with Merciless Enemies
Successfully Guided Sir Colin Campbell and His Army
To the Relief of The Garrison

On a lighter note we visited La Martiniere School in Lucknow, looking more like a palace than a school, it was founded in 1845 and is the only school to have been awarded battle honours for its role in the defence of Lucknow during the Mutiny. Because it was then and is still occupied and in use as a school it has been described as the best preserved colonial building in Lucknow - thank heavens.

Back now to Delhi where we did all the well-known tourist sites and were rather taken with the lawn mower in the public gardens. This consisted of a white bullock drawing the mower whilst the gardener rested under a tree and an elephant was piled high with clippings from trees that were being pruned. We visited St James' Church at the Kashmir Gate, not your usual tourist venue, but it was built by Colonel James Skinner in the early 19thC in the style of a small St Paul's Cathedral and he was himself buried there in 1841.

Patricia had been born in Mussoorie in the hills but we were unable to go there as it was then a closed military area so instead she wanted to visit Allahabad where her sisters were born and baptised. We flew to Varanasi (Benares that was) and TC had hired a car and driver to take us the hundred miles to Allahabad, and what a day's driving that was. It seemed suicidal on narrow roads where the sacred cows wandered freely, bicycles proliferated and huge gaily painted buses careered towards us down the middle of the road. But it was worth it. We went straight to the Anglican church and asked to see the vicar who was most hospitable if a little astounded at who we were and where we had come from. He found the baptismal registers from the '30s and '40s and Patricia was able to see the entries for her sisters. I know from my own family history research how affecting it can be to see these actual documents, it really is a connection to the past. Then it was back on those mad roads to Varanasi. This city is on the River Ganges and it is here Hindus come to bathe in what they revere as its sacred waters and also to burn their dead on its banks or to float the dead bodies down river. There are long flights of steps leading down to the water and I foolishly thought that I would put my toes in the river too until I saw what was lying on the steps at low tide! We watched a couple of bodies floating past and decided that was enough and did some shopping for handmade woven rugs instead.

Back to Delhi in time to catch the overnight Kalka Express train as we were heading to the hills in the manner of the civil service who in days gone by moved their centre of government to Simla in the summer to escape the heat of the plains. The Kalka Express was not the Palace on Wheels! The reservation list on the outside of the carriage showed that we had been allocated a four berth A/C compartment. A/C, air conditioning, being the only way to travel. As we settled in two gentlemen arrived to share our compartment! A brief exchange of words and rupees with the conductor and we were then left in peace. As we hadn't reserved any bedding we had to use our clothes as covers. The toilet facilities were exactly the same as on the Bosphorus ferry that I have already mentioned - not to be recommended. However next morning we arrived at Kalka station where porters dashed down the platform to assist the passengers, we said 'Simla 'and a smiling young man took our order and money for breakfast and off he dashed - never to be seen again? We went to the Ladies Cloakroom, bliss, and emerged clean and refreshed and then made our way across the station to the narrow gauge train that would take us to the hills. Our smiling porter then appeared with hot tea, hot rolls and a delicious omelette, his arrival reminded me of the tiffins in Bombay that somehow always reached the correct destination. The journey of 90 miles took six hours going through 107 tunnels and over 864 bridges, at every turn there were magnificent views of the Himalayan foothills. We stopped at several small stations en route, I think the purpose was to deliver provisions to the local inhabitants as no-one got on or off the train, each of these stations had beautiful gardens and in a photo Patricia stands by a sign saying 'No Plucking'. Nearing 7000ft Simla can be seen in the distance, buildings seeming to flow down the hillside.

All the buildings are on steep terraces amongst the cedar trees and from the railway station a porter carried our small bags and we walked up to the Clarks Hotel right in the centre of the town on the Mall. Can you imagine a vehicle free English village high street lined with small shops, an Anglican church at one end and even a Gaiety Theatre, this is Simla, with cedar trees and monkeys! The villas where the civil servants and their families lived during the summer were set amongst the trees and had typical English names, Laburnum Cottage, Cedar Villa, Sunrise House. With our background of stage productions in Maseru Patricia and I had to visit the Gaiety Theatre. We found it was now a private theatre owned by the army but a kind chap allowed us inside, and what a pleasure that was. It was built in 1877 and is a typically Victorian theatre with plush seats, velvet curtains and much gilt, the joy was to see framed photos of actors and visitors of the past including Rudyard Kipling.

Our last excursion in the hills was to Kufri about ten miles from Simla, a taxi from outside Simla took us up to 7,500ft to see Lord Kitchener's summer residence, Wildflower Hall. Then it was not possible to see inside but at the time of writing it is a luxury hotel and what a wonderful place it would be for a holiday, with views of the snow-capped Himalayas. Patricia's claim to fame was riding a yak at Kufri!

We left the next day for the train down to the plains, the two of us on the steep walk to the station followed by three porters, two carrying our bags and one porter with boxes of cheese sandwiches from the hotel for our lunch en route. One final contemporary message;

Simla October '83 on Hotel Oberoi Clarkes notepaper.
Dear Girls (As I don't know your names)
Sorry I missed you for a farewell booze up. Thank you for all our drinks yesterday.
Best Wishes, who knows we may meet again somewhere
Sincerely Anne L W.

On to Nepal with a flight to Kathmandu from Varanasi via Patna. Mount Everest was another 'must see' on my journey through life. I had immersed myself over the years in books about the mountain and its climbers from the tragic expeditions of Mallory and Irvine in 1922 and 1924, and yes I do believe that Mallory reached the summit, to the successful 1952 expedition of Hillary and Tensing which I heard about on the wireless at the time and then onwards with Chris Bonnington, Doug Scott and Dougal Haston and others who climbed and failed to return. In those days climbing the mountain really was an expedition which had to be undertaken by experienced climbers with the correct equipment and lead by the extraordinary Sherpas. Now, in modern times it seems that money can buy you a walk up Mount Everest which tends to diminish the exploits of those earlier adventurers.

Patricia and I had arrived in Kathmandu at the time of Diwali, the Hindu festival of lights. All the houses and temples were lit with lanterns and sacrifices of animals had been made and the blood smeared on the steps of these same houses and temples which meant it was best not to walk in sandals, rather wear closed shoes. However after a day of temples and archways and the saffron robes of the monks it was Everest that called.

In order to see the sunrise over Everest we had a very early morning start and the car took us 20 miles to Nagarkot where eventually the clouds lifted and the sun appeared in the far distance over the snow capped Himalayas and THE mountain - magical. We then drove for another 20 miles to Dhulikel where breakfast was ready for us in a small rest house. The scenery was stunning, rows of foothills rising higher to the mountains and the hills around Dhulikel were terraced, I am not sure what crops were being grown.

Next day we took 'The Mountain Flight' in a small aircraft, what type I don't know but the registration was VT-ECB it took eighteen passengers and the flight lasted for an hour. We seemed to be right alongside the mountains, first the pilot flew one way for half an hour and then he turned round and flew back the other way so that everyone had the opportunity to see Mount Everest close up and take photos, and of course not just Everest, but those other magical names associated with the climbs, Lhotse and Makalu and then further along Kanchenjunga.

Our three weeks in India and Nepal had come to an end, it had been a physically and emotionally tiring experience. Patricia flew back to Delhi and onwards with Zambia Airways to Johannesburg whilst I went on to Bangkok and Hong Kong. I was making an inspection visit to look at hotels for a forthcoming group and had two days in Pattaya at the Royal Suites of the Royal Cliff Hotel. Such luxury. The individual suites were vast with a bedroom, bathroom, lounge and a huge verandah overlooking the beach. Sumptuously furnished with orchids in abundance. At the poolside which was virtually on the beach the sun loungers were lined up, each bearing a brass label with your name - so no rushing down early in the morning to reserve the best seat with a towel! I was sorry that I was on my own with no-one to share this luxury. I went on to Hong Kong for twenty four hours to see the hotel planned for the prospective group, here my memory lets me down, but I think it was the Royal Garden Hotel, I know I had tea at the famous Peninsular Hotel and was taken to the Jockey Club in Happy Valley, another iconic HK institution where we planned to have a function for the group.

After almost a month away I returned to Johannesburg. Some heated discussions followed and after some soul searching Cliff and I decided to part and were soon divorced, to be fair it was probably two thirds my fault but there is no point in mulling over the issues. Cliff and Blanche were married soon after and it was sad that she died not many years later.

My journey now took a different route.....

Grandparents
George & Harriet Thatcher
Wedding Day 1899

G.G. Grandmother
Harriet Daisy Adams
born 1817

G. Grandmother
Elizabeth Sarah Berryman
as a child c.1823

Grandma B
& her parents The Emerys
c1900

Dad & Mum 1948

Mary & HM The Queen 1954

Aden

Goldmohur

Sira Island

The Harbour

Aden

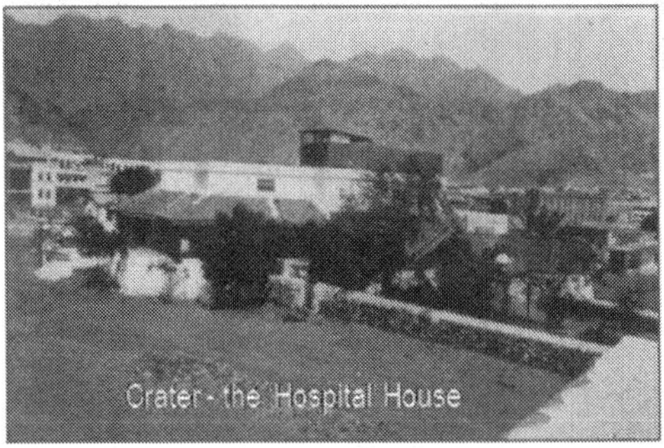
Crater - the Hospital House

Khormaksar - 11 Downing St

Aden

At work and at play

Lesotho – mountain road picnic

An Isandlwana commemoration

Some 'educational' destinations

'Boissevain' Chinese dinner - 1958

Greek Islands cruise - 1992

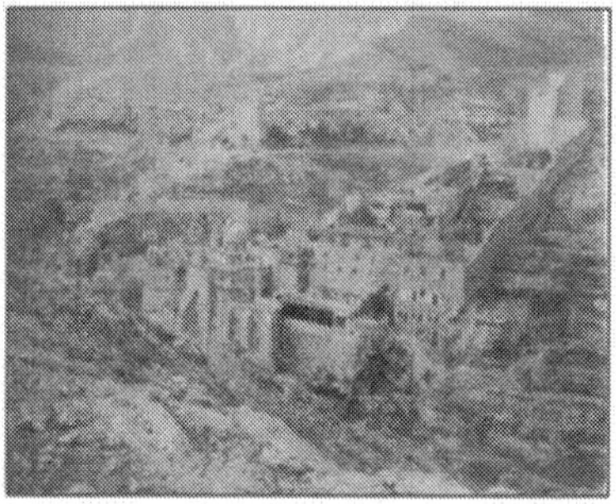

Israel – St George's Monastery - 1996

New York - 1989

Berlin Wall - 1985

Lucknow – The Residency

Bombay – Tiffin carriers

Delhi – lawn mower

Simla – The Mall

Moscow – snow collector

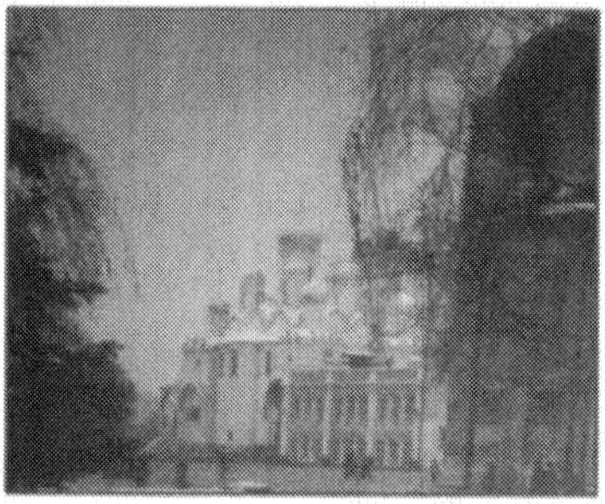

Inside the Kremlin walls

Palace on Wheels

Sonoran desert
cactus

The Three Rondavels

In the Umfolozi River

Madikwe – Coming down the mountain

Okavango – bedroom & lunch IN the river

Faroes - Funningur where the Norsemen landed & Gjogv

Cornwall – Kynance Cove

Portugal – Ferraguda Castle

Lewis – The Teardrop

Peru – Macchu Picchu building

At the end of Africa

Peru
Machu Picchu

Brazil/Paraguay
1982
Construction of
Itaipu dam on
Parana River

Vernacular Architecture Class - 2004

MSc Graduation - 2012

A successful project

Conservation?
Restoration?
OBLITERATION

CHAPTER 7
Track into unknown territory

'Looking back isn't going to help you. Moving forward is the thing you have to do'.
McKayla Maroney

The usual progress through life is school, qualifications, independence by leaving home, career, marriage, children and retirement. My life missed out on the important part of leaving home and becoming independent, I left school, briefly worked whilst living at home then married, had children and resumed my career, I was therefore never responsible for myself, there was always someone else whom I could rely upon to provide the home, the car and all that living entails. Now, at the end of '83 I really was on my own and responsible for myself for the first time since that brief period of separation in Lusaka.

I found a small flat in Yeoville, then a rather trendy suburb of Johannesburg and set about establishing my new life. It is strange that friends that you have as a married couple suddenly don't want to know you when you are no longer married, I think the wives fear for the safety of their husbands which doesn't say much for the security of their own marriages or maybe it upset the seating arrangements around the dinner table by having an 'odd' female. So I was dropped by most of my previous so-called friends but fortunately had my friends and colleagues from Thomas Cook. The company gave me a car so I was able to continue with my work life and a reasonable social life too and with more and more overseas trips connected with work. Sarah was living in Johannesburg so we met frequently and I visited Su in Natal too.

In February '84 UTA, the French Airline invited a small group of agents to 'Semaine Mondiale' in Paris. This was a trade fair for travel agents from all over the world. This was my first visit to Paris and I paired up with another girl who knew Paris well and after we had made our appearance at the trade fair took in some sightseeing. On the steps of Sacre Coeur were many painters and I bought a water colour, not of a Paris scene, but a tranquil river view. I also spent a fortune on a genuine Christian Dior small handbag which turned out to be utterly useless as it was so small - a few more francs would have bought a more suitable size. UTA then hosted us for a few days on the French Riviera where we visited and dined at some of the best hotels in Cannes and Nice, the most memorable being the Ritz Carlton in Cannes. I loved the flower market in Nice, my photo is of all the Spring flowers. But my favourite place was the hilltop medieval village of St Paul de Vence where we spent a day. We couldn't afford to eat at La Colombe d'Or, the notable celebrity restaurant but settled for a local café where elderly men were playing boules on the grass outside. I have never returned there but given the choice between Paris and St Paul de Vence I know which I would choose.

In May came another invitation to a travel fair, this one was the American annual International Pow Wow to be held in Seattle and as I had also to visit Hawaii on an inspection visit I made a quick fourteen days grand tour. Flying into New York for just twenty four hours I have a photo of the Twin Towers at the World Trade Centre (one day this will be a valuable item) and of the Stature of Liberty surrounded by scaffolding for renovation. A stop in San Francisco and the Golden Gate bridge and then on to Seattle home of the iconic Space Needle, a relic from the 1962 World Fair. Pow Wow was enormous, thousands of people in the conference halls, the only worthwhile event was an outside function where the Beach Boys played. One of the excursions arranged for delegates was a day's boat trip into the Puget Sound to see some of the islands, this was more my scene.

I flew on to Hawaii, or rather the island of Oahu, the capital of Hawaii. Waikiki Beach is backed by many high rise hotels but the beach itself was almost free of tourists and very beautiful with golden sands and fringed with palm trees. I stayed in two hotels, the Hawaiian Regent on Waikiki and then the much more luxurious Turtle Bay on North Beach. My only purchases on this trip were a couple of hula hula skirts as requested by one of the TC girls for a fancy dress party. Although I took no photos of Pearl Harbour I do remember the visit as being a solemn and sad experience. And then the long flight back to South Africa, half way around the world. As it happened the company that had been planning an incentive group to Hawaii and for which I was undertaking the inspection of hotels changed their minds and decided on a different country so I had made that long journey to no purpose but at least I saw Hawaii!

In September I took a client to the Algarve for four days to look at hotels for yet another proposed group and yes this one did materialise. There were several large and suitable hotels along the coast and we settled on the Balaia, with its gardens and golf course and perched on the cliffs by the sea it was the best that we had seen. As I knew the Algarve fairly well from my previous visit we spent some time driving to see the sights and I was particularly interested to see how the harbour at Vilamoura was progressing. At my last visit it was in a sorry state, the marina was full of yachts but the buildings surrounding the marina which were going to be flats and shops were half built and remained derelict. There was the odd café but otherwise no infrastructure for tourists or sailors. At this visit things were looking up, construction of the buildings was continuing and there was an air of prosperity about the place. I was amused at a sign over the hand basins in the public wash rooms which said 'no hair washing', I can only assume that this was directed to the yachties who on making landfall wanted a good wash and brush up.

The final stop on our journey along the coast was at the harbour of Carvoeiro which I came to know so well in later years. Here we had a delicious lunch at a beach restaurant of 'cataplana' which is a mixture of mussels and other shell fish in a tomato sauce cooked in a small metal dish. Oh dear. That night I was very ill and the next morning we had to fly to Lisbon and home. I was unable to walk so at Faro airport I was wheelchaired onto the aircraft but by the time we arrived in Lisbon I was fine. I should mention Faro airport - it was just a large shed in those days with a couple of check-in desks and a baggage carousel for arriving passengers. Now it is a large international airport and it reminds me of the transformation that took place over the years at Jan Smuts airport.

Back on track and November sees me in Israel for a week with an insurance incentive group. Just getting to board the aircraft of El Al Airlines to Israel is a journey. As you queue to check-in every passenger is interrogated and asked why are you travelling, where are you staying, have you been to Israel before, do you know anyone in Israel, what will you be doing in Israel? The same procedure takes place again when you land at Ben Gurion airport. You can understand why they are so thorough. We stayed at the King Solomon's Palace Hotel in Eilat, a high rise property right at the waterfront. There was a Bedouin themed evening for our stay, the guys seemed to like the belly dancing! With only being in Israel for seven days we had a busy schedule and after a day sailing on the Red Sea we returned to Jerusalem. The guys wanted to see the Golan Heights on the border of Israel and Syria, scene of much fighting so we went there in army command vehicles, at our destination was a burnt out Israeli truck and also some good scenic views, I doubt that tourists can go anywhere near this place now.

A day's drive into the Judean desert took us to St. George's Monastery, spectacularly set clinging to the red sandstone cliffs in a gorge and seeming to grow out of the rocks, the only colour provided by the brilliant cerulean blue on a dome. I found this day in the desert very nostalgic, the sands and the colours reminded me of Aden and I thought to myself Aden isn’t too far down the road from here, just go back to Eilat and continue sailing down the Red Sea.

You must realise that between all these visits away from Johannesburg I was still actually working in my office, visiting clients, seeing my daughters and friends and generally getting on with being a single woman. Sol Kerzner. who at this time was married to Anneline Kriel, an ex Miss World, had developed a luxury hotel complex in the bush of Magaliesberg in Bophuthatswana, an state independent from South Africa and therefore able to have casinos and risqué shows. Although over the top in terms of style and luxury it had a large theatre which hosted worldwide celebrity concerts and with a group of friends we tried to attend as many shows as we could. Who can forget Queen, the incomparable Freddy Mercury and the whole stadium consumed by Bohemian Rhapsody. Frank Sinatra's voice was very dodgy but his charisma was undiminished. I fell in love with Julio Iglesias and yes the ladies in the front row really did throw their knickers on stage - I was not in the front row. Rod Stewart has always been a favourite performer, he was as glamorous as ever at Sun City and during his performance an unexpected guest walked onto the stage and started playing the piano - it was Elton John. As he played 'Candles in the Wind' the whole audience lit matches or cigarette lighters and waved them during the song. The next time I heard him sing this was in Westminster Abbey at Princess Diana's funeral.

Leonard, Anthony and I stayed in a small safari lodge not far from Sun City in March '86, being in the bush and far from any light pollution it was the ideal place to see Halley's Comet which was making its once in 76 years pass through our skies. It was not spectacular! Just a bright light high above with a tail of star dust. It could almost have been the International Space Station passing over.

I suppose that I was in that enviable position in my career when I had others to do the hard office work and I could take advantage of the offers of free travel and to act as a tour leader for incentive and conference groups travelling abroad. These groups were no walk in the park, there was a responsibility to make sure that all the arrangements proceeded smoothly and that everyone was happy. It was on the pre tour inspection visits that all the potential problems could be sorted out with the ground handlers and it was most important to have complete trust in all the local people, coach drivers, restaurateurs, hotel staff etc.

In May '85 Lufthansa, the German airline invited a group of travel agents to visit Germany. The view of East Berlin across the wall is one of the brutalist architecture of blocks of flats. My photo shows the wall itself (only dismantled in 1989) covered with graffiti, across the barren no-man's land to the further wall on the eastern side. Tall lights march down the centre of the bare space. How did anyone ever manage to cross safely from east to west? We passed through Checkpoint Charlie and visited the 1936 Olympic Stadium, friend and colleague Vera H posed beneath the five Olympic rings. What I found astonishing was the grandeur of some of the buildings in East Berlin and the beautiful gardens at the imposing Russian War Memorial. There was little road traffic and few people around, in contrast with West Berlin where on the same sunny day hoards of people were sitting outside enjoying a beer and a chat beneath the ruins of the Memorial Church - aptly named 'the lipstick' for the shape of the ruined tower.

The train journey from West Berlin to Hamburg took us through East Germany, it was very apparent that we were travelling though a militarised zone, there were armed guards walking continually up and down the corridor so it was a relief when we eventually moved into West Germany. From Hamburg the train took us to that delightful town, Baden Baden and the sumptuous Brenner's Park Hotel. There are beautiful gardens along the River Oos, blossom and azaleas were flowering. The town itself is picturesque and we visited the thermal baths and the casino. Lufthansa had offered various add-ons to the main part of the educational trip and Vera H and I decided on a couple of days in the Black Forest at Hotel Adler in Hinterzarten. It was all you would expect of a village known as a ski resort with steeply pitched roofs to the chalet style houses with their window boxes of red geraniums. It had been an excellent educational visit to Germany, I was fortunate to see Berlin before the Fall of the Wall and to appreciate the beauty of Baden Baden which I returned to again later.

The insurance group for which I had made the inspection visit travelled to the Algarve and the Balaia Hotel in June, because it was a large group Connie and Theresa from TC came with me too and I needed their support as it was not all plain sailing. Unknown to me the insurance company had booked air freight for a large consignment of equipment and goodies that they wanted for their conference. Books, T shirts, pens and paper, films, banners, projection equipment and so on. When this arrived in Lisbon, at the same time as the group, Customs would not clear this freight unless a large amount of duty was paid. To cut a long story short I sent off the group by coach to the Balaia and with the ground handler tried to sort out the problem, eventually with guarantees that everything was going to be taken out of the country the goods were released, but only early in the morning of the day the conference was due to take place. We got it all there in time but it was very stressful! I made another picture purchase, this time from an artist on the beach at Albufeira. It is a modern scene of the sun rising over a typical Portuguese fishing boat and it features a liberal application of sand in the picture, as I pass it at home it exudes the feeling of the sun, sea and sand of the Algarve.

This year, 1985, Sarah decided to leave South Africa and return to live in England permanently, it was a brave decision for her and one that turned out to be immensely successful, her decision made me ponder my own future and what it would be if I stayed in South Africa and did I have the courage to up sticks and leave Africa for good. I felt that being single in South Africa and getting older was not a good idea and at the back of my mind was the realisation that I should leave before my fiftieth birthday as I might then have the chance to start another life and career in England. Changes were afoot in TC which caused me to leave and I then worked for another travel company with Vera H. I also gave up my flat and for a few months rented a flat over the garage of a house in Parkhurst. Here I saw my friends Jean and Roger, who lived not far away and Leonard and Anthony who lived in Victory Park. One Sunday morning is particularly memorable, I awoke to much smoke from a fire in the bush grass along the Braamfontein Spruit which ran just a house away from my flat. Someone must have phoned the fire brigade for they arrived and commenced to put out the fire - using their helmets to take water from the spruit (stream) and throw on the flames!

So I passed my forty-ninth birthday with no decision as to my future. The impetus for change came with Leonard and Anthony who had also decided to leave South Africa in September and go to live in Portugal. They suggested that I accompany them and live in Portugal for while to help them settle and this would provide a transition period for me. In July they gave me six weeks to decide and on the final day I said yes! August saw me in Hillcrest, Natal to say goodbye to Su, Terry and the boys, Leonard and Anthony left at the end of August and I had moved into Graham's flat for my final couple of weeks. My last Sunday, 7 September, was spent on a nostalgic trip around Johannesburg. I'd lived in the city for twelve years but as is the way, never taken any photos of my surroundings so now I have some lovely mementos of that Sunday. Jean, Christine and I went to Zoo Lake and had a picnic and then followed many photo opportunities of a quiet Sunday in Johannesburg, I am so glad I took them as much has changed since then. No-one could have had a better farewell. Jean, Roger, Christine and Graham gave me a super party at the airport and as I boarded the Lufthansa flight for Frankfurt and London I wondered if I would ever return to South Africa.

I was only in England for two days, a brief catch up with Sarah and the family before being collected by Leonard and Anthony in their BMW convertible, and we were off by ferry and road to Portugal. It was a fairly leisurely journey of about seven days through France and Spain, we stayed in pensions en route where Leonard was sent on to negotiate the best rates for us. One of the highlights on the journey was San Sebastian in Spain where we spent two nights. Anthony parked the car outside the pension on the main road and next morning the car had gone, he had parked in a no parking area and the car had been impounded, with a lot of our gear in the boot. Eventually we found the whereabouts of the car pound and managed to negotiate its release. San Sebastian has a beautiful beach, a charming old quarter and some excellent fish restaurants, it is well worth a holiday visit.

Another highlight was Salamanca. As we walked into the Plaza Mayor a trio of pan pipers were playing their soulful music, it echoed around what is thought to be Spain's most beautiful square, it is grand almost beyond belief. Our rooms for the night were in an old monastery and my room was high in the building overlooking the square. When we reached Lisbon the boys said it was my turn to find our rooms for the night as I knew Lisbon. This was all very well but it was the weekend of the Formula 1 Grand Prix at Estoril so space was at a premium. I thought it best to aim high so marched into the Sheraton Hotel, asked for the Manager, explained I was from Thomas Cook (no longer strictly accurate) and asked for two complimentary rooms - which he gave us. It was marvellous to have all mod cons after the budget accommodation of the previous few nights.

We travelled onwards down the west coast of Portugal which is very wild and unspoilt until we reached the Algarve. Here the boys had a couple of timeshare properties lined up for our first two weeks. In Vilamoura it was a lovely flat near the marina which I was pleased to see was starting to look more prosperous with building work ongoing in the apartments surrounding the marina. Then we moved to a cottage in a holiday complex on the hill in Carvoeiro - no cataplana for me this time, or ever again.

As the timeshare weeks came to an end by the beginning of October we rented a very small house in Sesmarias, just a couple of miles from Carvoeiro and Leonard and Anthony started looking for their own future work opportunities. They very kindly funded my stay with them in return for being head cook but of course I needed pocket money for personal stuff. I allowed myself £5 per week and I even managed to buy paperbacks from the local second-hand bookshop and have the occasional hairdo.

There was a tiny golden sand beach about a mile from the house, there was no access by road or even a proper path, we found it by going up and down the hills through the bushes of oregano which released their herby smell as you brushed past them and then after about 20 minutes a negotiation of some rocks and there was this pristine bay, no more than 100yds wide with hills almost enclosing it on both sides. Sometimes the water was calm, sometimes rough but it was the perfect place to swim and relax. I usually went on my own, just being careful on the one day of the week when hunters were allowed to shoot birds, I think it was a Wednesday, they then wandered over the same area that took me to the beach. One morning after a fairly wild night with wind and storms I walked down to the beach expecting a quiet time lying on the sand and to my horror there was no beach. Nothing, no sand, just a jumble of huge rocks which had been brought in and upturned by the heavy seas. It seemed impossible that water could move such rocks, these were not boulders but rocks the size of small houses. Years later I was further along the coast at Ferraguda where the concrete angled crosses of the sea defences had similarly been swept from their precision line of defence into a jumbled mass of concrete.

By December '86 L and A had sorted themselves out and I knew that I had to get on with living my life, not idling away in the sun on the Algarve. Sarah and Ian, who was to become her husband, came for a short holiday, we all squashed into the tiny house and then I returned with them to England and Christmas 'at home'.

I had some savings from South Africa, and I had been frugal in my spending in Portugal however I knew that I had to earn my living as soon as possible. Come the New Year I visited the local travel agent in Evesham and borrowed their travel newspapers to see what vacancies there were. I signed on at the local employment bureau and although nothing was forthcoming from there they did refund my train fares to other interviews, one of the benefits of the Welfare State! I had mentally given myself six weeks to find work in the travel industry and if I was not successful then I would answer advertisements in *The Lady* magazine for housekeepers and home helps. I went to an interview in London with Jules Verne who did really interesting tours worldwide and I would like to have worked for them but I was 'too highly qualified!'

In the meantime I wrote to the MD of a coach touring company in Kent whom I had met in Johannesburg asking if he know of any vacancies in my field, he replied asking me for an interview at his Kent office. Apparently I was just the person they needed to prepare a completely new set of itineraries for coach tours in the UK, I could approach the task with fresh eyes. So by mid January I had a job, a car and a company credit card and was told to travel for as long as I needed to and just return to the office occasionally to write up my suggestions. However I needed somewhere to live, Evesham was too far away to commute and I was so fortunate that a neighbour of my mother had a basement flat in Bloomsbury not far from the British Museum which was currently not being used by any of her family - I could have it and just pay the utility bills. Frankly it was in a bit of a state having been empty for a long time and needed a good clean and liberal amounts of anti-cockroach powder before it was habitable, but I realise I was a very lucky girl having a virtually free home in the centre of London. The problem was the car, when I was travelling there was no problem but as soon as I got back to base where did I park it - there was no parking at work and certainly none in London that was affordable, so I had to leave the car in Evesham and use the train to London and Kent and then when I needed the car do the journey in reverse.

Sarah came with me on my first foray in fact finding for the proposed coach tours. Ludlow Castle, Tintern Abbey, Raglan, Caerphilly and Carnarvon Castles, Llandaff Cathedral and the little known ruins of Carrig Cennen Castle. We stayed in the Victorian Metropole Hotel in Llandrindod Wells, as the only guests for dinner in the vast dining room, why did we whisper?

I spent two weeks in the Republic of Ireland as it had so much to offer, the countryside is beautiful and unspoilt, Dublin is very cosmopolitan. I had been told to drive around the Ring of Kerry which I apparently did in the wrong direction , you are supposed to drive in a clockwise direction to make the most of the views! There were many abandoned white painted thatched cottages dotted around the countryside, perhaps by the time of writing the situation in Eire has improved and these are once again homes. The spectacular Cliffs of Mohur, Bunratty Castle and Folk Museum - there is so much to see. I carried on around England and into Scotland, and on my way to John o Groats (having 'done' Land's End) I drove over the high plateau of Sutherland and there I felt I was in Africa with the vastness of the horizon.

By April I was writing some thoughts in my little black book.
10 April 1987. Five months in England after 30 years out there.
Home Thoughts from Home, or Out There from Here.

The passage of time blurs the first impressions
So I offer now my thoughts on relocation
An African daisy for a lifetime and now an English rose.
Uprooted from the brilliant sun and great horizon of the veld
To the soft green fields and gentle rains of England.

The one question that never fails to be asked
'How can you leave it all behind'?
'Don't you miss the sun - the servants and that marvellous way of life'?
Uprooted from the red, red soil and bright dry air of Africa
To rain and snow and never ending grey, grey skies.

Another asks what difference between life OUT THERE and here
The only answer is...nothing, the difference is so great.
One life is finished, ended, and another has begun
Uprooted from the ease and cushioned comfort of white South Africa
To the ease and comfort of the Welfare State.

To be amongst the family after years of being away
To share their joys and sorrows in person and not by mail.
To once again be mother, sister, aunt and not just Ann
Uprooted from my dear, dear friends who've been my family

To....no-one   I miss them so.
A walk in London on a Sunday, it's a joy to re-explore
To see the famous buildings unhindered by the crowds
I've photos of the world to show but nothing of this city.
Uprooted from a golden town with roots deep in the mines
To a vibrant living city built lovingly on centuries of change.

Politics in England are a more relaxed affair
It's red or blue or yellow and here's a green one too.
What difference does it make, little to you or me
Uprooted from a land where I could never vote
To a land where my X will help.

Politics OUT THERE are an all consuming passion
We know the Nats will win but there's left and right as well
Conservatives and PFP and the AVB.
Uprooted from a land where I would probably vote Nat
To a land where CND doesn't mean that much to me.

The weather to the English is of paramount importance
It's a subject of such pessimism it would be best forgotten
They says its overcast and grey but always mild, mild, mild.
Uprooted from the drama of a thundering highveld storm
To the mild grey skies of a mild grey day.

If I have to say I miss something it would be storms and sunsets
The deafening clashes and bright flashes that race across the heavens,
The orange, red and purple streaks found only in an African dusk.
Uprooted from the high drama of Africa
To the grey mildness of England.

Here everyone speaks English, a joy you can't believe
It could be slightly flavoured with a hint of rural slang,
But here we are the ones in charge, the others them to us
Uprooted from bilingualism where English is second best.

The countryside is wonderful, there is so much of it

There really isn't quite as much of town and grime and grit
There's mountains, lakes and valleys and empty vistas too.
Uprooted from a land where all these words apply
To a land where all these words are true.

It is difficult to put in words the frenetic Joeys life
It's all hard world and play and living for today
to hell with bombs in Wimpey bars and empty litter bins.
Uprooted from the necklace horrors and clashing tribal strife
To TOXTETH, BRISTON, BLACKWATER FARM....

There are other parts of Africa which have a hold on me
Which must not be forgotten in this settling of my past
I'll write about them all in turn to settle any ghosts.
Uprooted from the darkest South
To the enlightened West.

The early days in NR are now blurred by time
But a melange of thoughts and pictures come through
Of fair-haired daughters, the NRP in blue,
Rhodes statue now gone to the Cape and the mighty Falls
Transplanted from the tropics
To the temperate South.

Lesotho gave to all of us a temporary colonial life
Maseru Club, Maseru Prep, Maseru Bridge et al
Collier and Yeats and Tully's Stores they are all still there
Transplanted across the river
To the dark mountains beyond.

And so I've laid the ghosts to rest, it's all still there and not forgotten
The people, places and good times we shared will be part of me forever
But life goes on, and forward, and changes, and I must keep going too.
Each country in its own way has the very best of scenery and people and that good old way of life
It's not a question of good and bad but what's best for me right now.

Uprooted from my past OUT THERE
To continue life right HERE.

Strange I did not think to mention Aden. I must have been in the mood for writing (I hope I am not as boring as FJB) as in May I was invited to travel by train to Glasgow which resulted in the following:

May. London - Glasgow - celebrating 21years of B.R Intercity 125.
Dashing north on the 125
Cocooned in first class comfort
Smells of kippers and coffee or the traditional English grill
Envelops the city businessmen
Restrained and unspeaking in their neat grey suits
Off to Crewe and Wigan, to spread their London logic
Or off to Glasgow and Aviemore, to subdue the natives?

Outside the scenery changes
The speed of the 125
Takes us through lush green fields and blinding yellow rape seed
To the Industrial north
On past the Roman fortresses of Lancaster and Carlisle
Beyond Hadrian's Wall

A glimpse of a hare
Factory workers on time off
A sight of snow on Skiddaw
Lorries on the motorway square-dancing with saloons
Lambs hop skippety jump startled by the noise

Rivers, canals, bridges and houses
Laundry on lines, lines on roads
Towns and villages, limestone, brick, concrete and granite
Rush, rush, rush...

Dashing north on the 125
This island becomes so small
A kaleidoscope of images of life as lived in Britain
Or is it in reality only the face that shows
To prove that dashing anywhere

You miss the spirit underneath.

By early July I was back in the office writing up the really exciting and different itineraries for coach tours all the while being advised by coach drivers just how far they could and wouldn't drive each day. All to no avail as the company decided they couldn't afford the programme for the UK and would rely on their European programme instead. I wasn't upset after all I had seen England, Scotland, Wales and Eire all at their expense. The company proposed that I should take charge of the hotel reservations system for the European coach tours which was in a mess, this was not my scene so whilst trying to implement new procedures I scoured the travel papers for opportunities in an area that would be near the family, not miles away in London or Kent.
An advert appeared for a group tours manager at a retail travel agency in Abingdon, near Oxford, I applied, had an interview, was accepted, left Kent and moved to exactly where I wanted to be. I found a small flat in Abingdon in an old brewery building which had been converted and was within my price range, I had enough money for the deposit and on the strength of my job offer the bank gave me a mortgage. So eleven months after leaving South Africa I now had, in August '87, a position with prospects, my own home, a company car and daughter, sister and mother all within a reasonable distance.

The company that I was working for, Harvey Thomas Travel, was a long standing retail travel agency in Abingdon with a large client base of top commercial companies in Oxfordshire and Berkshire and it was because of the requirements of these companies for conferences and incentive tours that they had to expand to meet their clients' needs. I was extremely busy for the following couple of years, until I had an assistant, seeing these companies and selling them the ideas for their incentive programmes and conferences.
I was able, work and travelling permitting, to spend most weekends in Evesham with my mother and to see her also for an evening midweek. Time is the most precious thing you can give someone and for the first time in my adult life I was able to spend quality time with Mum and to see my sister too of course. Sarah lived fairly close by so I was grateful to have close family contacts once again. With

my own home, albeit small, friends from Africa came to stayso I had a busy and fulfilling life.
The following year, 1988, turned out to be one of frantic work and travel once again. My ideas had borne fruit and one large commercial company in Slough decided to offer as an incentive to their sales agents a holiday in Thailand in October. As a result in February I did the first of two inspection visits with the client to Thailand to see the hotels and what I could suggest for touring and special events. We were only away for four days but travelling with the luxurious Thai Airlines made the journey a pleasure. March saw me once again in Greece with a client on an inspection visit which resulted in a group on the *MTS Pegasus* of Epirotiki Lines for a seven day cruise in July.

You may remember that in 1949 on my way home from Aden to England I stayed overnight with my parents and sister at the Phoenicia Hotel in Malta and also had lunch there in 1954 with my parents and Colin. Now in '88 the hotel was managed by Trust Houses Forte and it had undergone an extensive restoration which THF wanted to show to UK tour operators, hence my invitation to fly to Malta for a night in May at the hotel. It was only a brief visit to this special island but the hotel was just as I remembered it externally and in the public rooms and gardens but the bedrooms had been modernised.

Sylvia, my school friend from St Paul's whom you have met previously retired with her husband to live in an ancient cottage in rural Dorset, you will hear more of the cottage later, but I was able to spend weekends with them whenever work or family allowed and I could dash down the A303, past Stonehenge on a Friday afternoon and relax until the early hours of Monday with a fast return to work. I tell you this now as the journey provided me with an unexpected meeting place. I had received a couple of 'out of the blue' telephone calls from Don who wanted to meet and talk and the grounds of Longleat provided the ideal place, just off my route to Dorset and not too far from where he lived with Ethel. We had two meetings and talked about so many things and there was a glimpse of the Don from Aden days but then I think his conscience got the better of him and there were no more meetings. I wrote my thoughts in my little black book, I would like to have sent them to him but that was impossible.

Recollections. D.G.G. May 1988
Why recapture the past, the essence of lost youth?
Back to the days of desperate teenage emotions.

What is the purpose of remembering those days?

Because they are there.
they are the foundation stones of the years that followed,
Wanting to be remembered

I had thought those days were lost
Apart from a stray glimpse of the past occasioned by a melody or a perfume -
Family remembrances with just a touch of sun and sand -
And thoughts of my very first love.

First love and the emotions it generated-
Always waiting - for a phone call or the sound of your land rover travelling the tracks to Khormaksar.

It is only now after seeing you again
That the closed door of that time past has been opened
Allowing a rush of memories to come through.

How strange that we each have different memories
But only of the good times when we were
enveloped, engrossed, enmeshed by those days of the desert,
the Scottish coast, the Welsh mountains -
Such contrasting surroundings to our early years.

Indeed our memories are so different we could be remembering separate lives.
Should we also not remember the bitterness and pain that caused our parting?
Was it inevitable that the children, each with their own problems,
should be the reason for our meeting again after so many years?

What we least expected was the turmoil in discovering that we still cared for each other.
Will this time, in time, become another sweet memory hidden in gentler surroundings than those of long ago?

Endless woods of pine, acres of bluebells sparked with wood anemones
And a farm gate overlooking fields of fresh spring green.
What a wonderful end to our beginnings or a beginning to an end
Or perhaps just a perfect interlude in May.

Only time will show how this Spring
Affects the pattern of our lives.

We had further meetings in later years connected with the our daughters but the magic had gone. When I telephoned him on what was to be his final birthday he asked why I was calling and said he had nothing to say to me. He was a complicated man!

I had been working hard in the office with early mornings and late nights and the bosses said I should take a short break so courtesy of Olympic Airways and my friends at Epirotiki I took a five day cruise of the Greek Islands. Apart from Patmos where I wanted to see the monastery I stayed on board at all the other stops and relaxed. It probably sounds as though life was one long holiday but I was working hard. In August I took my annual holiday and Mary and I went to Portugal to stay with Leonard and Anthony in their newly acquired house in Sesmarias. Christine from South Africa flew in to join us for the two weeks and it was a holiday of sun, sea and good food. We spent many hours at the beach that I told you about earlier, although some of the huge rocks were still there parts of the sand had re-appeared and made for good sunbathing and the swimming was excellent.

Early in September KLM Dutch Airlines invited a small group of tour operators to visit India and I was thrilled to be included. We were only away for five days but saw much of Old and New Delhi, the Taj Mahal (full of tourists) and Jaipur where we had the elephant ride to Amber Fort. The hotels were not as luxurious as those that Patricia and I had stayed in previously in '83 but it was always good to see another standard of hotel to offer clients. On this occasion we spent more time in New Delhi as I wanted to see Government House and the Secretariat buildings designed by Edwin Lutyens and Herbert Baker in the early 20thC. The architects fell out over the position of these two important buildings and Baker's buildings dominate the view up the hill from Rajpath whilst only the dome of Lutyens Government House can be seen. Nevertheless they are a collection of beautiful and powerful buildings in a fusion of English, Classical and Indian styles.

I was hardly back from India when I did another four day inspection visit to Thailand mid September followed by the actual visit with the group for a week in October. I am amazed at myself for coping with all the time differences in these quick east west journeys!

We stayed at the Royal Wing of the Royal Cliff Hotel in Pattaya, it really is a most luxurious and beautiful hotel, and gazing from by balcony window over the gardens to the sea I wished that I had someone of my own with whom I could share the experience, it is all very well travelling with a group of people, some friendly of course some not so friendly, but with a companion there is always someone to share the experiences and to talk about them afterwards. I guess I was beginning to feel that it was time to leave this unknown territory that I had been in for a few years and find more settled pastures! But I enjoyed being at the Royal Wing, the staff in Reception knew me when I arrived and then my sun lounger was ready with its brass name plaque, a feature that the other members of the group thought was wonderful and made them feel special which is what this sort of Incentive tour is all about. We had a quick visit to the Floating Market at Damern Saduak the day we arrived and the rest of the time in Pattaya, relaxing and enjoying the hotel's facilities and also having a day by boat to an uninhabited island. I have never returned since that visit but looking at my photos I know it would make the perfect holiday.

So, three visits to Thailand in eight months, I was to pay for those stamps in my passport.

In November another principal, Princess Hotels invited a group of ten travel agents/ tour operators for a five day tour to see their luxury hotel in Scottsdale Arizona which was opened the previous December. I was delighted to be asked and to be able to see another part of the USA. My problems started on arrival at Los Angeles airport where we had to get a connection to Phoenix. At Immigration I had a lengthy interrogation to why I had been to Thailand three times recently, I suppose I should have said 'on holiday' but I said 'work related' and 'viewing hotels' which apparently sounded very suspicious and drug related. Anyway I got through immigration, all the time worried about making the onward connection as the rest of the group had disappeared. Then I collected my bag and at Customs was made to take everything out and the bag itself was searched thoroughly, however, hot and bothered I made the Phoenix flight.

The Princess Hotel, Scottsdale was large, many buildings spread through the gardens, all very grand and in retrospect the style reminds me of Sol Kerzner's Sun City in South Africa and his Atlantis Hotel. One morning we had breakfast in the Sonoran Desert, which reminded me of the tea party we had had in the Thar Desert near Jaisalmer, there tea had been set on cloths on the sands with the silver trays of food and sparkling tea urns; here in the Sonoran for breakfast we had tables and chairs, snowy white linen and sparkling tea urns. It is the unexpected which makes the experience so memorable. Whereas the Thar was sand the Sonora is scrub and cacti. The Saguaro cacti are over 250 years old and their height, judging by the photo of me standing beside one is over 20ft.

There was no time for us to drive to the Grand Canyon instead we had a morning flight by light aircraft. The weather was unseasonably cold and we had no warm clothes so we were kitted out in a variety of garments loaned for the occasion from the staff of the flight company and our ground agents. I had a very fetching fur waistcoat and a pair of very large gloves. The flight to the Grand Canyon South Rim was over the red rocks of Sedona and canyons with towering rock formations, followed by a short flight along the canyon itself. Am I allowed to say I was underwhelmed? Having read so much about the depth, the length and the majesty of the Canyon I was prepared to be awe-inspired. I think this was because you need to be a dot standing on the rim of the canyon to appreciate its immenseness, which was completely lacking by flying a few hundred feet above it.

The shopping malls in Scottsdale were very desirable but we had no time for purchasing. This was in the lead up to Christmas so the windows were beautifully decorated but the best decoration for me was a Christmas tree made from red poinsettias, twenty circular layers of potted plants making a tree over twenty feet tall. And so back to work and a family Christmas in Evesham.

During these last months I decided that I needed to make some effort to find a partner with whom to share my life. My travels had been with many males, single and married but none that appealed to me so I answered an advertisement for *Dateline* and sent in my credentials, mostly fairly honest, and the type of person I was looking for. This was all pre the computer age and eventually through the post I received a long list of 'matches'. Having weeded them out by place of residence or intuition I then had six meetings. Four were useless, not my cup of tea at all, one I saw a couple of times but he lived too far away and was into sailing and Damian I met in the car park of a hotel in Banbury halfway between where we both lived. Two disparate people you have probably never met but we talked for hours over coffee and then went into town for a curry lunch and continued to meet intermittently over the forthcoming months.

I knew that 1989 was going to be a turning point in my journey, I'd had five independent years, those same years that I should have had in my twenties, I now felt settled in England with my family and friends and was ready to go in a different direction. But firstly there was more travel to experience.

Pat and Peter were on holiday from Lesotho and I joined them for a weekend in Northumberland, a new county for me and so impressive. Warkworth Castle is probably not on every tourist's itinerary but it is a splendid ruined medieval edifice in glorious surroundings above the River Coquet. Nearby is the 12thC Augustinian priory of Brinkburn by the River Coquet in very tranquil surroundings. Visiting these ancient properties with architect Peter made the experience so much more worthwhile and started my interest in the origins of old buildings.

One of my clients was interested in visiting Morocco with a view to organising an incentive tour there and I was friendly with Jane who was their organiser so it seemed a good opportunity to explore what was for me an unknown country and to once again step onto the African continent. What a country of contrasts. Casablanca was a huge disappointment, commerce, skyscrapers and no atmosphere. The hotel was pleasant and the pianist serenaded us with . … you can guess, all very corny. Rabat, the capital of Morocco, was a surprise, it is by the sea, has lovely sandy beaches and a collection of Islamic and French colonial style buildings. My favourite photo is of the 12thC Hassan Tower surrounded by the ruins of a mosque.

In Marrakech we stayed at Hotel Tichka, it was built earlier in the '80s but its architecture and stained glass gave it the feel of a much older traditional style hotel. The market is not the place to go if you don't like crowds but it is very atmospheric with great opportunities for shopping providing you like bargaining. My photo taken from the upper floor of a restaurant in the late afternoon looking down onto the marketplace shows 'wall to wall' people.

The most enjoyable day was driving into the Atlas Mountains about an hour from Marrakech to the resort of La Roseraie. As the road weaves its way upwards to 700ft above sea level small boys stand on the roadside selling large lumps of crystals. The hotel is set in parklands and groves of olive trees and a large rose garden and is a perfect foil for a peaceful break after the bustle of Marrakech. I was sorry that the client did not decide on Morocco for their future journey.

When I was in Israel in '84 all the arrangements had been handled by Joey of Ophir Tours whom I had first met when I was with Thomas Cook in the early '80s, we had stayed in contact over the years, this resulted in an invitation to bring some clients to Israel in March '89. I took representatives from two of my top clients and with other agents and their clients we were a small party of only six plus the Israeli guide and Joey too. This was a more extensive visit than previously. Although initially we stayed in Tel Aviv it was fascinating to visit the old city of Jaffa, one of the world's oldest ports. Tel Aviv grew out of Jaffa but whereas this later city is skyscrapers and modern, Jaffa is old buildings and narrow alleyways with traditional food and vegetable markets. Then we went north to Caesarea, also on the coast, with ancient ruins of Herod the Great's palace and a beautiful beach by the Aqueduct. This area should be on every tourist's itinerary. Caesarea was the site of one of the most important cities of the Roman world but it had no reliable fresh water so in 22BC Herod commissioned the aqueduct to bring water from Shuni to Caesarea, a distance of 11miles. Emperor Hadrian built an additional aqueduct and they continued to supply water for 1200years. Very substantial remains of the arched aqueduct are on the beach, it was an impressive feat of construction and engineering. We had a brief visit to Lake Tiberias (Galilee), I gather that in recent times the water level has gone down but it was a very healthy lake when we saw it and quite able to support the 40 fishes.

The Garden Tomb in Jerusalem, thought to be the possible site for the Resurrection of Jesus has been surrounded by the trappings of tourists, necessary I suppose because of the hordes who visit here annually, but rather like all the other sites in Jerusalem I feel that money concerns outweigh spirituality. Much more my scene - we went out into the desert on a safari in an open jeep, on a jolly cold and wet morning! The destination was once again that extraordinary monastery of St George hidden in a the rocky valley in the Judean desert. I wish I could show you one of my photos. Golden coloured mountains in which there is a very narrow winding cleft and on one bend deep in the valley are a huddle of green trees. There is a flash of cerulean blue and only by looking closely can you see the seemingly hidden monastery buildings which fade into, or seem to grow out of the hillside. Magical.

Onwards through the desert to Massada, yet another place in Israel which makes it such a fascinating place to visit if you like history, archaeology, landscapes and buildings, add in beaches, excellent hotels and good food and why go anywhere else? Except of course for the airport security measures which we know we have to accept. Any way - Massada - one large plateau in the middle of the desert overlooking the Dead Sea accessible only by cable car or if you are fit by a very steep path. The epic story of how 960 people were besieged for three years by the Romans and who died rather than be captured to me symbolises the spirit of modern Israel. After a brief stop at the Dead Sea - no time for swimming, that comes on another visit - we continued by road through, to me, the stunning desert scenery of mountains and sandy wastes, so reminiscent of Aden, further down the Red Sea. We ended this journey at the King Solomon's Palace Hotel - again, for a relaxing couple of days before flying home.

Damian and I were continuing to see each other and I had taken him to Dorset to meet Sylvia and Dermott and I was delighted that they approved. He had also met my mother who was a little wary in her approval to start with. I was gradually introducing him to all my colonial friends and in July we spent what was the hottest weekend of the year on the Isle of Wight with Jackie W, my friend and neighbour from Maseru days, also her son Simon who was now a young man not a small boy. That same month Jann and Al, my Lusaka friends came to stay and we went blackberrying on Wittenham Clumps. These two wooded chalk hills were not far from where I lived in Abingdon and in those days the 390ft walk to the top was easily done. The summits of the Clumps are covered by beech trees dating from the mid 18thC making them some of the oldest beech trees in England. There is a good view from the top over the Thames Valley and their iconic appearance of grassy slopes topped by trees makes them a focal point for any train journey from Reading to Bristol.

In September I was invited to join a group of travel agents on a week's 'fam' trip to Egypt which would include a Nile cruise. It was an offer I could not refuse although I had passed through Luxor and Alexandria on earlier 'flying' visits and stayed in Cairo in 1955 when I was working for Aden Airways, I certainly wanted to experience the cruise. We were a group of eleven agents plus our tour leader and in Cairo we stayed at the Intercontinental Hotel. Nothing had changed in the Museum, it was still dark and dusty with the precious objects almost invisible in their cabinets, even Tutankhamen could have done with a clean. I was astonished at how Cairo had encroached upon the area of the Pyramids, on my previous visit they had appeared to be set in the desert far from the city but now they were part of the conurbation. Nevertheless we had the obligatory camel ride to the Pyramids and had refreshments in a tent serenaded by buglers.

We flew to Luxor and stayed at the Sheraton Hotel, a modern building on the banks of the Nile, we saw from the river the historic 19^{th}C Winter Palace Hotel where Agatha Christie wrote her 1937 novel, *Death on the Nile* and that would be my preferred place to stay! Before embarking we 'did' the local sights and sites including the Temples of Karnak and Luxor. In the dry and clean atmosphere it is still possible to see, after 2000 years, the paint colours on the underside of the stone cross-beams on the giant pillars. I am not going to give you the history of all that I saw in Egypt but Karnak is a special place, it is so large that St Peter's, Milan and Notre Dame Cathedrals could all fit inside its walls. It is impossible to write about the Egyptian temples and archaeology without saying incredible, majestic and fantastic. These adjectives apply to everything that I saw and my photos bring back the sheer joy of looking at the edifices and being made to feel humbled and overwhelmed by their size and the expertise and dedication in conception and building.

The four day cruise southwards from Luxor to Aswan up the Nile was on the *MS Nile President,* certainly not a five star vessel, just about three star, comfortable and clean, but the food was not great. Since meeting Damian I had become a vegetarian which was just as well as many of the meat eaters on the cruise became ill, even our tour leader succumbed for days to Delhi belly, or should that be Pharaoh's Revenge? However the journey and the stops en route were all that I imagined. There is something very peaceful about moving slowly along the Nile, you can absorb the scenery on both banks and wave to the feluccas as you pass them by. As it was between seasons the river and the tourist sites were not too busy. We visited Esna, Edfu and Kom Ombo where more than life-size figures were carved into the buildings as a frieze. There were many hieroglyphics and these came in two forms, one type that was carved into the face of the building and one in relief. The first, the carved in type, was crisp as new because it had been protected from erosion by wind, but the relief hieroglyphics were still perfectly readable (if you could) but the edges of the symbols were blunted by the wind and sand. We continued up the river to Aswan and the dam, sadly there wasn't time to go further to see the Abu Simbel temples which had been re-located in the '60s as the waters of the newly created Nasser Dam rose to cover their original site.

After a flight back to Cairo we spent a day with friends of the tour leader, who had recovered from her indisposition, at a large house right on the banks of the Suez Canal. In two respects it was a strange day. I had never expected to be sitting by the Canal that I had sailed through in '47 and '54 and watch vessels pass by so close you could almost touch them. I was sitting next to a stranger, a friend of a friend of the tour leader who talked about the Arab/Jewish conflict in some detail and with military knowledge, I somehow knew I should not ask his name as I doubt it would have been forthcoming but I think it would have been familiar……

My daughter Sarah had been suggesting for some time that we should organise a get-together for our old colonial friends and call it a 'When We' as that is how our conversations always seemed to start. So the first meeting of the When We Association took place at the end of October at Wigfair Hall near St Asaph in Clywd, North Wales. Wigfair is a Grade II Victorian building within its own grounds and terraces down to the river Elwy, we couldn't have chosen a better venue for our house party which must have been an echo of similar house parties in the Victorian era. There were grand bedrooms, many reception rooms, an imposing staircase, a panelled formal dining room and a huge kitchen with a table to seat twelve. I had hoped we would be a party of twelve but Damian couldn't attend so there was myself with Sarah and her partner Ian, Tess and Peter (Maseru days), Sylvia and Dermott (St Paul's), Jann and Al (Lusaka days), Rick (Sarah's host from Rotary, British Columbia), and James a friend of Tess and Peter.

Al cooked a full English breakfast every morning for all of us, Sylvia was chief stoker as there were several large fires which needed to be kept alight, the rest of the day we spent individually as there was much to see and do. Some went exploring the countryside or visiting the markets, Peter played golf and got stung by a bee which meant his arm was in a sling for days. St Asaph itself is interesting, it has a cathedral and is the second smallest city in Britain. For us Africaphiles there was an important connection as it was the birthplace of Stanley - he who 'found' David Livingstone. His name was actually John Rowlands and he spent time in the workhouse at St Asaph until he emigrated to America in 1859 and assumed the name Stanley.

Apart from the first evening, dinners were formal affairs in the dining room, black tie and long dresses, silver candelabra and a three course menu prepared and cooked by the ladies in turn. We had two themed evenings, Scottish, with haggis and neeps, and Halloween. Jann and Al prepared the Scottish menu and for the latter the tables were decorated with candles in pumpkins and we all had a splendid array of ghostly hats. Special effects were by Ian and included lights and masks in various places around the dining room. For after dinner entertainment there was a billiards room, table tennis and much wine to be consumed.

I have two particularly interesting photos, one of us all around the kitchen table, Al cooking, presumably breakfast, bottles of wine on the table and my caption is 'not breakfast, probably lunch, see wine'. The other is of an aproned James emptying a can of fruit salad into a bowl, two chocolate Swiss rolls on the side and captioned 'James making his special dessert'. I have no recall of the finished dish.

As a group we spent a day at Portmeirion, apparently the '60s TV series *The Prisoner* was filmed here, but we were all living in Africa at the time so it passed us by. It is a magical place to visit with its amusing collection of buildings in mostly an Italianate style. We had lunch at the hotel which is right on the Dywryd Estuary and is definitely a place to return to. Rick and I visited Harlech Castle, one of the castles that I had missed on my 1987 travels and from which there are magnificent views of Snowdonia.

Tess and Peter wanted a day out exploring, so we went first to the Aber Falls which are about 130ft high, quite spectacular in a wooded gorge, and this being Autumn the foliage had autumnal colours. We then went to the Ceiriog Valley as I wanted to see Dolywern where I had spent that long leave in 1963 with Don and the children. The house, the mill where we had our flat and the surrounding fields were all unchanged which was remarkable and brought back some mixed memories.

And so ended our Victorian House Party with promises to repeat it perhaps the following year.

The year was coming to an end and I was about to move from this unknown territory that I had entered with some trepidation six years previously into a more settled and calm part of my journey, but I had one more visit to make.

In November I asked Damian if he would like to visit New York with me for a long weekend as I knew that he wanted to see the various art galleries. We stayed in the Salisbury Hotel in midtown Manhatten and did the touristy sights. As you know I had been to New York previously but this time I went to the galleries that so interested Damian, and what a joy they all were. MOMA with its modern art, the Frick with the old European masters and gardens, Guggenheim an architectural masterpiece and the Met where we had a lovely lunch and the Whitney with its American art. I have a stunning photo of the twin towers taken from the water, another view of them from the top of the Empire State building and even a photo taken from the World Trade Centre looking north across Manhatten. Do I need to return to record the current skyline?

We took a morning Circle Line cruise around Manhattan which is surely the best way to assimilate all the sights and size of New York. We passed Ellis Island, the Yankee Stadium, South St Seaport, under bridges and past harbours with small and large ships and the outstanding, literally, riverside Church with its tower 20 floors tall. I understand the nave can sit a congregation of over 2000 but from the water it was the tower that was so impressive.

In a yellow cab on the way back to the hotel Damian asked me to marry him, I thought that was a good idea to we went to Macys where he bought me an emerald and diamond ring. And so my journey continues in a new direction.

CHAPTER 8
Travelling in a new direction

'The good life is a process, not a state of being. It is a direction not a destination'.
Carl Rogers.

Physically I am still on track in Abingdon in 1990, still working for Harvey Thomas Travel but now it is not just me, Damian and I can plan our future together. We planned to marry sometime in the year but first we had to find somewhere to live that satisfied the parameters that we both required. I needed to be near Abingdon and not too far from Heathrow airport because of my frequent travels and Damian wanted to be closer to Oxford as he spent time researching for his books in the libraries of the University of Oxford, particularly the Bodleian Library. We both wanted a house, not a flat, with a small garden and the most important feature was a decent sized room for Damian for his study, not just a small spare bedroom with a tiny window. We spent many weekends at housing developments in towns which suited our needs and it was only by the middle of the year that we found just what we wanted in Witney. It was a new development of three storey houses and on the plan the ground floor had a dining room and kitchen, middle floor a sitting room, bedroom and a shower room, top floor two bedrooms and a bathroom, We decided the downstairs dining room could be the sitting room and the middle floor sitting room would make a perfect study as it was large and had doors opening onto a small balcony. And that is the configuration that has remained, so far for twenty seven years. We made some changes in the kitchen which was opened out into a conservatory making the garden smaller but it has suited us perfectly. We both sold our flats easily and made a good profit and moved into the new house at the end of August, one month before we married. When moving day arrived I was sorry we had a three storey house after so many journeys up and down stairs to sort out all our furniture and belongings. But I am getting ahead of myself as there are more events in this year.

In January Damian and I went to Portugal to stay with Leonard and Anthony in their Sesmarias house and we returned again in June with my mother and sister Mary. That was such a lovely holiday and Mum even managed to enjoy swimming in the pool.

Remember my inspection visit to Morocco with client Jane who was looking for a venue for her company's incentive tour? She decided against Morocco and now wanted to visit Israel so Jane and I set off there in March, Damian too. In addition to the places that I have already told you about we had a fun evening dining at Cardo Culinaria, in the style of Ancient Rome, where we donned togas and laurel wreaths. This restaurant was under the Old City in the earlier city ruled by the Romans, the marble paving stones of their road is still there and the street lined with tall pillars. There was also a glass blowers stall where I bought some blue hand blown goblets in the Roman style. We paid another visit to the beautiful St George's monastery in the desert, my third visit, more beautiful photos, and then onto the Dead Sea where we had the obligatory swim and yes it is true you can lie in the water and read a book. En route to Eilat and the Red Sea a stop was made at Masada. Although I had made this car journey before, from Jerusalem to the monastery, to Masada and Eilat, each time the desert looked different and was so reminiscent of Aden it almost felt like a homecoming. The visit ended with a day's cruising on the Red Sea in a two-masted schooner and with Damian having a go at para-sailing!

Weddings were in the air this year, Sarah and Ian were married in March at Reading Registry Office and what a wonderful collection of guests there were. Many of Sarah and Ian's friends; all the family from Evesham, Mary and Michael and their children; Cliff and all his family from Southport; Don and Ethel, Damian and I, Tess and Peter, Jann and Al - all names you will recognise from past times. The reception was held at St Anne's Manor Hotel and most of the guests stayed overnight so the party continued into the evening. I don’t suppose many brides have their father, stepfather and prospective stepfather at their wedding!

In May Jean and Roger were married in Weybridge, it was a lovely sunny day and during the reception we were able to be in the garden of the hotel. Another wedding took place this year in South Africa, that of Terry, Su's ex husband and Beverley but it was to be a couple of years before they returned to live in England and our friendship could be resumed. Here it might be interesting to tell you of one of life's coincidences. Terry's first wife Dorothy remarried after her divorce from Terry to Paul my friend from Aden days, he of Peter and Paul that I knew from when I was fifteen and then seventeen in Aden.

Our wedding day was 29 September in the Evesham Registry Office and afterwards, as the invitation says *The Countess of Evesham casts off for a cruise on the River Avon.* Mum made my wedding outfit, it was blue again but a linen dress with a waterfall jacket edged in blue satin. Fascinator hats were just becoming the rage and I found one that suited me with a small veil and which didn't mess up my hair and I covered it in the same blue satin. I had satin shoes dyed to match. For a bouquet Mary and I had been to a local flower shop and I ordered a twiggy arrangement with lime coloured orchids.

Usually a day at the end of September can be sunny and dry, but this particular day it was grey and wet! We started the celebrations a couple of days earlier when friends from South Africa arrived and after the ceremony at the Registry Office we boarded the *Countess of Evesham* at Evesham marina, she is a 70ft barge turned into a luxury restaurant and we had hired it for our special lunch.

Menu

Watercress soup served with cream and chopped parsley
Fresh leek mousse served with a lemon sauce
Apricot sorbet
Chicken Supreme served with orange sauce
a selection of vegetables
Choux swans with fresh fruit and brandy sauce
or a selection of English cheeses
Coffee and mints

I must tell you about the champagne. On one of my journeys in the previous year to various conferences I had entered a raffle and won, I who never win anything had won a bottle of champagne, not just an ordinary bottle but a Jeroboam and I hoped that it would be drinkable at the reception. When opened I asked Dermott to sample it and he pronounced it acceptable and there was a bar on board for those who didn't like champagne. At one point on the cruise we had to stop to go through a lock and I had to go outside and kiss the lock keeper - in the pouring rain.

The guests were a mixture of Atkinsons, my family and our friends. Damian's best man was his brother Martin and my matron of honour was Jean. I would like to record the guest list:
Martin & Val Atkinson, Simon & Caroline Atkinson, Rupert Atkinson & Jill, my mother, Michael & Mary Haines, Bruce Haines & Nicki, Christine & Joe, Jean & Roger, Peter & Tess, Jann & Al, Sylvia & Dermott, Margie & Jimmy, Su & Rob, Sarah & Ian, Jane & partner, Jean & Jim, Astri & John, Anthony & Leonard, Edgar & Joan.

After the cruise most of us repaired to the Northwick Arms Hotel in Evesham for supper and reminiscing as it was not often that we could all be together. Our honeymoon was delayed until November when we flew to Singapore for a week to stay with Hilary and Ian, friends from South Africa days. They had a beautiful house in Adam Park an area that I didn't know at the time was on the site of a WWII battlefield and prisoner of war camp. No sign of that in modern times, just villas surrounded by lush gardens. Raffles Hotel was in the process of renovation so we couldn't see inside instead we had a Singapore Sling, served in a glass in the shape of a merlion on top of the then worlds' tallest building, the Westin Plaza, and a coffee one morning in Marks and Spencer!

The Kranji War Cemetery is another of those places so well cared for by the War Graves Commission, there are rows of head stones bearing the inscription 'A Soldier of the 1939-1945 War', so few with names. There is an interesting sign at the entrance:

WARNING

The use of vases or other water-bearing receptacles to contain flowers leads to mosquito breeding and is PROHIBITED. Flowers may be placed on the grave WITHOUT the use of a vase or other water-bearing receptacle.

Sentosa Island appears to be where Singaporeans go for a day out, rather like going to a theme park in England, but we went for the ride there by cable car which gave splendid views over Singapore and the beaches of Sentosa. We also went by boat across from Singapore Island to the mainland of Malaysia and the fishing village of Kukup. Just a short distance separates these two countries and the contrast is great, Singapore is all modernity and the small area we saw around Kukup was probably unchanged for centuries. Damian hated this day as the smells from the fishing village were too ghastly!

We went to Chicago for a long weekend at the end of February '91. Damian needed to visit one of the University libraries connected with his research so I found a hotel, The Mayfair, actually called a boutique hotel which was the first time I had come across that term, on the shores of Lake Michigan. It was a very, very cold weekend. Chicagoans seemed to exist underground, walking from one building to another via subways and I understood why when we returned one afternoon walking from the main street round the corner to the hotel and were met with icy blasts, in just minutes I felt frostbite forming on my face.

I decided it was time to introduce Damian to Africa so that he could understand what we were talking about on 'when we' occasions, so in May we went on a two week holiday to South Africa. As a fitting introduction on the first day we visited the Voortrekker Monument in Pretoria. It is a grand monument to the Voortrekkers who left the Cape Colony between 1835 and 1854, and has two very special features, the world's longest marble frieze depicting the exploits of the Voortrekkers and an opening in the roof through which a shaft of sunlight shines at the same time every 16 December, a public holiday which used to be called Dingaan's Day and is now the Day of Reconciliation. It is a place to admire and understand the spirit of the Afrikaner people. We saw the Union Buildings and on Sunday morning visited Emmarentia Lake for the monthly 'Artists in the Sun' exhibition. I would like to have added to my collection of paintings with some of the vibrant works done by African artists but baggage space did not allow.

After a catch-up with friends at Christine's house we flew to Skukuza for a four day stay at the luxurious Sabi Sabi Game Reserve on the edge of the Kruger Park. We stayed in Bush Lodge and had our own private guide, Witas, who was amazingly knowledgeable about the game and also where to find the animals. The Big Five are in Sabi but we did not see leopard, but there were many lion and I will never forget Damian's face when an elephant emerged from the bush in front of where we were driving, waved his trunk at the vehicle and then slowly ambled off. Witas took us on a evening walk at dusk, quite a scary experience, but it was so worthwhile as we saw and heard a magnificent Giant Eagle Owl which is the largest owl in the world.

Our journey continued to Natal where we stayed in Pinetown on the hills behind Durban with Su and her partner and this provided an ideal base to explore the Royal Natal National Park, it was here in the hotel that our Queen stayed with her parents and Princess Margaret in 1947, the year that she turned 21 and gave the speech that dedicated herself to her role 'whether her life be long or short'. I don't think the hotel had changed over the years, the rooms were quite basic but the joy was the dining room, also unchanged, the menu was long, you were expected to have every course, not to choose, and one that stands out in my memory is ' fish cakes with HP sauce'. Being winter the bush was very dry but the Amphitheatre, that well-known rock wall famous as the backdrop in the film 'Zulu' still stirred the imagination. It is three miles long and 546 yds high and contains the source of the mighty Orange river. We spent a day trekking into the bush away from the hotel with our guide who was over seventy and very fit! We went past Fairy Glen, discovered rock paintings hidden in a cave and saw the Sunday Falls which in spite of it being winter had two long curtains of water falling over a sandstone ridge down into the bush below.

In the Cape we were looked after by Janette, a friend from Maseru days and on a rather murky day visited Cape Point. This is not the southernmost point in Africa, I had to wait a few years before going there, but certainly the most treacherous where many ships have foundered on the Cape of Storms aptly named by Bartholomew Diaz who rounded the Cape in 1488. I have always been interested in Cecil John Rhodes and have a good collection of books relating to his life and work so I wanted see places associated with him. The small cottage in Muizenberg where he died in 1902 aged forty nine and one of the wealthiest men in the world is now a museum and the cottage is very simple in contrast to his extraordinary achievements. It is said that his last words were 'so little time, so much to do'.

The statue of Rhodes at the University of Cape Town was removed in 2015 as part of the 'Rhodes Must Fall' campaign but the Rhodes Memorial stands as a powerful monument to a great man. It was designed in 1912 by our friend Herbert Baker whom we have met before, he who designed houses in Johannesburg, the Union buildings in Pretoria and some of the Government Buildings in New Delhi. There are forty nine steps leading to the monument, one for each year of Rhodes's life and at the bottom of the steps is Frederick Watts bronze statue of *Physical Energy* and what an apt description for a sculpture that appears to be about to leave its plinth and bound away into the distance. At the centre of the memorial is a bust of Rhodes which was apparently also vandalised in 2015, but my photo shows him in a contemplative pose, inscribed over the bust with the words:

To the Spirit and life work of Cecil John Rhodes who loved and served South Africa

and below him words from Kipling's poem *Burial:*

The immense and brooding spirit still
Shall quicken and control
Living he was the land, and dead
His soul shall be her soul

To anyone interested in Cecil Rhodes and his times I would recommend three books, *Cecil Rhodes by His Architect* by Herbert Baker, *Randlords* by Paul Emden and *The Founder* by Robert Rotberg.

We left Cape Town for the 24hour, 1000mile journey to Johannesburg on the Blue Train, said to be one of the most luxurious train journeys in the world and it certainly is a wonderful way to travel. The train is blue, the compartments comfortable, the dining superb, and all these features are outclassed by the scenery. Leaving Cape Town mid morning we passed through the fruit and wine farms of Worcester and then stopped at Matjiesfontein to see the incongruity of the grand Victorian styled Lord Milner Hotel set by the rail tracks in the middle of the Little Karoo desert. Both the South African and British Union flags were then flying from the hotel. Olive Schreiner lived in Matjiesfontein as the cool, clear air was good for her health and she wrote here The *Story of an African Farm.* It was possible to enjoy the vastness of the Karoo travelling at the leisurely pace of the train and Olive Schreiner's words give life to this place:

The full African moon poured down its light from the blue sky into the wild and lonely plain. The dry sandy earth, with its coating of stunted karoo bushes a few inches high, the low hills that skirted the plain, the milk-bushes with their longer finger-like leaves, all were touched by a weird and almost oppressive beauty as they lay in white light.

It is these scented Karoo bushes which give Karoo lamb its distinctive flavour and also from here comes the restorative rooibos tea.

After travelling overnight through the Free State, with beds far more comfortable than the Palace on Wheels in Rajasthan, we arrived in Johannesburg mid morning at the end of our South African adventure.

And so it was back to work for both Damian and me. Damian was working as assistant to the Librarian at St Edmund Hall, one of the smaller University of Oxford colleges and I continued at Harvey Thomas in Abingdon but with more travel ahead. Jane, my client from the Morocco and Israel inspection visits needed to see a UK venue so in June we went to Torquay for a long weekend, together with her partner and Damian.

The Imperial Hotel in Torquay has a stunning location on a cliff top overlooking the bay, beautiful bedrooms with balconies and fine reception rooms too. But Torquay as a town re-enforces my view that England doesn't do good seaside town resorts. We had a day out to Dartmouth on the Paignton & Dartmouth railway pulled by Great Western steam engine 4555 and Jane eventually, in 1992, hired the Devon Belle saloon car on this railway for her group who also stayed at the Imperial. We took the ferry across the Dart to the town which is very picturesque and on the water's edge, against a hill. It was here that parts of the '70s TV film *The Onedin Line* were filmed and the18thC houses that line the river provided a backdrop to the 19thC sailing ships in the river.

In July I was off again on a 'fam' trip with Lufthansa to Baden Baden, the Brenner's Park Hotel again, and then the Black Forest and Heidelberg. It was a visit to superlative hotels, I have already told you about Brenner's Park, then came Hotel Buhlerhohe, in the style of a baroque castle in the Black Forest, set high amongst the tree with stupendous views. It was here that I had my first taste of a Peach Bellini cocktail - strange how the most inconsequential things can be the most memorable. The other hotel was not so grand but just as perfect. Hotel Hirschgasse in Heidelberg is a small 15thC Inn hidden away from the town. The group photo shows us sitting on the steps of the Inn with flowers cascading from the window boxes above us. We spent two days here and explored this beautiful town and the historic castle. The previous time that I had been here was when Cliff and I were travelling down the Rhine on a cruise.

The final event of the year was the 'When We' get together at Wigfair Hall in October. Some of the guests were as previously as well as the inclusion of Damian; Sylvia and Dermott could not make it and were replaced by Janet and Peter H, friends of Tess and Peter and once again Rick came all the way from Canada to be with us. An excursion this year took us to the summit of Snowdon, by rail, not walking, and jolly freezing cold it was too but the views from the top made it all worthwhile. Damian and I had a marvellous walk around the Lleyn Peninsula, it is a wild unspoilt area, the walk started along the beach and then you gradually rise up to the top of the hills, crossing small streams as you go. At one point on the top we were deafened by low flying military fighters out on manoevres.

One afternoon whilst everyone was watching rugby on TV I took myself off for a walk and came to the terraces in front of the house, I slid/jumped from one level to the next and misjudged the height, consequently landing badly and damaging my knee which was the start of many knee problems.

April '92 saw Damian and I off on our holidays to Greece for two weeks. The lady who had always looked after my groups, Lena, let us stay in her flat in Glyfada for a few days, this is a pleasant suburb away from the rush of Athens and near to Vougliameni where I had stayed previously. We were able to take the bus into Athens and explore the Plaka district with its markets and small restaurants, and then join the tourists on the Acropolis. Lena took us to the Vorres Folk Art Museum as she wanted to show me the property as a potential venue for a special evening for groups. The museum buildings are set in lush simple gardens not far from the centre of Athens and I did indeed later bring a group here for a farewell dinner in the gardens to the accompaniment of traditional music.

Damian and I then embarked of *MTS Jason* of Epirotiki Lines for a seven day cruise. It was a wet and windy day in Istanbul as evidenced by the umbrellas in my photos but we saw the other needle - the twin of Cleopatra's on the London embankment, this one being in far better condition because of the cleaner atmosphere. Topkapi and the Mosques and then on to Kusadasi where there was no time to look for another Clarice Cliff cup and saucer as we took the tour to Ephesus. It was good to be going somewhere new to both of us. And what a splendid place it is, an ancient Greek city originating from the 10thBC. The Library, of which the facade still stands, is rather similar to that at Petra, without the sandy surroundings. The public toilets of the city, the Scholastica Baths are in perfect condition and a photo shows Damian having a seat there. In Mykonos I was able to show Damian how to find the path along the water's edge to the un-touristy part of Little Venice. This time on Santorini there was a cable car to take cruise passengers from the harbour up to the whitewashed town of Thera, the donkeys were long gone which was probably just as well as with cruise ships getting larger an army of donkeys would have been required for the conveyance of passengers. A new stop for me was Heraklion on Crete from where we took a tour to see the Palace of Knossos dating from 1900BC. The ruins are grand and are a tribute to the archaeological investigations of Sir Arthur Evans in 1900, just a few hours there did not do the site justice.

Back home in July we travelled to Leicester University for Damian's Graduation Day where he was awarded a PhD for his work entitled *Some unpublished letters of William Ernest Henley (1849-1903)* 4 vols.(1991). It was the culmination of many years research and inspired him to continue writing.

In the travel papers in the summer Cox and Kings were advertising a short tour to India for travel agents and partners at a reasonable cost so I booked for Damian and I to go at the end of September as it gave Damian the opportunity for an elephant ride to the Amber Fort in Jaipur. The tour consisted of two nights Delhi, one night Gwalior, one night Agra, two nights Jaipur and one night Delhi. The standard of hotels was three star, not the luxury hotels that I had stayed in during previous visits and therefore located in other area of the cities, and this produced some different photos for my album of many downtown places full of people, rickshaws, cars and cows. In Delhi there is an impressive bronze statue of eleven life-size figures lead by Gandhi to commemorate The Salt march which took place in 1930. This had not featured in my earlier itineraries and should certainly be included for tourists to see both for its historical and sculptural appeal.

In Gwalior we stayed at the Usha Kiran Palace Hotel, built over a hundred years ago in a style I would call Indian Art Deco! The bedrooms in the hotel were very basic and I was so glad I had brought mosquito coils to burn overnight as there were plenty of the little beasts. Two good features of the hotel were the nine acres of beautiful gardens and a run of intricately carved wooden screens along one side of the first floor of the hotel. I see that now, in the 21stC it is called a luxury five star hotel so I guess much money has been spent to upgrade it. Our sightseeing day was to the Mansingh Palace outside Gwalior, and what a splendid, magnificent vision it was and it should be included in all holidays to India. For me it equalled the grandeur and beauty of the Taj Mahal, Amber Fort and Red Fort. The sign set in a wall explains:

MANSINGH PALACE
THIS FAMOUS PALACE IS FINE EXAMPLE OF HINDU ARCHITECTURE IN INDIA. IT WAS BUILT BY RAJA MANSINGH OF TOMAR DYNASTY OF GWALIOR IN 15TH CENT. A.D. HAVING TWO UNDERGROUND FLOORS. IT CONSISTS OF TWO OPEN COURTS SURROUNDED BY APARTMENTS WITH CARVED STONE PILLARS AND BRACKETS. THE FAÇADE STANDS ON A LOFTY CLIFF OF THE RUGGED FORTRESS AT A HEIGHT OF 300FT. ABOVE THE GROUND LEVEL BELOW. ITSELF ABOUT 300 FT. LONG AND ABOUT 80FT. HIGH BEING RELIEVED AT REGULAR INTERVALS BY SIX ROUNDED TOWERS OF SINGULARLY PLEASING DESIGN CROWNED BY DOMED CUPOLAS
THE WALL IS INLAID WITH ENAMELLED TILES BLUE, GREEN AND YELLOW FORMING BANDS OF MOSAIC CONSISTING CHIEFLY OF CONVENTIONAL FIGURES OF MEN, DUCK AND ELEPHANTS,

CROCODILES, TIGER AND BANNANA (sic) TREES, AT THE SOUTHERN END OF THIS FRONTAGE IS THE MAIN GATE OF THE PALACE, CALLED THE HATIA PAUR OR ELEPHANT GATE WHICH IS ITSELF A PRODUCT OF GREAT ARTISTIC MERIT. DURING THE MUGHAL PERIOD THE FORT WAS USED AS STATE PRISON.
ARCHAEOLOGIAL SURVEY OF INDIA
BHOPAL CIRCLE, BHOPAL

It is such an imposing complex of red sandstone highlighted by the brilliant colours of the tiles. We travelled on to Agra by the Shatabdi Express train, fortunately a short journey as the only memorable part of the journey were the cockroaches rushing around the floor. You've visited the Taj Mahal with me on previous trips so I won't repeat myself but we celebrated out second wedding anniversary here with a special dinner in the hotel. Then on to the deserted city of Fatepur Sikri which was far more deserted than my previous visit with Patricia in'83. In Jaipur we stayed at the Jai Mahal Palace Hotel and this really was worthy of the Palace name. Built in the mid 18^{th}C with glorious gardens, water features and swimming pools. It was such a pity that Damian could not enjoy the two nights here as he was felled by a virus, the doctor couldn't prescribe any medication so he was in bed for the two days and so missed his long awaited elephant ride to the Amber Fort. I gave it a miss too and between playing nurse lazed in the pool. Fortunately he was well enough to continue on to Delhi and then home.

Lufthansa and Kempinski hotels invited me to join a small group of agents for a few days in Moscow at the end of November, probably not the best time to go north, everywhere was covered in thick snow and it was fairly treacherous underfoot. However I was amazed at the snow clearing equipment, basically a lorry which went along the road scraping up the snow and depositing in the back of the lorry. To start with we went out without head covering which prompted the locals to stop us and point to their covered heads, so we got the message and covered up against the cold.

The Kempinski Baltschug Hotel was across the road from the Kremlin and Red Square and St Basil's so could not have been better located as we were able to walk, carefully, everywhere. I found the opulence of the hotel at odds with the obvious poverty in the area of the city away from the tourist attractions. There was a large market full of stalls selling anything and everything and from an elderly lady I bought some hand knitted shawls for USD5 each, she was so grateful for the dollars and in retrospect I should have given her more. Inside the Kremlin walls the buildings are magnificent and again painted with the same shade of yellow that I was to see in Sweden and Finland and here it matched the gold of the many turrets that topped the buildings. We have all heard of the interior decoration of the Moscow metro, and I can confirm that at the stations we visited there were roof and wall paintings and sculptures too.

I know it seems as though my life was flitting from one destination to another staying in luxury hotels and taking cruises but remember this was mainly for work and where the journey encompassed holidays I was fortunate to get discounts and complimentary accommodations, for most of the time I was working hard. It had escalated to such an extent that I now had an assistant, Stuart, who was able to keep the office on track whilst I visited clients to discuss their future programmes. I should mention that at this time I was still not computerised! Stuart and I wrote our letters, proposals and itineraries by hand and these were typed by the secretarial staff. The fax machine was the extent of our modern equipment as well as a mobile phone, rather large and cumbersome which we shared between the two of us depending on who was going out and about.

At home Damian was taking the bus to Oxford every day for his work at Teddy Hall as St Edmund Hall is affectionately known and I had the daily drive to and from Abingdon and then usually up and down the M4 visiting clients. Weekends were busy too. We liked walking so for some years, before my joint problems became too severe, we roamed over the Cotswolds and further afield in whatever the weather decided to be. Many a picnic lunch we have had sitting in the rain on a Cotswold stone wall. Also I tried to visit my mother at least twice a week, midweek and at the weekend, one of the reasons for coming to live back in England in 1986 had been to see more of the family and this I had achieved and it was good also to see my sister's family growing up. On visits to my mother she would talk about her ancestors and this was the beginnings of me being interested in my antecedents. I even taped some of her conversations although she would say 'turn that damn thing off'!

We had our friends come to stay and many a good 'when we' party took place in our small garden and we paid return visits to them, and many to rural Dorset to stay with Sylvia and Dermott in their ancient cottage. So although it might appear that my life was all work, foreign destinations and no play in fact it was a very balanced life.

It was time for me to catch up with Susan and her partner so in February '93 I spent five days with them in their house in Pinetown. I had someone to accompany me - Mary's son Ross aged16 was on half term holiday from school and it seemed a good idea for him to meet his cousins Simon and Robin. This was the only time in all my travels that my suitcase was seriously lost from a flight. It was an exceptionally heavy case as Vera, my ex travel colleague had asked me to bring some brochures from England for her; anyway Ross and I arrived in Durban but not my suitcase. Fortunately I have always travelled with a handbag large enough for some essentials so it wasn't a disaster but we had arrived on Thursday, the case arrived on Sunday - delivered to the door, and we left for Johannesburg on Monday.

The teenagers went surfing and visited Waterworld and we had a particularly gruesome visit to the Natal Sharks Board at Umhlanga where we were given a demonstration of dissecting a shark. Our final day was spent in Johannesburg at Gold Reef City which was an opportunity to show Ross how Johannesburg appeared in the gold rush days before the city became covered in skyscrapers. It is actually a theme park on an old gold mine and has many iconic buildings that date from the start of the gold rush in the 1880s. Ross went down a mine shaft, we saw an exhibition of dancing by miners in their gumboots and then had lunch with some of my old friends, Lily and Paddy P, Rina and her partner, Connie, Graham and Christine. I hope these few days gave Ross a new perspective on South Africa - remember he had been here as a child when he had almost drowned in the swimming pool in Parkhurst!

In April Damian and I went to Florence for a long weekend and stayed at a very super hotel - I can't recall the name - but we had a large suite, the dining room was terrifyingly grand and we could not afford to eat there except we did have one continental breakfast at £15 each, just to say that we had been in the dining room. We visited the Uffizi gallery and marvelled at David but best of all I liked the Ponte Vecchio as it was how I imagined the original London Bridge must have looked in medieval times, with its shops and stalls and markets all taking place in the buildings along the bridge. We bought a oil painting of the Florence skyline from the artist by the Ponte Vecchio.

Entertaining continued at home, Easter was spent in Witney with all my sister's family and mother coming for lunch and Graham from South Africa was staying with us too. Simon and Robin came from South Africa for the month of July and stayed with Sarah and Ian and they visited Scotland. Damian and I stayed in Yorkshire with Jim and Jean from Lusaka days, and had a glorious day out walking the dales in the Ingleborough area. It is interesting to compare the Yorkshire stone walls with those of the Cotswolds, they are of similar construction and have a similar purpose, that of defining a boundary and/or containing livestock but the Yorkshire walls are of rougher and larger pieces of rock and do not have the defined horizontal lines of the Cotswold walls, more a random construction. I read somewhere that Cotswolds walls are considered twee and Yorkshire walls are rugged.

British Airways invited me to go to Washington for a weekend in October, on Concorde, how could I refuse? It was a journey of a lifetime even for me who had travelled so much and even more special if I had known that by 2003 Concorde would be no more. The sound and strength of this aircraft was still with me from when it flew overhead on one of its test fights, whilst I was sun-bathing on Glyfada beach in 1972. You knew that you were about to experience something special when you checked in at the Concorde desk at Heathrow Terminal 4. On entering the aircraft it seemed so small compared with the other wide bodied aircraft that I had flown in - I remember the first time I entered a 747 and that seemed vast, compared to that Concorde was almost cramped. The seating was 2 x 2 and the headspace was low and the aisle narrow. A friend of Jean used to be a Concorde hostess and she said the trolleys were especially made to fit the narrowness (not the width!) of the aisle and

I guess the hostesses were similar constructed! On the bulkhead was a digital display showing the aircraft's speed and when we reached Mach 2.04 or 1345mph it felt as though someone had thumped the back of your seat. The flight only lasted for under four hours and we arrived in Washington before we had left London, time wise. We stayed for two nights at the Ritz Carlton near the Pentagon and did some sightseeing before flying home Business Class, not even First Class - how spoilt can one be?

What to do on Christmas Day? This year we decided on a picnic by the seaside - yes in December, in England! Sarah and Ian, Damian and I went to the South coast and had our picnic lunch on the beach at Seaford followed by a visit to Brighton Pier where we had our photos taken inside the cardboard cut-outs, Damian as Prince Albert and me as Queen Vic. It was not a traditional Christmas but certainly memorable.

In February '94 South African Airways invited me on a familiarisation trip to South Africa - as if I wasn't already familiar with this beautiful country, however I accepted as it fitted in nicely with me being able to attend a wedding in Johannesburg beforehand and see Su in Natal. Pat and Peter H's daughter Fiona married Jason at the Hertford Inn just north of Johannesburg, it was a lovely country venue, a small hotel with its own rustic stone built chapel. For me it was a lovely day as I met up with many friends from Lesotho days. I then joined the SAA group in Cape Town where we went to the top of Table Mountain in a cable car, took more photos of Cape Point and then stayed in the Grande Roche Hotel in Paarl. This is a stunning hotel in a restored 18^{th}C farmhouse in the traditional Dutch/South African style with views over vineyards and towards the mountains. As a group we then flew to Johannesburg and on to stay at Sun City, a world of glitz and bling as far away in style from the restrained elegance of Grand Roche as you could possibly imagine. Our stay was in one of the four hotels at the Sun City complex, The Palace of The Lost City where the words opulent and lavish are particularly apt descriptions as well as 'over the top'. You wouldn't believe my description of The Palace, so I give you the words from the official website:

This magnificent palace, so legend tells, was built for a king by an ancient civilization from the north of Africa, who made this idyllic valley their home until it was destroyed by an earthquake. Now restored to its former glory, this unique establishment specializes in extending a royal welcome to the discerning guests who come to call. The Palace offers opulent accommodation, fabulous architecture & decor details, the finest cuisine and incomparable sporting and leisure facilities. The Palace wants for nothing - it has no equal. Faux elephant tusks, sculptured bronze and crystal, richly woven colours of Africa, mystery-scented air and jungle cascades fuse into an atmosphere fit for a king. With frescoed ceilings above and ancient tiles below, you are left to stand in awe at the sheer scale of this masterpiece. The craftsmen who fashioned this breathtaking Palace used equal quantities of art and nature in soaring columns and intricate mosaic, capturing wild elegance and savage beauty in bronze and stone, culminating in a life-size sculpture of the mighty elephant Shawu, who takes pride of place in the Shawu Court.
http://www.eyesonafrica.net/south-african-safari/sun-city-palace.htm

It is truly unique, my photos are captioned 'Some of the most extraordinary parts of The Lost City'. There is the volcano which belches forth smoke at regular intervals, the Bridge of Time which as you walk over it shakes from an apparent earthquake every minute or so and most bizarre of all is the sandy beach with 6ft waves, all 700 miles from the coast. To complete the South African experience Sun City is close to the Pilanesburg Game Reserve and on an early morning drive we saw a pair of lions ambling along the road.

In July British Airways, bless them, invited me to join a small group of agents on a short trip to Sydney, we were there for five days and four nights, with three of the nights spent in different hotels, to say it was exhausting is no exaggeration as there was no time to recover from the jet lag, one just had to carry on regardless! The four hotels that we 'inspected' are just a blur but you might like to hear what I actually remembered.

Instead of the usual sightseeing tour of the city by car or coach this one was taken on the pillion seat of a Harley Davidson motorbike, it was scary but certainly memorable and we toured the harbour area and went to see the Opera House. Then a lunch on a private launch around the harbour and out to the Heads which form the wide entrance to the harbour. It was the lunch that was special. I was a vegetarian at this time, the others had fillet steak on toast with a sauce, my dish looked exactly the same but it was aubergine sliced and rolled to resemble the steak with the same sauce on toast so it looked exactly like the meat dish, I thought that was very clever. Another foody first was in a Japanese restaurant on the top floor of a hotel where there was a sushi bar which revolved and you just took what you wanted as it moved around. Another hotel that we didn't stay in but visited was the Observatory Hotel with an exceptional indoor swimming pool with a star lit roof.

Somehow we managed to include day out into the Blue Mountains where the scenery is spectacular and a walk through the forests to see tree ferns in their natural habitat. My only purchase was not a painting but a small toy koala bear with corks dangling from his hat. As a parting present from the Sydney ground handler we were all given a Drizabone waxed coat, which was such a generous gift. I think we flew home via Singapore but I was too tired to notice.

The Witney garden looked lovely this year, as we hosted lunch parties for all our friends in August. This was before the conservatory was built so there was still some lawn and many creepers over the fences, before these had to be taken down as damaging the fences especially Russian Vine or Mile a Minute which threatened to overtake the neighbour's fences too. I had planted a fir tree when we moved in - Jupiter Skyrocket, and rocket it did into alarming proportions and that too had to go. The laurels and ivy all made for a lovely green garden but they were also too invasive. I've never pretended to be gardener.

Damian and I had a two week holiday in South Africa in September - doing what we wanted to do, no inspections and no familiarisation trips. We took the ordinary train for an overnight journey from Johannesburg to Durban, in no way did this resemble the Palace on Wheels or the Blue Train, and it was infinitely better than the Shatabdi Express, it was basic but clean and our compartment was adequate. The best part was the breakfast, vors and pap for the meat eaters and eggs and beans as well. Several other passengers were also enjoying their liquid breakfast as they had entered the dining car carrying six packs of lager.

Su took us on a day out sightseeing, starting at World's View, just outside Pietermaritzburg. It does have the most stunning views over the city and towards the Drakensberg mountains. It is a site of great historical interest for South Africans and I make no apologies for quoting the website for World's View.

In 1837-8, the wagons of the Voortrekkers were brought down the slopes of the Drakensberg mountains into Natal, and many came through here, into the future Pietermaritzburg. Signs of the old route can still be seen. There is a magnificent view of Pietermaritzburg, table mountain (the Natal version) and the surrounding country. The old Voortrekker road is a national monument.

(Editor's Note) As I had completed the photos and was heading back towards Hilton along the narrow road away from the Worlds View area, I almost sensed an Ox Wagon just ahead of the car and a child not more than ten years old looking back from inside the wagon right at my car. He had blond hair, it was as if he was staring at this strange creature on four wheels from across the gulf of two centuries. It was the strangest sensation. There are so many untold stories of ordinary people who achieved extraordinary things on a daily basis so long ago, of families who really just wanted to survive as best they could. We are their legacy and how we remember them is by memorials such as the one we have at Worlds View.

http://www.pietermaritzburgtourism.co.za/worldsview/

The memorial says;

OLD ROAD
WORLD'S VIEW
THIS ROAD WAS USED BY THE VOORTREKKERS
AND LATER BY OTHER PIONEERS
AND TRANSPORT RIDERS.

It is said that you can still see the marks made in the rocks from the wagon wheels in the flat rocks to the left of the memorial but I did not find them. I think the writer of the above did see a child on an ox wagon from across the centuries, rather like Patricia and I saw dancers in the Banqueting House at Lucknow.

We passed through Hilton on our way back to Durban, you may remember Hilton as the place where Cliff and I were going to run the Hilton Hotel all those years ago. This time as we rounded a bend in the road a steam engine passed the level crossing going into a siding, Damian leapt out of the car and before you could say 'good heavens' he was on the footplate and off into the distance. He has always been mad about steam engines and this was too good an opportunity to miss. Su and I waited at the Natal Railway Museum whilst the engine went back and forth hooking up to a line of trucks bearing logs for Japan.

Under our own steam now with a car we went into the Drakensberg and spent five days at the Mont Aux Sources Hotel. It was a perfect place for a relaxing break, no high-rise, just two storeys of lovely bedrooms, ours was on the ground floor and we could walk straight out into the gardens and see the views of the mountains which went on forever. From the hotel we walked to find the bushman paintings, as in a previous visit to the Royal Natal National Park, these were hard to find but my photos show the underside of an overhanging rock bearing ochre and white painted animals - aurochs and deer - who knows? We followed a river and came to the bridge with the iconic view of the Amphitheatre and again thoughts whizz round the brain of the films about the Zulu wars which have used this view as a backdrop.

As part of his research Damian wanted to find a particular grave in Ladysmith cemetery as it bore the words of W.E. Henley, whose letters he was editing. It is a poignant memorial;

IN MEMORY
OF
GEORGE WARRINGTON
STEEVENS
WAR CORRESPONDENT OF THE DAILY MAIL
HE DIED OF ENTERIC FEVER DURING THE SEIGE
OF LADYSMITH IN 1900 AGED 31 YEARS
THIS CROSS
IS SENT BY HIS BROKEN-HEARTED WIFE
FROM THE COUNTRY HE LOVED SO WELL
HER HEARTH IS LEFT UNTO HER DESOLATE

'WE CHEERED YOU FORTH BRILLIANT AND KIND AND BRAVE:
UNDER YOUR COUNTRY'S TRIUMPHANT FLAG YOU FELL:
IT FLOATS DEAR HEART OVER NO DEARER GRAVE.
BRILLIANT AND BRAVE AND KIND.HAIL AND FAREWELL'.

W.E.HENLEY

The church in Ladysmith has many memorials to all who died during the siege. We went to Chieveley Cemetery between Colenso and Estcourt to see the grave of Lord Roberts's son Fred who was mortally wounded on 15 December 1899. He was awarded the Victoria Cross posthumously, his father who was Commander-in-Chief during the Boer War, was awarded the Victoria Cross in 1858, a brave father and son.

Our final Boer War site before heading back into Zulu War territory was to the place where Winston Churchill was captured in November 1899. By walking along the track and away from the road you come to a very small cemetery of the four soldiers who were killed during that incident, I do hope it is still maintained sensitively.

I have told you already about previous visits to the Zulu War battlefield but this time we had a very special stay at Fugitive's Drift Lodge, overlooking the Buffalo River and owned by David Rattray and run by his wife Nicky, whom he called pie-head! David was an historian and knew the history of the Zulu Wars from an English and also a Zulu perspective, he was brought up with Zulu friends and together they explored the battlefield which was on the door step of his home. He had that gift of bringing to life history through words. We had an en-suite cottage at the lodge with a view to the hill of Isandlwana in the distance. We were privileged to have David take us out for the day, just us, to Isandlwana and to follow with him the course of the battle on 22 January 1879 as we sat at the site of the regiment's last stand. Even now I find it moving to look at my photos of the battlefield, the white-washed stone cairns marking where soldiers fell standing starkly in the surrounding bush so brown and parched after the summer and the one stone and brick memorial to the 24th Regiment seeming abandoned in this vast space. You look across to the Nqutu plateau from where the Zulu impi commenced their attack - the whole area is redolent with the ghosts of 1350 soldiers who died in a few hours trying to defend their camp at Isandlwana.

In the evening David took us with some other guests to Rorke's Drift to have drinks as the sun was setting and for him to relive for us through words the heroic defense of this mission station which started in the afternoon of 22 January. Since my previous visit the area had been 'tidied up' and the old hospital turned into a museum, it had become more for the tourists and less for the historian.

Before we left the Lodge we walked to the graves of Lieutenants Melvill and Coghill who had died crossing the Buffalo River whilst trying to save the Queen's Colour of the 24th Regiment. Coghill and Melvill were amongst the first soldiers to receive the VC posthumously in 1907. They lie together overlooking the river where they died, the grave surmounted by a cross erected by Sir Bartle Frere 1879.

David Rattray was murdered at Fugitive Drift's Lodge in January 2007 but I understand that his sons and the guides trained by him continue to bring alive the stories of this remarkable place.

Sarah's work took her to live in Finland in1995, she and Ian had a house outside Helsinki and we went to visit for Easter '95. It is such a beautiful country with so many trees and much water. Their white painted house was of two storeys in a modern style, with the living space upstairs to take advantage of the views into the woods and the bedrooms below. There was a house nearby in a more traditional style painted a pale yellow with a grey tiled mansard roof, a French influence? But most extraordinary was a house of brick with a gabled roof completely covered in glass through which you could see the timber roof structure.

We had a day out to visit Porvoo, a medieval town from the 14thC about thirty miles east of Helsinki. It is most attractive and thankfully unspoilt. Along the riverside the wooden buildings are painted red and these were originally houses to store goods brought in from afar. Away from the water the wooden houses were painted various shades of yellow and grey with white features. The narrow cobbled streets were still edged with snow and there were sheets of ice on the river.

Helsinki in contrast is very grand with three and four storey buildings surrounding the harbour, painted again in various shades of yellow, I presume this is to give a cheerful aspect during the dark days of winter. The University buildings below the Cathedral are particularly fine and to me are a replica of the Palace in Athens on Syntagma Square. The Cathedral, close to the harbour has a Russian influence with its cupolas.

To add another country to our journey we spent a day in Tallinn, capital of Estonia, travelling there by hovercraft. On arrival at the harbour the hovercraft was met by coaches to take the passengers who wanted to on sightseeing tours of Tallinn, we headed to the coach for English speakers and were the only occupants so we had the lovely lady guide to ourselves for the day. Tallinn is a mixture of ghastly Soviet inspired concrete boxes and the glorious architecture of the walled Old City, whose walls date from the 13th and 14thC and the pastel coloured buildings around the Town Hall Square are from the 15th to 17thC. We walked the cobbled streets of the Old Town and the coach took us around the new city and further afield with our guide giving an excellent commentary on the sights and the history. We had lunch in a restaurant that she recommended, very small with no menu in English or any recognisable language so 'omelet's appeared to be understood and we four had a good lunch with dessert and wine for which I magnanimously said I would pay the bill, it came to the equivalent of £15. At the end of the day as we left the guide we gave her £50 which seemed fair for four of us for the day. She was overcome and in tears and said it would help her to finish building her house.

We returned to Finland again in September but this time we spent a couple of nights in Stockholm, I loved the old town, Gamla Stan where Stockholm was founded in the 13thC. The cobbled streets are so narrow that you can touch the houses on each side with your arms spread, the houses are painted various shades of yellow and gold, these colours seems to be a feature of northern towns. We travelled on to Helsinki by ferry, a huge affair of many storeys, we had an inside cabin which had a window looking down several floors to a shopping mall with restaurants and shops. In spite of the window it was very claustrophobic and I made sure we had an outside cabin for the return journey a few days later. We spent a day walking along the lakes and in the woods of Espoo before an evening with the neighbours sampling their homemade wines from local berries. Damian surprised us with demanding strawberry wine for breakfast the following morning!

We returned to Finland in April '96, this time it was to a white winter wonderland. Where before I had walked along the edge of the sea now that sea was frozen over I literally walked on water - or ice. Sarah and Ian did not have a garage at their house, instead the car was parked outside, in the snow, and plugged into a post which provided heat to the vehicle, so there was never any problem starting it in the morning and the car was always warm inside, what a good idea. We were sad when they left Finland as we had enjoyed our holidays there.

However I am getting ahead of myself as in July we paid the first of many visits to Orford in Suffolk. We had first seen Orford when we had stayed in Ipswich with John and Astri years previously and loved its position on the river and close to the sea as well as being small and totally unspoilt. Our home in Orford became the Crown and Castle Hotel, it must be good as we have stayed there five times over the years. The 12thC Orford castle is opposite the hotel and the River Or a ten minutes walk, along which the old barges with large red sails amble down river. Orfordness is a spit of land between the river and the sea and has some extraordinary buildings that were used in the 1950s and 1960s for testing military weapons.

Nearby Dunwich Beach has almost everything for a perfect seaside holiday, miles of golden sand, hardly a person in sight but a freezing cold North Sea.

Photos for August show our garden looking full of flowers for the annual summer lunch party for all the friends and family and my mother looking well and happy at meeting again friends that she had made on her earlier visits to Lesotho and South Africa.

Toward the end of the year changes were afoot in work - most of my clients were nearer to our Slough office than Abingdon where Stuart and I were based and it was deemed more suitable to move the tours office to Slough. This was fine for Stuart as he lived in that direction but certainly not for me, I was given the opportunity to move or to take voluntary redundancy; there was no way I was prepared to spend at least an hour each way travelling to work so I chose the latter and I would therefore end my days at Harvey Thomas Travel at the end of December. I was going to wait until January to decide whether or not I wanted to continue working and in the meantime Damian and I decided to spend Christmas at Victoria Falls.

We were away for eleven days and spent Christmas at the Intercontinental Hotel on the Zambian side of the Falls. This was a rambling, two storey hotel 300yds from the Falls, it has since been replaced with a multi storey high rise built in its place so I am glad that we stayed in the original hotel with its charm and beautiful established gardens. At this time of the year the Falls were not 'the smoke that thunders' more a gentle curtain of water over the main part of the Falls, this low volume of water was due to a severe drought in the catchment areas of northern Zambia and Zaire. The bonus was we could get very close without getting soaked in spray and could walk warily almost to the point where the river falls over the edge. Livingstone Island in the middle of the river was perched almost at the edge and at this low water season it was possible to get there by boat and picnic or even camp for a night but we were not brave enough to do that. It was a relaxing few days around the pool and walking in the bush heeding the sign ' Beware of wildlife outside the hotel premises'. Christmas dinner was a leisurely buffet on the verandah and I managed, with difficulty to phone my mother little knowing that this would be the last time I would be able to wish her a Happy Christmas.....

Remembering the time when I lived in Northern Rhodesia/Zambia I wanted to go into Livingstone to see how it had changed and Damian wanted to see the Railway Museum and the steam engines graveyard. We hired a taxi for the day and the driver was most accommodating, taking us wherever we wanted to go. Just outside Livingstone are twenty-five abandoned rusting hulks of Beyer-Garratt steam engines, these were given to Zambia when Rhodesia Railways split into Zambia and Zimbabwe Railways in 1965. Most are upright but some are on their sides, and the bush is gradually encroaching to cover them, even for a non steam enthusiast like me it was a sad and sorry sight but Damian was overwhelmed at the waste of these magnificent beasts. The Railway Museum in the town was greatly in need of funds as the exhibits were sparse and randomly displayed - it reminded me in a way of the neglected Egyptian Museum in Cairo. The only thing to buy in the shop was a saucer bearing the crest of Rhodesia Railways. Outside the museum stood an unrestored carriage of Rhodesia Railways and alongside it a restored version. The Government bungalows that I remembered on the road into town were still there, most of them dilapidated, paint peeling from the corrugated tin roofs and the bougainvilleas overgrown in the gardens.

We took the touristy sunset cruise on the Zambezi on *M.V. Makumbi,* it was a peaceful way to pass an evening and to glimpse elephant almost hidden in the trees on the river banks. It was possible to walk across the iconic railway bridge between Zambia and Zimbabwe, this was part of Cecil Rhodes dream of a railway from Cape to Cairo and was opened in 1905 three years after his death. The memorial plaque on the bridge had been defaced, and at the centre of the bridge bungee jumping was taking place. We walked on into Victoria Falls town and what a shabby place it had become, catering for backpackers with camping sites and fast food restaurants. We had no time to go into the Victoria Falls Hotel but I am sure it was still the epitome of elegance.

Onwards to Kasane in Botswana, just 50 miles from Livingstone to the Cresta Mowana Lodge on the banks of the Chobe River, a delightful small thatched property built around an 800yr old baobab tree. I have a photo of this tree and it is not nearly as large as some of the trees I've seen in Zambia and Zimbabwe so they must have been really ancient. Close by the hotel is the Chobe Game Reserve which has the big cats but we only saw waterbuck, bushbuck, hippo, warthog , monkeys and more elephants than you can imagine. It was said that 45,000 elephant are in Chobe and I hope this is so today. We went out for the day on the Chobe river and on each side were groups of elephant and at one stage we had to stop the boat for the six of them to cross from one bank to the other, at mid river only the top of their heads, tusks, trunk tip and back were visible.

So to 1996 and the question 'to work or not to work'? I visited the local travel agents and looked in the weekly travel papers and found an advert from a company in Abingdon who arranged tailor-made tours to sporting events and who were looking for temporary staff to cover the '96 Olympic Games in Atlanta in July. At the interview I was asked if I was computer literate and I replied that to me a mouse was what the cat brought in! I was offered the job and promised two weeks of one to one tuition on computers, something for which I have always been so grateful.

I started work mid February, worked for a couple of days and then it was Saturday the 18th and time for my visit to see Mum in Evesham. We had our usual long chat, in retrospect I could see her colour was not good, but after coffee I went to the shops to buy us some goodies for lunch. On my return at 12.30 I poured us each a sherry and put out the lunch, Mum didn't feel like anything and I got quite cross and said she must have something. She got up to go to the bathroom, after a minute she called my name, I went in and she had fallen onto the floor, I tried to lift her but couldn't so I made her comfortable leaning against a chair and rushed to phone my sister Mary who lived up the road and told her Mum had fallen and could she come to help. I went back into the bathroom and sat on the floor and held Mum, I knew then what was happening, I made myself remember the feel of her and her woollen cardigan, I talked to her and said Mary would soon be here, she hadn't spoken at all, gradually her breathing lessened and as Mary arrived her breathing stopped, it was 1pm. It was all so sudden and unexpected and dreadful. I won't dwell on all the arrangements that had to be made but she was buried at Norton church on the following Friday. My friend Laura, you may remember from Aden days, who I hadn't seen for years came to the funeral and at the graveside she said the loss would get better, it doesn't, but it does become easier to bear.

Up to then I had considered myself immortal, after all there was an older member of the family and I could certainly live forever whilst she was still alive, now I was the oldest member of the family and no longer immortal, it was a sobering and life adjusting thought.

I had to get back to my new job so I went to Atlanta with another girl from work at the end of February and again in May to check out the hotels we would be using for the Olympic packages. There is not much to say about this capital of the state of Georgia, skyscraper and shopping malls abound. Even in these months before the Games started the done thing was to exchange Olympic country badges - we had been given a few and in the malls a stranger would stop and ask if you would trade badges. We were taken out for a day away from the city which was a blessing, into the countryside to see one of the historic Civil War houses, the Tullie Smith House in the grounds of the Atlanta History Center. I went back to Atlanta in July with a large group from the company before the Games started to make sure that all was in order. Not being one for crowds I wasn't that interested in the Games themselves but I did sit through part of the rehearsal for the opening ceremony. Once the Games started I stayed for a few days and then flew back to the office in Abingdon. There wasn't much to do there until the final winding up of all the admin and accounts and by the end of October I was un-employed once again!

My journey now continues along several tracks as the various strands of part-time work and outside interests such as family history research, National Trust volunteering and getting to know Oxford run together concurrently.

Damian celebrated his 60th birthday at the end of September with a party in the garden and it was a great gathering of the family from Evesham, the Atkinsons and our friends from Africa, Peter & Pat H, Astri & John, Judith & Jack, Al & Jann, Tess & Peter and Hilary H. This was Damian's wine making period and there was a series of flasks and tubes in the kitchen but I don't think any of it was consumed on this occasion.

Towards the end of this year with time on my hands I decided it was time I got to know Oxford, to learn which college was which and something of the history of the University. A lovely elderly lady, Sheila Phillips, ran a six-weekly programme of one afternoon walking tours for two hours, each series of walks had a different theme and over the next year I took part in seven of her walks often repeating a particular theme and in this way I visited all thirty eight of the Oxford colleges. Because Sheila had good relations with the porters at each college lodge we were able to go into the dining halls, chapels and gardens - good relations with the porters was essential as they appeared to be the titular head of the colleges! Not only did

Sheila give us the history of each college but also her personal anecdotes from when she was a student. We never did get to the bottom of which is the oldest college, University College, Balliol and Merton were established between 1249 and 1264 and all three claim the title but the dispute rests with whether you allow for the date of commencement of teaching or the charter being awarded. A University existed in Oxford in 1096, the other place - Cambridge - came later. It was during these walks that I became interested in the architecture, building and stone of the colleges.

After the Olympics work finished I still wanted to earn some extra money for Christmas so I went to 'Past Times' an online catalogue company which sold jewellery and knick knacks especially for the Christmas season, their office was in Witney and they needed staff to take telephone orders for the three weeks leading up to Christmas. With my newly acquired computer skills I worked there in December '96 and '97. It was not like anything I had done before, we clocked on and off and there was a supervisor who sat on a raised dais to keep check that you were answering the phones immediately and weren't wasting any time chatting. Still it was only for three weeks, the pay was good and there was the opportunity to purchase sale items at a discount.

The next advert I answered was for an assistant with a company who made tailor-made tours to Africa for wealthy clients, I went for the interview with Josie and found that she worked from home which was a small cottage. The 'office' was a small shed in the garden, unheated, no window, just the door for fresh air. It was very basic and in retrospect I am amazed that I stayed there for almost three years. But the hours suited me, I worked usually about four mornings a week and was paid on an hourly basis with no holiday money. I often thought that it was as well that the wealthy clients couldn't see where their holidays were being planned. I enjoyed doing the work even if the surroundings were cold and dirty; clients went on walking tours in north Luangwa, camped in the Makgadikgadi and paddled in mokoros in the Okavango. During '97 Josie sent me on two trips to become familiar with some of the lesser known places that clients wanted on their holidays. These two trips made working in the cold and dirty shed worthwhile.

In May '97 I went to Namibia for a Skeleton Coast fly-in safari of four days and three nights. The small Cessna single-engine aircraft took five passengers plus the pilot, Helga. One of the passengers was Julie from New York, she and I got on well and she is still a friend after all these years. Alongside the printed itinerary I made notes as to animals that we saw and because it was all so special I will give you the full story:

Day One: 1000 departure to the Skeleton Coast via Conception Bay. The Kuiseb Canyon and adjoining red dunes are a spectacular view from the air. The flight includes an aerial view of the famous Eduard Bohlen shipwreck at Conception Bay. After landing and refuelling at Swakopmund we continue with a low level flight north along the Skeleton Coast past the seal colony at Cape Cross for a light picnic near the beach. As we flew over Sossusvlei we saw oryx and springbok and at Cape Cross seals and flamingoes. *After lunch we cross the desert by aircraft to the Ugab formations, a nearly lifeless moon landscape of numerous black ridges, in stark contrast to the white desert floor, from here we cross to our camp Kuidas in the Huab Valley where we stay for the night. Amongst the rocks within walking distance are ancient rock carvings.* The dining room was an open sided tent, we each had an igloo tent for a bedroom with its own chemical toilet. There was a separate shower tent. Outside each tent was table with a bucket of water and a bowl for early morning ablutions. It was all very comfortable. The engravings were incised onto a flat slab of rock and looked like a form of hieroglyphics.

Day Two: After breakfast we depart by Landrover (after a puncture was fixed) *to explore the colourful red lavas and yellow sandstones of the Huab River formations and to be introduced to the ecological aspects of this environment, with its wide diversity of flora and fauna. This includes the Welwitschia mirabilis, a tree that has been dwarfed by the rigours of the desert climate.* This tree/plant covered an area of about five feet in diameter with thick curled leaves and seedpods, it looked prehistoric. Helga took pieces of the red stone and ground it to a powder to show how the Himba tribe use it to colour themselves. *After lunch at Huab camp we depart by aircraft along the coast for Terrace Bay in the Skeleton Coast Park. The most prominent shipwrecks along this part of the coast are the Montrose and Henrietta, still relatively intact.* Landing on the beach was a hairy operation, Helga flew up and down for about fifteen minutes to check the sand for rocks and seals before finally making a landing. There were hundreds of seals along the edge of the water and in order to get close and not disturb them we had to crawl forward on hands and knees. I have a photo of a jackal a short distance from me also going towards the seals. *At Terrace Bay we access the roaring dunes by Landrover, which has always proved an exhilarating experience.* It certainly was! Up a steep dune, poised on the top before tipping down the other side. Because tyre tracks can stay on the dunes for decades with only the wind to perhaps cover them, there was just one dune that the company used for the dune experience. *We also visit the beach with its profusion of multi-coloured pebbles consisting of agates, lavas, granites and others. It is interesting to see old whale bones scattered along the beach above high tide mark. We return to the airfield and continue north to our camp Purros in the Hoarusib Valley where we stay the night.* As we flew over the scrublike bush we had been warned to look out for the desert elephant, rare creatures and not often seen, I saw a glimpse of two desert elephant and also a giraffe. Our camp for night was in individual tiny wooden chalets.

Day Three: After breakfast (which was set up on a hilltop away from the camp because of flies) *we take a scenic drive along the Hoarusib Valley to visit a settlement of nomadic Himba people. From here we continue north along the Skeleton Coast by aircraft to the perennial Kunene River on the Angolan border. The Kaiu Maru shipwreck and pieces from old sailing vessels lie scattered along this part of the coast. From the airfield we take a scenic drive by Landrover to our favourite lunch site.* (on the airstrip!)*After lunch we continue through the mountains and dunes of the Hartmann Valley, which extend to the Kunene River, arriving at our camp next to the river in the late afternoon where we spend the last night.* Bedrooms were the igloo tents again and in a photo Julie stand in her pale blue nightgown outside the thatched shower. The dining tent was in a superb location on the hillside overlooking the Kunene River. My notes for this day give the wildlife sighted as springbok steenbok, jackal, seals, oryx, crocodile, leguaan. blacksmith plover, dune lark, weavers, finches, and mountain chat.

Day Four: An early morning boat trip on the Kunene River as it flows through scenic desert landscape observing birdlife and some crocodiles. Birds vary from aquatic species on the perennial waters to endemic desert varieties and those which inhabit dense riverine vegetation. After the boat trip we depart by Landrover through the mountains of the Hartmann Valley to a shady lunch spot, then fly back to Windhoek arriving in the late afternoon. We actually flew back via Etosha where we dropped off Julie who was to spend a couple of nights there. I spent a night in Windhoek and then flew home.

The second trip which Josie kindly send me on was to Botswana and the Okavango in November '97 for a five day mobile camping safari. I flew into Maun and joined five other agents and then set off in a Landrover into the bush. Mobile safaris move from camp site to camp site depending on where the guides decide to stop and importantly not camping in the same place where others may have done recently, this keeps the bush pristine and does not disturb the wildlife and also keeping as far away as possible from other mobile safaris, in fact in our five days we did not see another person accept for the pilot flying in extra fresh food. The safari moves into fresh territory every two or three days to explore the most untouched wilderness.

The 'removal truck' preceded our departure from Maun, this carried everything necessary for a mobile camp and when we eventually arrived the camp was set up, tents with their own adjacent bucket shower tent, a long drop loo surrounded by a tent and an open sided dining tent. Each tent had one or two beds, bedside trunk for clothes, lamp, rug, and colourful covers and outside a table with an African print table cloth with a basin and bucket of water for washing; they were very comfortable without being over the top luxurious. When we left the camp the removal truck packed up everything, filled in the loo and left the site as it was before we had camped there.

Our first camp was Mboma in the Moremi Game Reserve, very shady under the fever and sausage trees with the lagoon close by. Two chefs prepared the meals and cold beers and soft drinks lay in canvas troughs to keep them cool. Before we left Mboma further supplies were needed and we spent an hilarious time in the Landrover shooing elephant and zebra from the airstrip at Xakanaxa so that the single engined aircraft could land, seemingly with boxes of bananas but I am sure there must have been other produce too. A lagoon was in front of the camp, my tent was at the end of the line and during the night I heard grunting and heavy footsteps as various hippo went past en route to the water. Moremi is known for its large population of lion and we saw many, usually lying down on the track in the very place that we wanted to drive and because it is not ecologically good to go off track and make another track we had to wait until they dispersed, it made for excellent photo opportunities.

The second camp was at Bodamatau, miles from anywhere and right on the edge of a lagoon which was full of dozens of hippo. We crossed the lagoon by mokoro for an excursion but stayed well away from the hippo. During the game drives away from Bodamatau we had punctures, got stuck in the mud and then when crossing the supposedly shallow river went in so deep that the water came up to my knees where I was sitting in front of the Landrover - we had to make a hurried exit and wait for another vehicle to come and pull us out. This whole area was full of lagoons and rivers and in the rainy season this would become part of the Okavango Delta.

A small boat took us for a cruise on the Mauna Chera river, part of the Okavango River, where we stopped for lunch in the river, yes in, not on! The water was around knee deep, chairs and tables with lunch were put in the river as well as the cool box for drinks and all this resulted in a really cool lunch on a very hot day. We saw all the animals that you could possibly wish to see on a safari but the best was to come early one morning at Bodamatau. During dinner that night we heard lion roar in the distance, probably quite far away as that eerie sound carries on a clear night but at 3am the guide came to wake us up to say that the lion was close by and we should go in the Landrover to find him. Which we did, just as it was beginning to get light he was there, close to the camp, obviously fat from a kill and refusing to acknowledge our presence or even move. So we left him and as we were up and about so early the guide carried on driving into the bush - no tracks now as it was complete wilderness. My photo shows the front of the Landrover in the early morning light with a cheetah sitting on an ant hill perhaps thirty yards distant. My heading of this photo says 'there is an interesting story to this cheetah' and there is.

Bear in mind how close we were to her and that she made no suggestion that she knew we were there. We sat there motionless for three hours whilst she groomed herself from top to tail and then she too sat alert, waiting and watching the trees about five hundred yards away. Eventually, after the three hours, a line of springbok came into view through the trees at the rear of which were some young ones, from a sitting position to full stretch took only seconds, her speed was extraordinary and she caught her breakfast too so her wait had not been in vain and for me it was one of those moments which make Africa special.

This mobile safari ended with a farewell dinner during a beautiful sunset over the river and a final camp coffee which was actually a bottle of Camp Coffee sitting beside a can of water heating on the ash remains of the camp fire.

During the time that I worked for Josie there is one episode that annoys me - one morning the bailiffs called at the cottage demanding £500, I don’t know what it was for but Josie did not have the money so I said I would lend it to her, and dashed back to Witney to withdraw it from my bank. She did repay it within a couple of weeks. There was never much to do in December so that December '99 I may have worked only a couple of mornings. On January 1st I phoned to ask when she wanted me to start again and she said she didn’t need me anymore! I thought this was rather a high handed way to deal with someone so I went to the Citizens Advice Bureau to ask for their advice and was amazed to find that I was due a substantial sum for unfair dismissal and even though I had worked on an hourly basis I was still due holiday money for the three years that I had worked for her. I sent a solicitor's letter and of course she disagreed so I prepared to take her to court, a week before the case was due to be heard she agreed to settle the money owing but could only pay it over six months.

On my spare days when working for Josie I became a National Trust volunteer at one of their Gloucestershire properties which was being restored before its public opening. I was at Lodge Park from '99 until early in 2002 and how I enjoyed my time there as it furthered my interest in architecture, architects and building materials. With the death of Lord Sherborne in1982 his 4000 acre estate, excluding the house that had previously been sold, was offered to the National Trust. The bequest was accepted because of the outstanding national importance of the shell of a surviving 17thC Lodge overlooking the one mile walled enclosure used for chasing deer, with a park for corralling the deer to the rear. I joined Lodge Park just as the restorations were being completed and was able to see some of the underlying archaeological features on which the restoration was based. The Lodge has many similarities to the imposing Banqueting House of Inigo Jones in London where Charles 1st lost his head in 1649, in fact it looks like a smaller version. I subsequently discovered that the mason who worked on the Banqueting House was Nicholas Strong, he and his family of masons came from this part of Gloucestershire and were responsible for many well-known buildings in Gloucestershire and Oxfordshire including the Danby Gate to the Oxford Botanical Gardens where the rusticated pillars are similar to those of the loggia at Lodge Park, but don’t let me bore you any further with this remarkable building.
Once the Lodge opened I eventually progressed to doing talks with the aid of a slide show and went to meetings in local village halls to talk about the history and building of the Lodge. I stopped volunteering in 2002 as there was a change of management and they only wanted door keepers at the property with no talks, you know, those fearsome ladies who stand guard as you enter a NT room and make sure you are not trespassing onto the carpet or touching the china, not that there were any such artefacts at the Lodge.

Let me recap, for some months I was taking walking tours of Oxford, I helped at the Olympic Games in Atlanta, I survived working for Josie and I was a National Trust volunteer. By the beginning of '97 I have explained in Chapter 1 how I began researching the family history. But there was another area that I wanted to investigate, my daughter who had been adopted at birth. Since this had taken place in

Northern Rhodesia it did not seem likely that I would find any information in London however one February morning Damian had to go to Somerset House (the records had not yet moved to Myddelton House) for his own research and whilst he was busy I found myself by the shelves of volumes of marriage certificates. I knew the surname of her adopted father (from the papers that had never been shown to me when we were on leave in Shropshire in 1965) and guessed that in arranging the adoption, parents would have been found as close in age and background as possible to the birth mother and father. Quite by chance I found what I hoped was the correct marriage certificate of a London marriage but that really didn’t get me any further. I spent some time in the local library looking at for UK telephone numbers for that surname but found nothing.

Quite unknown to me at the same time my daughter had started to look for her birth parents, her quest is a story in itself and not for me to tell but she finally found her father through Colonial Police records and then we spoke to each other in June. Alex came to England in August to meet her mother and sister for the first time, it was an emotional time. We had a gathering of all the friends in the garden and then at the end of her visit Sarah went back with her to Johannesburg for a few days. This is not the place for me to say how I felt about meeting my 33 year old daughter for the first time but I think we both agreed that the past has gone, it can't be changed, and what was done was for the best for both of us as far as I was concerned, thankfully there were no recriminations and we have the rest of our lives to be mother and daughter. When I see some of the harrowing stories on the TV programme 'Long Lost Family' I know that I am incredibly lucky to have been re-united with my daughter who has only love and forgiveness in her heart. It would be so easy to go down the track of 'if onlys' especially when I see the girls together but I appreciate the nurture that her adoptive parents gave her and am grateful that the nature shines through.

Damian and I went to South Africa to meet all the family in March '98 and spent a short holiday with them in their house at Hartebeespoort Dam. We then went onto Cape Town where we stayed with Janette who took us to Franschoek to see the Huguenot Monument, dedicated to the French Huguenots who emigrated to the

Cape in the 17th and 18thC. It is a simple and elegant monument and I like the words expressed in the official website:

The three lofty arches are a symbol of the Holy Trinity. Above it the Sun of Righteousness shines, and above that the Cross as symbol of Christian faith is mounted. The water pond, reflecting the colonnade behind it, expresses the undisturbed tranquillity of mind and spiritual peace the Huguenots experienced after much conflict and strife. www.hugenoot.org.za.

With Christine we had a few days away in Natal and a memorable visit to the site where Louis Napoleon, Prince Imperial was killed on 1 June 1879.As a Frenchman, Queen Victoria, who was a friend of his mother Empress Eugénie, allowed him to join the British Forces in the aftermath of Isandlwana. He was part of a reconnaissance party that was ambushed by Zulus and when he died so did the Napoleon dynasty. The site is not easy to find, it is not far from Dundee on the Jojozi River. His body was taken back to England for burial. What made this day particularly memorable was that Christine was driving on a dirt road, we were talking away, and none of us saw the STOP sign at a crossroads so we drove straight across a busy main road. It was a miracle that we did not end up with the Prince Imperial.

Talking of memorable journeys, Alex came to visit in September 2000 and as a surprise we booked cabins for ourselves and Mary on the ferry from Portsmouth to Santander. This entailed a night each way on the ferry and a day in northern Spain. The Spanish day was great fun, Mary and Alex went off to do the markets and Damian and I wandered hither and yon soaking up the atmosphere and sampling the food. The ferries are amazing in that they resemble cruise ships in what they have to offer, several dining rooms and cafes, cabaret shows in the evening and a cinema with the latest films. Our cabins were basic but comfortable, situated quite low down on the ferry. What made the journey unforgettable was the weather on the outward journey! In the middle of the night waves were slamming against the hull seemingly right at our cabin, the noise and juddering were alarming. Damian and I stayed put but Alex and Mary were so alarmed that they quickly dressed and went

up a few decks and spent the night on the floor of one of the public areas. On arriving back home we discovered that we had been lucky to be on the edge of a depression that had caused damage to the 69,000 ton P and O liner *Oriana* as detailed in the official enquiry:
The passenger cruise ship Oriana was on passage from New York to Southampton at a speed of about 19.5 knots when she was struck by a large wave amidships on her port side. As a result three cabin windows on deck 5, and three cabin windows on deck 6 were breached, injuring the occupants and causing extensive damage to the cabins and fittings. Storm covers had been fitted to the damaged windows on deck 5 but these were also breached. The ship was experiencing storm force conditions and very high seas.
assets.publishing.service.gov.uk
I think the ferries weigh half as much as the *Oriana* so you can imagine how we were tossed about!

My New York friend Julie, from Namibia days, came to visit in 2000 and 2001 and it was fun showing her our area of the Cotswolds and then the Welsh castles. In just two villages near us on the River Windrush, Swinbrook and Asthall, there is so much history. The Mitford family have a long association with the area having lived at the 17thC Asthall Manor in the1920s.Unity, the Fascist, convalesced at Swan Cottage in Swinbrook after a suicide attempt in Germany in 1939 and in the simple churchyard of St. Mary's Swinbrook are buried Nancy (author), Unity (friend of Hitler), Diana (Mosley), Pamela and their parents. There is a memorial to their brother who was killed during the war inside the church. Julie particularly liked the 17thC Fettiplace tombs in the chancel. It is worth visiting the church just to see these fine Elizabethan and Stuart gentlemen, wealthy local landowners, seemingly nonchalantly lying on their sides, one above the other as though about to engage in conversation. Outside in the churchyard and indeed found in other Cotswold churchyards are the samples of the wool bale tombs, these stone tombs of wool merchants have carved roll tops in the form of wool bales.

In Wales we took Julie to Raglan Castle, it is one of the later Welsh castles being built in the mid 15thC and enough of the buildings survive to show just how grand it must have been.

Our friends Sylvia and Dermott were great travellers by sea and had taken container ships to South Africa on two occasions, in 2002 they suggested that we join them for a three week journey from Southampton to Durban on the *Heldeberg* of Safmarine, one of four ships known as The Great Whites. We were assured by Sylvia that we would enjoy the experience and she was correct, it was an idyllic three weeks. There were five cabins but only eleven passengers on this voyage, the cabins were very comfortable and large, ours had windows facing to the rear towards the funnel and open deck, there were two larger suites facing forward which was fine if there were no containers but as the ship took on freight so the containers eventually came right up to the cabin windows. Our meals were taken in the officer's dining room and the food was very good and plentiful. After dinner we all retired to the bar and sang songs, played games or just chatted and enjoyed the drinks at 20p a time.

Somehow the days passed quickly, there was a small swimming pool but the water was too cold for me. Visits could be made to any part of the ship including the bridge and the engine room but the best part was going forward, squeezing past the containers and reaching the prow of the ship and sitting there gazing at the sea. We saw dolphins and birds until we left all sight of land behind and for ten perfect days we saw nothing, not a bird, a fish, a boat or a plane, we really were the only people on earth. Eventually another ship came in sight, it was another Great White so there was much hooting and waving as we passed by. We were due to stop in Cape Town for a day and night and had made arrangements to see Janette, but as we neared the Cape word came that there were no berths for us in the harbour so we continued on to Port Elizabeth. The four passengers who should have disembarked at Cape Town had to travel by road from P.E. We had an excellent two days there taking a tour to the Addo Elephant Park and then having a day's shopping with lunch at a garden restaurant that Sylvia and Dermott knew from previous visits. The shopping was crucial for me as I had forgotten to pack mascara so for two weeks had existed with pale and uninteresting eyes! We then carried on along the coast to Durban where we said a sad farewell to all the lovely stewards who had looked after us. Su met us and from there we went to visit Sylvia and

Dermott's relations who lived at Zimbali on the Natal north coast. These same relations left South Africa this year as I write and I expect they miss their beautiful home and the glorious white sandy beaches.

You will recall that I finished working as a volunteer with the National Trust in '02, just before our voyage to South Africa but I was so fortunate to continue to have paid part time employment with Sarah from 2001 to 2008. She now had her own company and I helped by finding venues for conferences as well as small meetings all in the U.K. and handling the admin and accounting side. I enjoyed doing all this work from home and on occasions being at the venues to assist with the arrangements. One really large conference was held at a hotel at Canary Wharf over three days in 2004 and Su, who had just returned to live in England came to help on the final day. It was on the last afternoon of this conference that I had to leave early to return to Oxford in time to take the new direction that I was about to pursue.

CHAPTER 9
Taking the 'up' line

"Anyone who stops learning is old, whether at twenty or eighty. Anyone who keeps learning stays young."
Henry Ford

According to Oxford Dictionaries ' up' means at or to a university, especially Oxford or Cambridge. Various factors sent me to study in Oxford between the commencement of the academic year in 2004 and graduation in 2012. Apart from working occasionally for Sarah until 2008 and of course continuing travelling it was the walking tours of Oxford and volunteering at Lodge Park that gave me an interest in the whys, hows and whodunnit of architecture and I wanted to study this in more depth. I am going to take you though my years of study first and then return to see where the travels took Damian and I during the same period.

For the first five years my Oxford home was the Department of Continuing Education in Wellington Square, Oxford. Conted, as it is known, is part of the University of Oxford providing continuing education for part-time and mature students, courses range from one day, weekly over 10 weeks, weekends and summer schools and online courses; current enrolled students are 15,000 worldwide. Some courses range from Level to Level 3 and most of them are awarded points which can be accumulated, other courses gain certificates, diplomas and eventually degrees.

Before I started my serious studying I had already taken three courses in '02 and '03 for one afternoon a week for 10 weeks each these were concerned with Christopher Wren and his architecture, 17^{th}C and 18^{th}C town planning in London and Five Great Architects, so my mind was being stimulated in the right direction towards the course in Vernacular Architecture starting in Michaelmas term '04. Twenty students assembled that first Thursday evening, four eventually dropped out, sixteen completed the two year course of which ten of us with our partners still meet at regular intervals usually an annual weekend away, to discuss such erudite matters as a squinted butt or bare-faced soffit tenon! One of the students, Jacky RW came from Devon, she drove up every Thursday, stayed with friends and drove home on Friday morning, she only missed one lesson because of bad weather during the two years, quite amazing. But what is vernacular architecture? It is the opposite of polite architecture, that also doesn't explain it. Vernacular architecture uses local materials, local traditions for local needs and in the original did not use architects but relied of the skills of local builders. Think back to what I told you about Lodge Park - that is actually an anomaly as it is a polite building, in other words grand and not for local needs, but built using local materials and not by an architect but by a local mason. Perhaps the best extreme explanation is Anne Hathaway's cottage is vernacular and Buckingham Palace is polite.

Over the two years we covered a fascinating range of subjects and I knew that at the end of the two years coursework would be required for assessment so I decided to focus on Sylvia and Dermott's ancient cottage in Dorset. What did we study? Here are the assignments, *my titles* and comments:

1.Find out what you can about a traditional building material in your local area, such as where it came from, when did its use become common, how was it transported and used, and discuss with examples from the area how it has contributed to the local distinctiveness of the buildings.

A traditional building material from the Windrush Valley.

Living on the Cotswold limestone belt its use is all around in buildings and stone walls.

2.Choose a rural parish in your locality and prepare a set of sketch-maps, with accompanying notes and illustrations, showing how the pattern of settlement and the buildings might have developed up to 1530. *The Parish of Asthall – From Bronze Age barrows to Medieval Manor.*

The manor house was where the Mitfords lived in the 1920s.

3.Looking at a specific medieval rural domestic or farm building identify and describe its main features and show how the architecture and other sources can indicate how the spaces in it might have been used when it was first built.

Swalcliffe Barn - A 15th Century Symbol of Collegiate Wealth.

4.It is now over 40 years since Pantin produced his typology for the medieval town house based on adaptations of rural hall houses. By considering subsequent work and your own observations of the similarities and differences between rural and urban buildings in the medieval period, how far do you think Pantin's findings remain valid today?

The medieval urban house: A country house in a town, or a planned 'town' house?

5.For a town of your choice which has some remaining medieval evidence, use available sources to show how it developed, its size and population in the Middle Ages, the location and types of medieval buildings, and how much of the evidence of medieval plots and buildings remain visible today.

Witta's Island – Wyttannige – Witenie – Witney

This town where I live still shows its evolution over the centuries in the landscape and buildings.

6.Recording a Building: Investigate & describe the study building and/or selected features, including its phases of development using personal observation and knowledge. Identify the features, which contribute to the building's special character. Carry out a photographic survey of the building, internally and externally, and its context, including details of features of particular significance. Carry out measurements on site and make a drawn record of the building, to show elevations, sections and floor plan as appropriate.

We were all taken to Wood Eaton to record the house and farm buildings.

7.Choose a house feature, either internal or external and describe its development in the post-medieval period in a rural locality of your choice, giving reasons for any changes, and the sources and dates of stylistic or decorative changes.

From 'Wind-Eyes' to Sashes in Rural West Dorset.

Just a short distance around Old Rectory Cottage in Dorset are examples of windows from 15^{th}C to modern times. Windows are an important feature as they can suggest a date for a house, not including the current trend for replacement windows.

8.In 1953, W.G. Hoskins produced evidence for a "great rebuilding" in rural England between 1570 and 1640, and an explanation for that phenomenon. Discuss what later research has told us about the nature of the evidence and whether his explanation stands up.

A general view of post medieval England.

9.By looking at a non domestic building type, (e.g. a farm or industrial building) in a rural area of your choice, discuss how the main changes (e.g.

in agriculture, industry, transport.) affected this building type from 16th century onwards.

Little Toller Farm Barn 1550-1890.

Not far from Chilfrome the collection of buildings at Toller feature strongly in much of my subsequent work.

10.Choose a non-domestic building type and discuss its development from the 16thC onwards to the point where it ceases to be 'vernacular' in concept or execution.

Tipplers, Taverns& Inns of Witney.

I had plenty of choice here as there were originally a hundred inns in Witney. Witney has been at or near the crossroads of major thoroughfares since the Romans built Akeman Street; 12 miles west from Oxford, 25 miles east from Gloucester, and a resting place on a major route from the north southwards to the River Thames. The main road from Oxford to Witney came via Woodstock and entered Witney at Wood Green. In 1769 the completion of the Swinford Bridge opened the road to heavy traffic westwards from Oxford, entering Witney from the direction of Eynsham. The better quality of the new road, paid by the Turnpike Trust, brought the carriage trade into Witney

11.Choose a vernacular building which is open to the public and discuss critically the way it has been renovated and presented in terms of the period or periods shown, the removal of earlier or later phases, interior decoration, furniture and features. Does the presentation enhance or confuse our understanding of vernacular buildings?

Lodge Park Sherborne. Gloucestershire. A re-creation by the National Trust.

I have already told you something of Lodge Park from when I was volunteering and you can probably now appreciate that it is difficult to decide whether this is a vernacular or polite building.

12.The final assignment was our own choice -

Old Rectory Cottage Chilfrome Dorset, and my introduction said:

In the 1970s the owner of Old Rectory Cottage accidentally put his foot through the bedroom floor of his newly acquired property thereby exposing the heavily moulded beams and the joists in the room beneath that were almost concealed under board and plaster.

Since then the exterior and interior fabric of the cottage have been painstakingly restored and the remaining original interior features have been revealed.
My own interest in the owners' progress has covered 20 years and participation in the Vernacular Architecture course has helped me to prepare this history of their home by using stylistic and documentary sources to date the various phases of construction.

I was able to unravel the evolution of this cottage, using its remaining physical features and using documentary evidence from the late 15^{th}C to the 21^{st}C. Dermott and I had many discussions concerning changes that had taken place and he provided a sounding board for my theories. He was delighted when I could prove that the beams in one of the downstairs rooms could be dated to 1480, this was not done by dendrochronology but by a comparison with similar beams in a nearby house where the date had been confirmed. This cottage also conformed to the typography of a medieval priest's house in this part of the west country so Sylvia and Dermott decided to re-name their home *The Priest's House.*

It was a very satisfying experience to be able produce a comprehensive history of the cottage and a copy of my work is in the Dorset History Centre in Dorchester. Some years later the cottage was sold and the new owners made many alterations internally despite this being a Grade II* property. I understand that English Heritage were advised of the changes to be made and allowed them to proceed, a criminal act in my view as the historical integrity of the cottage has been completely compromised. Restoration, Conservation, Obliteration - there is a fine line between the acceptable and the criminal.

So ended in mid '06 this two year course and the gaining of a Certificate in Vernacular Architecture. Rather like the engine on the train of my journey my brain was now fired up and ready to continue.

Looking through the upcoming courses at Conted I found one for a Post-Graduate Certificate in Architectural History, just a year's course starting in Michaelmas term '06. This course covered English architectural history from the Anglo-Saxon period to the present and included the practical skills of recording and analysing buildings. *Settlement, Landscape and Medieval Buildings* concentrated on the medieval period. It provided an introduction to the evolution of the landscape and the major elements of architectural history in England up to the 16thC.*Post-Medieval Buildings* analysed the major architectural developments from the 16thC to the present century. The final part of the course was an evaluation and survey of a site which was a skill-based unit designed to develop expertise in understanding the special architectural and historical characteristics of a particular site, building (or group of buildings) and to develop techniques for its representation through research, measurement, and drawn/photographic recording.

This was a more serious academic course than the Certificate, there we had sat round a table and the atmosphere was informal, here, Monday mornings were spent in the lecture theatre at Conted. There were over thirty students, none that I knew and not being face to face with the others there was no opportunity for getting to know anyone added to which it was necessary to make notes throughout the lectures with no time for interaction.

Towards the end of the course there was a discussion as to what sites we would each be using for the site evaluation and survey, one young man decided on the Grade II listed gates of Lord's cricket ground, my proposal was an architectural and historical survey of Lower Toller Farmstead, Toller Fratrum, not far from Chilfrome. The aim was to prepare a history of the farmstead to include all the farm buildings and to discover the original use of the building now called 'the stables'. The history of the land could be traced to the early 14thC but the earliest structures *appear* to be of the 16thC. The so-called stables are listed as being of national importance for their age, design and function but were in danger of collapsing. I had hoped to persuade the owner to apply to English Heritage for funding to conserve this building but more of this later

Surveying this farmstead and all its buildings, the Grade II* manor house, Grade II* stables, barn, cart shed, milking parlour and granary was a large project which I could not do on my own, I needed someone else to hold the other end of the measuring tape and who could climb into small spaces! I asked my Vernacular Architecture class if anyone was interested in helping me and probably because it was such an interesting collection of vernacular buildings I had six responses! Jacky RW, Dr Chris, Martin W, Sue O, Sue J, Paul C and Sue O's daughter who worked for English Heritage. This was going to take some organisation so I arranged for us to have working parties over two weekends in March and June. Accommodation was arranged for the Saturday nights and I prepared picnic lunches for all of us for four days. I am not going to give you the whole story of what we found - the documents are in the Dorset History Centre for you to read- but we did have a couple of OMG moments and some findings went beyond what I expected.

As an overview the farmstead was not in a particularly good condition even though it was still a working farm, the manor house had seen better days internally and the so-called stables in which I was most interested were being used as a barn and storage space with used hay and silage piled in some places three and four feet deep which made access inside quite difficult, in fact on our first morning there was a dead sheep inside -OMG- which Dr Chris was able to remove and place elsewhere.

I should explain that the stables were thought to be the preceptory/refectory of the Knights Hospitallers whose headquarters were in London but they had communities throughout the country to show hospitality to travellers and pilgrims and maintain divine services in their chapels. Toller is the name of the river nearby and Fratrum refers to the Brothers of the Order. In 1309 Toller Fratrum had to pay 12d quarterly to the London headquarters, so we can say that this is an historic site but externally the earliest evidence was for a 16thC building. I made an in depth study of the construction of the rear wall of the building which faces the small church of St Basil and from evidence in the stone placements put forward the premise that the building had originally, in the 14thC, been two buildings with a passage between the two leading to the church. At this time, 2007, the stables/preceptory/refectory, call it what you will, looked in good shape from the facade facing the farmstead with its arched casement windows, hamstone mouldings and stone initials and crests of later owners. The rear façade, only seen from the church, was in a rough vernacular style. The problem even then was the roof, although the timber structure was still in place the thatch was being covered by ivy which encouraged moisture to be retained in the thatch and eventually permeate and rot the timbers. We, the working party, spoke to the owner and suggested that it was a simple matter to cut the roots of the ivy in order to save the roof. In 2014 the roof collapsed and today, in 2017 this historically important Grade II* building is shrouded in scaffolding and flapping plastic sheeting.

The manor house externally still conformed to the comments of John Hutchins in the 19thC who called it 'one of the most picturesque manor houses in Dorset'. Internally on both the ground and first floor the layout of the rooms had changed over the centuries and with no sign of a 16thC chamber on the upper floor with a decorated plaster ceiling as one would expect in this type and age of building. The attic or roof space was a cornucopia of delights for all of us, various ages and types of timber and bracings, struts and rafters showed evidence of all the changes that had taken place in the house. You might be able to remove internal walls and change room layouts but the roof structure is fundamental to the integrity of the building so any changes will overlay earlier forms and with care it is possible to 'read' the history of a house in its roof. I won't go into all that we found except for two things, the house had been extended in the late 18thC and in the roof space we found three partitioned small dark windowless garrets which would have been for servants, still with their bell pull mechanisms. At the earlier end of the roof space, lying in a corner was a piece of white plaster about 24 x 18 inches, OMG, it was a piece of moulded ceiling plaster with typical 16thC decoration and would have been part of the ceiling of an upper chamber. We were so tempted to remove this piece of plaster but it may have crumbled when touched and it deserved to be left in situ as further evidence to future researchers of the age of the building.

However, in 2015 there was a fire at the manor house, part of the upper floor and all of the oldest part of the roof were completely destroyed, together with the decorated plaster, and whilst the roof will be reconstructed to a modern design it will have none of the history that made this property unique. I used to enjoy going to a service at St Basil's church when I was in Dorset but now the sight of these two ruined buildings is more than I can bear. I received the Post Grad certificate and the learning bug was upon me, so what to do next?

I had my eye on an online course starting in Michaelmas term 2008 but I needed something to keep my brain oiled from mid 2007 until then. Fortunately Conted offered four ten week courses which were interesting, Rural Landscapes, Urban Landscapes, Industrial Architecture and Architecture of London and the Home Counties.

A very respected tutor Trevor Rowley gave the Landscape courses and I was able to build on my knowledge of Chilfrome for the final Rural Landscape assignment which I entitled *The Landscape surrounding the Hamlet of Chilfrome, Dorset.* Using old maps, photographs and my personal view of the landscape I was able to document it from the Bronze Age c2350BC, through the Iron Age, late Anglo-Saxon and medieval periods through to the present day. I will just share with you one of Trevor's theories-the elements in the landscape required for a viable community from pre-historic times. For a village site five elements are necessary for life and he weights them according to relative importance, 10 being absolutely necessary and 1 not so important.
10 = water, 5= arable land, 3 = grazing land, 3 = fuel, 1 = building materials.

For Urban Landscapes I came back to my home town with the assignment entitled *Witta's Island – Wyttannige – Witenie – Witney: The development of an Oxfordshire market town from Saxon to Modern times.* Again ancient and modern maps showed how the town had developed, I have already told you about how it was at a crossroads of main routes which led to the establishment of so many inns and taverns, and sheep on the hills and the availability of water all contributed to the expanding wool trade and its associated buildings.

The Industrial Architecture course was given by Hubert P whose courses I had been studying since 2002, with his slides we explored a vast range of industrial buildings, particularly the mammoth mills in the north. My final assignment was *The buildings of the woollen industry in Witney.* In its heyday there were seventeen mills in Witney, some have been demolished but most have been converted in homes and offices whilst still retaining their industrial heritage.

For the Architecture of London and the Home Counties I decided investigate the suburb where Grandma B had been born and my final assignment was *From country villa to terrace house, the Growth of Muswell Hill from the nineteenth-century.* I wasn't sure how interesting I was going to find the research for this but it turned out to be fascinating, lots of old maps which showed how the suburb developed and the emergence of privately built housing estates and an abundance of photographs of houses which truly did show the villas through to the terrace houses. I contacted the local history centre and they sent me many leaflets and booklets which brought Muswell Hill to life and I could imagine Grandma living there with her parents.

These short courses had filled in the time but it was now time to continue with the online course for an Advanced Diploma in Local History which started in Michaelmas term 2008. I wasn't sure how I could cope with an online course but decided to try and it turned out to be easy and it was good to be working from home, I thought I would miss the interaction with other students but in fact online interaction was easy and made more interesting because the students were coming from many countries worldwide and not just from England. There were about forty of us in total and we were split into smaller tutorial groups of six to eight students each with a tutor and we had certain times for chat rooms to discuss the week's assignments and readings. We had a chat room Christmas party when all forty of us were online which was amazing, 'speaking' to students from all over the world who were celebrating in their own particular way. One girl from California was having problems with house subsidence due to an earthquake and another, Tim, was snowbound. I became friendly with Linda who shared my love of chocolate and who lived not far from Oxford and with Melanie. She was not in my tutor group but I found that she was living in Yemen and having understandable difficulty in obtaining the text books. I asked her if she had been to Aden and she said she was accompanying her husband who was taking the salute at the Armed Forces Silent Valley Cemetery in Little Aden on Remembrance Day. This was very special for me and the first time I would have news and photographs of Aden since my family had left in 1957.
The course contents were fascinating, bear in mind that 'local' meant local for any of us whether from UK,USA or wherever. 'The agenda

for local history arises from a concern with people, place and community. It includes such basic and shared questions as who lived here? How many of them? How, when and why were settlements made? Did they grow, decline or shift? How has human agency moulded the landscape? Did the physical setting, in turn, affect people's lives? What work did men, women and children do? How were they governed and educated? Did they take part in religious worship? What were their social relationships and attitudes?'

Just to give you an idea of the subjects covered these are the titles of my assignments:

'The internal structure and relationships of the family and also its relationships to the wider community'.

'Discuss the strengths and weaknesses of the sources available for studying the English family c. 1600-c. 1800'.

'A short comparative review of excerpts from the works on the history of Thame, an Oxfordshire market town'.

'A quantitative and qualitative analysis of the burial statistics for Stroud, Gloucestershire featuring the mortality crises occurring between 1625 and 1837'.

'Who were the inhabitants of Cumnor in the 1860s and were they equipped to withstand economic recession?'

'Design a data table or set of tables from selected Old Bailey records, the historical relevance of the project'. (This was fascinating as the Old Bailey records are all online and you can follow the cases of those poor individuals who were in court for, say, stealing a handkerchief worth ½d, the story of their life, addresses, names of witnesses and then the sentencing, often to be transported to Australia).

'Is there evidence to explain the form and function of domestic space in the houses of 17thC Woodstock?' (For those of us who lived near Oxford and Woodstock we all met for a pub lunch in Woodstock so it was good to meet some of my fellow students in the flesh including Linda, the fellow chocoholic).

For the final assignment I returned to Dorset and began assembling a database of all the census details for the various villages, my title was *'What impact did the advent of the railway have on the population of Maiden Newton and Frome Vauchurch in West Dorset in the mid nineteenth-century?'*

At the end of this course Linda, Melanie and I decided to forge ahead and apply to the University for acceptance on the Master of Science degree course in English Local History.

Don't worry I am not going to subject you to two years of the course. We were fifteen in class almost half male/female and we met every Thursday evening at Conted in term time for two years. I was the only student without a first degree. Not only did we have to pay the course fees to the Department of Continuing Education but we had to join a college and pay their fees too, the total cost was about £6000. Most of us joined Kellogg College which was geared towards mature and part time students but some preferred to join the more traditional colleges. In October of 2009 we had to matriculate, in other words to join the University and this took place at a ceremony in the Sheldonian Theatre in Oxford - one of Christopher Wren's masterpieces and designed in the 1660s when he was Professor of Astronomy at Oxford. Graduate matriculating students wear black trousers or skirt, white blouse, black ribbon tie, graduate gown and cap. I had been to the Sheldonian previously when I was awarded the various certificates but the matriculating ceremony was much more serious. When we graduated two years later Graduations took place again in Sheldonian and the ceremony, in Latin, was following in the centuries tradition of graduation. We were received into the Theatre in our graduate gowns, then had to process out of the Theatre and into the Divinity Hall where we changed into the splendid Master's gowns and caps. The MSc gown is of heavy silk with rich black braiding on the side and back, I have mine as a souvenir and I can wear it to college functions. The collar/hood is of blue and black and the colours denote the discipline of the degree.

We studied English local history from medieval though to modern times covering in much greater detail subjects from the Advanced Diploma syllabus, with some religion, statistics, architecture, rural change, enclosures etc added to the mix. I found it all very difficult to start with due to not having done a first degree and through that learning the structure of essays, however with some help from my friends I eventually got going. My first assignment was barely a pass, this was a shock as I had almost always had distinctions in all my previous courses, however succeeding work improved dramatically and the MSc was mine, although not a degree with distinction as my first assignment mark pulled all my other marks below the distinction threshold. But I didn't care, fifty eight years after leaving school I had a degree! Just for the record my 82 page dissertation was entitled *COMMUNITY AND KINSHIP: A STUDY OF THEIR INFLUENCE IN SIX PARISHES IN THE FROME VALLEY, DORSET IN THE NINETEENTH CENTURY;* you can find a copy in the Conted library.

Even though I was studying, holidays and other events still occurred. Our good friends Jean and Roger had a diplomatic posting to the divided island of Cyprus and we spent two holidays with them. Their house was in the Greek side of the island but as they had CD plates on the car we were able to cross into the Turkish side without difficulty and visit the northern part of the island which is very different from the tourist haven of the south. Nicosia is a city divided into the Greek south and Turkish north, separated by the Green Line which is manned by the United Nations. It is like going backwards in time to 1974 and seeing buildings abandoned and gradually being consumed by vegetation. Our brief glimpse of Greek Nicosia was of modern buildings and traffic, but on the Turkish side the ancient buildings prevail; the Ottoman Kervansaray, a resting place for travellers and traders has been conserved and now offers modern day travellers refreshments and artefacts in the sympathetically restored archways and rooms of the original building. What intrigued me were the rooms on the upper floor, clearly bedrooms for those Ottoman travellers, with a small fireplace in each room, so similar to rooms in the medieval abbey in Abingdon, Oxfordshire and in English medieval inns that catered for travellers, with accommodation in rooms on an upper storey, each containing a small fireplace. The necessities for travellers of all cultures in medieval times, including Ottoman and Christian was the same, a warm room for the night and somewhere to eat and buy provisions.

The joy of the north is the picturesque harbour of Kyrenia, still a working harbour but with more boats taking tourists out for day trips than fishing vessels, but it still retains the integrity of a small harbour, even the restaurants and bars which line the harbour are in old Venetian warehouses. We visited the remains of the ancient city of Salamis dating back to 1100BC. It was an extraordinary experience in several ways, the young man on the 'ticket desk', a table on the road side, was wearing a Manchester United shirt and more interested in asking us about MU than telling us about Salamis. The ruins are magnificent in the way that ruins are, columns and an amphitheatre, bath houses, mosaics and tiles, all there to be walked over, sat in and climbed if you wished, with no thought to conservation, maybe the situation has changed since our visit but obviously money would be needed to conserve what is such an important site for future generations.

Division is part of life in Cyprus, a divided island; Nicosia a divided city; and most chilling and eerie, that part of the city of Famagusta which remains isolated after the military coup of 1974 when Turkish forces invaded and all the Greek inhabitants of this part of the city fled. It is not for me to go further into the history of this coup but I saw the result when we stayed in a hotel on the beach in Turkish Famagusta adjacent to the barbed wire and netting that restricted all access to what had been a vibrant international holiday destination. I quote from a newspaper article; *In August 1974, 40,000 inhabitants of Famagusta fled as Turkish troops advanced leaving the town an emblem of divided Cyprus.*

The resort is still cordoned off from the public. Along the beach were the abandoned shells of what had been luxury hotels and stretching behind them as far as we could see were the buildings of the infrastructure of the resort. The climate has ensured that at first glance the buildings could be habitable but looking closer I am reminded of the skeletons of homes and workplaces that I saw in London during and after the war. Those who fled from this part of Famagusta were not at risk of death from war but how life shattering to perhaps be living now in Greek Cyprus and able to see the abandoned buildings of your earlier life.

On a more cheerful note we spent a few days at a hotel in Bellapais, a delightful village on the hillside just outside Kyrenia. Our old friends Jann and Al were holidaying on the coast and joined us for lunch in one of the tavernas and we explored the grounds of the 13thC Abbey. Our hotel nestled against the walls of the Abbey and had a beautiful swimming pool, my happiest memory of Cyprus is of Roger and Damian, neither of whom enjoyed swimming, relaxing in the shallow end of the pool, reading, and calling to the bar-man at intervals for a top-up to their brandy-sours! Yes, I remember the strawberry wine at breakfast in Finland too!

September 2005 saw us going to Belgium with Terry and Bev for a long weekend to explore the WWI battlefields. Terry liked driving and made some jolly good roadside picnics so he was just the person to be in charge. I had seen photos of rows and rows of iconic white headstones in the cemetery sites but nothing prepared me for the overwhelming emotion of pain and sadness when you are actually there.

At Delville Wood it is said that birds never sing, and we certainly didn't hear any on the warm and sunny day that we visited this site sacred to South Africans. The graves and lawns were immaculate as at all cemeteries looked after by the War Graves Commission. The memorial hall has a sandstone beautifully sculptured frieze bearing the figures of soldiers and horses reminiscent of the similar marble frieze at Voortrekker Monument in Pretoria. It is said that the most moving memorial is the Wood itself and we walked only to the edge of the site which had been left to re-juvenate itself after the desecration of the trees during the 1916 battle. The sign put into words just how sacred is this area:

Dellville Wood is hallowed as the resting place of those South Africans who made the supreme sacrifice to preserve freedom. The Wood is also the grave of thousands of British and German soldiers who died bravely.

Please help us to maintain the beauty, dignity and tranquillity of these surroundings.

On to Tyne Cot Cemetery which is so large that it is difficult to come to terms with how many men are buried here, it is also sublimely beautiful, the memorial having been designed by our old friend Sir Herbert Baker, he of the large sandstone houses in Johannesburg and the Government Building in New Delhi. There are 11,956 graves, of which 8,373 are unidentified. The curved stone walls of the Memorial of the Missing bear the names of 35,000 officers and men including this plaque;

Lance Corporal Henry John Martin
Royal West Kent Regiment
born Islington 14th October 1880
I was mobilised from the reserve in August 1914 and fought at St Ghislain, Mons, retreated down to the Marne, raced towards the sea via the Aisne and survived Neuve Chapelle despite being almost surrounded.
With C Company I helped to take Hill 60 on 17th April 1915, fought through 2nd Ypres and was wounded at High Wood, Somme on 22nd July 1916. I spent 14 months convalescing in Blighty only to return to Passchendaele and be blown to pieces at Poelcapelle on 27th November 1917.
I have no known grave, only my name on this panel and a plaque dedicated to me at St George's Memorial Church, Ieper.
I did my best
Please Remember Me

The Thiepval Memorial commemorates the Battle of the Somme in 1915 and was given world-wide prominence as the focus of commemorative ceremonies in 2015. It has a very strong presence overlooking the battlefield, a tall brick and stone structure of arches and colonnades which give it the surfaces on which are inscribed the names of 72,246 missing British and South African servicemen who died in the Battles of the Somme. Edwin Lutyens designed this memorial, and whilst it is not in the slightest bit like his work in New Delhi (with Herbert Baker) to me the arches have an echo of his architecture in India. Seventy two thousand, two hundred and forty six names, it is almost impossible to imagine them all being carved here in stone but to many families this carved name is their only remembrance of a lost loved one.

HERE ARE RECORDED
NAMES OF OFFICERS
AND MEN OF THE
BRITISH ARMIES WHO FELL
IN THE SOMME BATTLEFIELD
JULY 1915 FEBRUARY 1918
BUT TO WHOM
THE FORTUNE OF WAR

*DENIED THE KNOWN
AND HONOURED BURIAL
GIVEN TO THEIR
COMRADES IN DEATH*

The only way to end a sombre weekend was to attend the evening service at the Menin Gate, Memorial to the Missing at Ieper/Ypres. Here are inscribed 54,000 names of British and Commonwealth soldiers who died on the battlefield of Ypres. A service has been held here every evening at 8pm since 1928, apart from during the German occupation of WWII. On 9 July 2015 the 30,000th Last Post ceremony was held so we were there just ten years previously. It was an immensely moving experience. It is astonishing that every evening whether or not there are visitors the road through the gate is closed and volunteer buglers play the Last Post. When we were there it was quite crowded and at the end of the ceremony many were laying wreaths. The strains of the Last Post played anywhere bring me to tears but coupled with the aura of the place made for emotions difficult to control.

Let me lighten the mood by visiting some family events that took place during all this studying period. My sister Mary's two sons were married. One ceremony was at the Sandhurst Military Academy Chapel, and a grand affair it was. What is it about young men in full dress uniform, they ALL look so handsome. My friend Sylvia's son-in-law Jimmy who makes cakes for fun, made a wedding cake covered in edible butterflies, with more butterflies suspended on wires over the cake which 'flew' in the draughts of air. The other wedding was a typical country affair in a beautiful Cotswold church, the reception in a garden marquee and the bride and groom left for their honeymoon on 'a bicycle made for two'. Mary's daughter was married a couple of years earlier at Christmastime, the village church was decorated for the festive season and the green of the Christmas tree perfectly matched the long velvet hooded cloak that the bride wore over her wedding gown. Three family weddings, each different and each so special.

The year 2010 was a cause for the celebration of the 20th wedding anniversaries of Sarah and Ian, Jean and Roger and Damian and me so it seemed sensible to have a joint 'do' for all our friends and families. We hired a train!! And not just any old train, this was a Great Western pulled by a steam engine on the heritage line from Toddington to Gotherington in Gloucestershire. There were about forty of us, a mixture of all our friends whom you have met in previous pages, lots of family, Sarah and Ian's and Jean and Roger's friends too. We arranged a picnic lunch on board, there was a bar, and the children had balloons. Jimmy made a large cake featuring our six names and it was covered with edible sweet peas - a masterpiece. It was one of those wonderful days, the weather was perfect and friends who hadn't seen each other for years were able to catch up, or 'gobble and gossip' as dear Leonard would say.

There have been some notably good holidays without having to leave these shores, we have been to Suffolk several times and apart from Orford and the coast there are two churches which deserve a mention as they are so different from each other yet both outstanding. St Botolph's church at Iken is found in a field. It has a thatched Norman nave and 15thC additions although it is said to be on the site of a Saxon monastery. Standing in this isolated position close to the River Alde you are aware of the history surrounding this tiny place of worship. A 9thC Saxon cross was found in a field nearby and is now placed inside the church.

Whereas the Iken church is simple, almost homely, 15thC Holy Trinity Blythburgh is very grand. It is called the Cathedral of the Marshes for good reason, it stands on a rise above the Blyth estuary and can be seen for many miles. Inside, flying along the high nave ceiling are twelve carved angels, wings outspread, I believe there were more but they suffered during the 17thC destruction of churches, we are fortunate that some survived. The pew ends are medieval and feature beautifully carved monks and creatures. The Suffolk Churches website says: *You may be reading this in a far-off land, or perhaps you are here at home. Whatever, if you have not visited this church, then I urge you to do so. It is the most beautiful church in Suffolk, a wonderful art object and is always open in daylight. It remains one of the most significant medieval buildings in England. If you only visit one of Suffolk's churches then make it this one.* And I would add visit Iken too!

Just a few thoughts of other hols at home! We visited Astri and John at their home in North Wales, how lucky they are to be living on the coast with such glorious views, looking out of a window on our first morning I was amazed to see Isandlwana - actually it was called Madryn which has the same outline as that iconic mountain in Zululand.

Now a brief foray into Norfolk and King's Lynn. This city is a paradise for an architectural student, my photos show St Margaret's church founded in 1101 and the Customs House of 1683. The latter has a resemblance to some of Wren's work in London and even a nod to Inigo Jones' Banqueting House. Pevsner called the Customs House *one of the most perfect buildings ever built* but I would reserve that accolade for the Banqueting House.

King's Lynn was a great trading port from 14th to 18th C as it evidenced by the jettied brick and wood Hanseatic League Warehouse. Until I saw this building I was not aware of the importance of King's Lynn to the merchants of the German Hanseatic League. I was under the impression that the Hanseatic League cities were only in Germany but my interest in the architecture of the building led me to discover a proliferation of Hansa cities throughout northern Europe and around the Baltic Sea, and yet another one in England, Kingston-upon-Hull. This is an example of lateral thinking - a building's architecture, why is it there, its history, delve into King's Lynn history, also that of the Hanseatic League, where are the other Hansa cities, what did they trade and so on - before you know you have followed a whole new avenue of interest.

We spent a few days near St Ives in Cornwall and there are some stand out memories, good and not so good! For not so good, St Ives is very touristy but there is extension of the Tate Art Gallery which good! As for Land's End, it reminded me unfortunately of John O Groats, lots of cafes, tourist shops and amusements for children. But perhaps the most glorious place on the sea in England is Kynance Cove, I was unprepared for its beauty. Sapphire blue and emerald green seas, sandy coves, rocks and rock pools, all unspoilt. I sat on a rock for hours and just gazed at the scene below. There is a path down to the sand and sea but it was too steep for me to negotiate. Returning to the buildings theme, we visited Chyauster

Ancient Village or what remains of it. The village of eight houses was built in the Roman period between 1st and 3rdC, the walls of some of the houses remain at head height, built of large blocks of stone and you can still see the outline of gardens and terraced fields. It is another quiet isolated place with a considerable walk to reach it. Just wandering through the ruins you can imagine the local Cornishmen living here, I think the buildings would have been far too primitive for the Romans who liked their 'mod cons'.

Time to travel further afield. Although I had been going to South Africa almost every year since Alex had returned into my life, 2010 saw me off to experience their new house in the bush at Hermanusdoorns in the Waterberg about three hours drive north west of Johannesburg. It is a world away from the conurbation of Johannesburg and Pretoria, and is perched on a hill on a game farm with almost 360° views across the surrounding bush with no signs of human habitation. The other houses on the game farm are hidden as their thatched roofs blend in with the surrounding trees. The house it sited on the rocks of the hillside and supported by stone built pillars and posts of gum trees - it is African Vernacular at its best!

There are no predators and none of the Big Five on the farm but many different types of buck such as blesbok, kudu, nyala, red hartebeest, klipspringer and wildebeest, giraffe, warthog, zebra and a huge variety of birds. At whatever time of the day there is the thrill of seeing different species on a game drive and then relaxing with drinks by one of the dams to watch the sunset. I hadn't seen Wendy, my friend from Lusaka days for a long time and Alex arranged for her to come to the farm to stay, it was a lovely holiday for her away from Durban and very special for me.

Back in Johannesburg we had a Thomas Cookies 25 year Reunion, where had the years gone since we all worked for that august company? Renee, Christine, Gaby, Connie and me -it was a jolly good evening of reminiscing.

Back in Oxford there was a fascinating exhibition in front of the Natural History Museum called 'Ghost Trees'. I had driven past it on many occasions and seen what appeared to be stumps of trees on plinths and decided I needed to make their acquaintance. The emphasis was on the enormous upended stumps with their twisting and seemingly riotous roots trying to either knit themselves into more complex patterns or break free. A nearby board explained: *The Ghost Forest trees are from a commercially logged primary rainforest in Western Africa and were bought to Europe in a gargantuan logistical task by the artist Angela Palmer. They are intended as 'ambassadors' for all rain forest trees, and highlight the alarming depletion of the world's natural resources. Today a tropical forest the size of a football pitch is destroyed every four seconds. When the artist embarked on her journey she had no idea of the epic journey ahead.* These stumps were from trees up to 61m high - taller than Nelson's Column and only three were logged, the rest falling due to weather conditions. It was moving to see these forest giants laid low but they had a powerful message to impart.

The power of the people, or rather just Roger and me! I don't usually do projects but one presented itself as a result of reading a book about the life of Sir Francis Younghusband. Roger and I have similar reading interests relating to India and Nepal and to the history of those countries in the 19thC, add in my passion for Mount Everest and you will understand. We approached the project from two sides, mine and Roger's.

In Chapter 6 I introduced you to the climbers Mallory and Irving and the 1920s expeditions to Mount Everest. The man who set up these expeditions and encouraged the climbers was the President of the Royal Geographical Society, Francis Younghusband. In the way that I have of wanting to know more I discovered that he was not only an old India 'hand' but had been the first European to enter the closed city of Lhasa in Tibet in 1904. I read his extraordinary biography *The Last Great Imperial Adventurer* where he is further described as soldier, explorer, mystic, guru and spy, he also became a radical visionary and preached free love to his followers.

I discussed this with Roger who was then a member of the RGS and he introduced me to the books which further revealed the history of 'The Great Game', a confrontation in the 19thC between Britain and Russia over Afghanistan with India caught in the middle geographically. These books are exciting adventure stories but all are true and Younghusband was at the centre of talks with the Russians,

Afghans and Chinese. In the 1880s he sailed to China and then proceeded overland from Peking to Kashmir. Just look in an atlas and see the distance covered during this epic journey. Roger found almost nothing at the RGS to either mention or commemorate Younghusband and we decided that something needed to be done. His biography said he was buried at Lychett Minster in Dorset so Damian and I set off one day to investigate. During the first visit to the churchyard we could not locate the grave in spite of searching thoroughly so I then contacted the church warden who gave me a more specific location. On the next visit we found the grave and in such a sorry state, the name and the representation of the Potala Palace in Lhasa which was carved into the top of the headstone could hardly be seen under mould and dirt.

The RGS was contacted with a view to funding the cleaning and repair of the headstone, to no avail. Roger and I then started a fund via the church who contacted Younghusband's regiment now the 1st Queen's Dragoon Guards, and they agreed to pay for the work required. Eventually after two years we returned to the churchyard for the official 'unveiling' of the beautifully restored stone, Sir Francis rests under the frieze showing the outline of the Potala Palace backed by his beloved Himalayas.

There were three great events to end 2012, I have already told you about my Graduation, there was also the Queen's Diamond Jubilee and the London Olympic Games.

The day of the River Pageant was grey and wet, just like the Coronation Day sixty years previously, then the Queen wore the magnificent Coronation Robes over a white and gold dress, for the Jubilee she was equally beautiful in a white coat and hat covered with jewel-like studs. In 1953, her Coronation year, she travelled in a golden coach pulled by eight horses, in 2012, sixty years after her accession to the throne, in the barge *Spirit of Chartwell.* The royal procession of 1000 vessels of all shapes and sizes on that day was led by the golden royal barge *Gloriana* powered by eighteen oarsmen. In my album for that year I have a photo of the river and the skyline from St Paul's eastwards downriver underneath a Canaletto painting of exactly the same stretch of river and skyline painted in 1756, the previous time that 1000 boats were in a pageant on the Thames. The only difference is that Wren's City churches are now hidden behind glass and metal office blocks, the vessels on the river look much the same.

There had been some concerns that the Opening Ceremony of the London Olympic Games could not possibly live up to that of the Beijing Olympics which showcased a cast of thousands doing movements of almost mathematical and gymnastic precision. We need not have worried, our Opening Ceremony was spectacular. I will just mention my favourite items.

The Olympic Cauldron had an extraordinary effect when it was lit. There were 204 metal petals representing all the nations taking part, they were lit as they lay on the ground and then they rose up symbolising the coming together of the nations for the Games.

Who can forget HM The Queen walking with her corgis and James Bond along a Palace corridor and then seeming to parachute from a helicopter into the Stadium, the timing was perfect, just a brief drop through the sky and then she appeared in her seat!

The depiction of the Industrial Revolution rising from a green and pleasant land was incredible, 100ft chimneys belching smoke, flames, rivers of molten steel, sparks everywhere. Danny Boyle who created it all wanted to show that the Industrial Revolution was a key moment in our history. How did he make it happen - you can look online for the full story:
London 2012: How the might of the industrial revolution was created in stage. http://www.telegraph.co.uk/sport/olympics/london-2012

The closing ceremony was musical and fun, the Spice Girls my favourite, so good to see them back together again.

This 'up' line of studies and travels has come to an end and it is time to continue on the final part of my journey.

CHAPTER 10
Nearing the Terminus

"It is good to have an end to journey toward; but it is the journey that matters, in the end."
Ursula K. Le Guin

In University speak I came 'down' but even though I had finished with serious studying the need to learn was still there. Everyone should be introduced to MOOCs! Massive Open Online Courses ranging from four to eight weeks, offered by Universities worldwide and free. The range of subjects is vast and if you have the appetite for learning there is a subject of interest to everyone, historical, geographical, philosophical, mathematical and many more 'icals.

Over the past two years I have taken twelve courses including looking at the Roman way of life on Hadrian's Wall, explored Portas, the ancient port of Rome, had a disagreement with the tutors on a course concerning Empire (I like to think I was better informed than they were!) and looked at shipwrecks above and below the water as well as an introduction to geology which I should have taken all those years ago when I should have gone to University. The most interesting have been those concerning climate change, the weather, and monitoring climate from space, all offered by the European Space Agency. There is no reason why anyone, at any age, anywhere in the world, with a computer and a quest for knowledge should be denied the opportunity to learn. I will be continuing with MOOCs on what is left of my journey so I might see you on a course too.

According to that delectable star-gazer Professor Brian Cox
'curiosity has no age limit'.

What is a life or indeed a journey, without an animal friend? When I was a small child my mother had a black Persian cat called Peter and then we had a lemon and white Cocker Spaniel called Beauty and she was beautiful. My two Springer spaniels, Sandy and Rufus were with me on the earlier part of my journey, but since Damian and I married we have had feline friends to accompany us. Notable amongst these furry creatures was Henley, a roly poly black and white ball, Agapanthus who thought she was a Siamese and treated all the neighbour's houses as her own, there was no window that she could not climb through. Midnight joined us one year whilst we were away on holiday, the house was shut up and our cats in the cattery. He must have been left behind when the local 'travellers' departed, or maybe he had had enough of their peripatetic way of life so he broke through our cat flap and came to stay and fortunately the other cats tolerated him. One of these was Monet, a handsome marmalade cat who became my shadow and who was sadly only with us for three years. He came as a kitten and would sleep on my shoulder and as a 7kg ginger tom that was still his preferred place to sleep. We now have Rusty, the Maine Coon and Jess who both came from the Blue Cross rescue cats' home ten years ago, they are now fifteen and sixteen so I fear their journey is slowing down, when they depart the train we will have no more.

I recorded my thoughts when Monet died:

My Ginger Boy
You fill the house with your presence....
Framed by the window, gazing at passers-by,
Willing them to greet you nose to nose through the window.

Enjoying the warmth of the glass topped cooker
An expression of bliss on a gently toasting body...
Careful! Your paw will burn on that hot patch,
Just recline, stretch out and relax.

At the end of the garden path you sit guarding your domain,
Keeping it safe from the strays and the phanTOMS
or keeping a watch for your friends.
A fierce pose from a large ginger Tom
But you turn tail and abandon your post
at the first sound or sight that is strange.

There is an apricot silk cushion which perfectly reflects
The tones and shades of your soft velvet fur,

From deepest marmalade through ginger to the apricot fluff on your tum.
Here you lie back in the day and ponder the sunbeams
That shine through the study door.

Curled on my pillow, headless and tailless
Just a tight ball of ginger cat, fast asleep.
But a lion-like purr ready to burst forth
At the sound of a friend.

Now the window frames an empty picture
Passers-by go unwatched.
Some of your hairs are scattered atop the cooker
The silk cushion shows its pattern but looks unfinished without you
There's a large round dip on my pillow, empty, silent, no purr.

The garden is unguarded, strays appear unchecked,
The birds have returned.

Monet, I miss you.

There's a thump on the stairs this evening,
And a shadow passes the doorway,
I find a stray hair on my jumper,

Monet, is it you?

On safari with the Ross family after Alex's special birthday in 2014. Madikwe Game Reserve in the North West Province of South Africa close to the border with Botswana has all the Big Five and many of them in abundance. I am not going to tell you all that we did and saw except for three special moments. Remember my special time watching the cheetah in the Okavango? I was hoping to see one again as they are my favourite wild animal, so sleek, beautiful and athletic.

During a night game drive we saw three cheetah slinking through the bush, almost invisible, I managed to capture just one in a hazy photograph. Also I had never seen a leopard and this time we saw several both by day and at night, I find them sinister looking, so strong and alert, whereas cheetah to me look feminine, a leopard is definitely masculine - even if a female!

One afternoon, sitting on the patio of our cottage there was an increasingly loud sound of branches being broken on the side of the steep koppie just yards from the cottage and the tops of the trees waved from side to side. Gradually the backs of elephants appeared as they made their way so slowly down the steep side, occasionally stopping and then continuing, the reason for this stop/start became obvious as six adult elephants appeared surrounding three young ones, the adults apparently helping the young ones negotiate the treacherous going underfoot. You could see the adults lift one foot, wait, lift another and then move, the epitome of a measured tread, all the while to the noise of branches crackling and the inevitable sound of these huge beasts as they moved through the trees. After forty five minutes the group stopped briefly at the waterhole below the cottage and then they ambled off into the bush, the whole episode had taken more than an hour. Another day twenty elephant came to the waterhole - it is impossible to describe the joy of being within yards of these magnificent creatures, of being part of their world but not impinging upon it.

Before my journey ends there is a loose end that needs to be tied. I always wondered what happened to Colin, my first innocent love from Aden days? Over the years since Google arrived I tried to find him using a combination of his name, New Zealand, Kew Gardens, but with no luck. When I started to think about this journey I found all the shipping passenger lists for the journeys that my family had taken in order to confirm dates and ships' names. On the *Kenya* passenger list Colin's occupation was given as horticulturalist which is of course what he was but I had never thought to use that term in my searches. So into Google went his name and occupation and - bingo- I found an article by his daughter Carol who lives in the Caribbean regarding her own 'green fingers' inherited from her late father. I contacted her via Facebook, and then we had a tearful telephone call, she said I could be her mother! I was sad to hear that Colin died so young at 50 in 1980. After his marriage (not far from where Grandma B lived) he and his family lived in the Caribbean and Carol said that they knew of me as Colin's mystery woman!

Colin's wife Dorothea Whitehorne (she remarried) wrote of her meeting and marriage to Colin in her autobiography *Part of the Ocean.*

Perhaps if the Red Sea had not been a barrier to our relationship we might have gone on to have a happy life together. How fortunate that I am the one to be in a loving marriage in my later years.

There were many Battle of the Somme commemorations in 2014 which reminded me of our earlier visit to the WWI battlefields. Sarah and I had our own emotional visit to the Tower of London to see the 'Blood Swept Lands and Seas of Red' installation of ceramic poppies. They fell in a waterfall from a window in the Tower and then flowed around the moat. Each of the 888,246 poppies represented a British military death. It was impossible not to be moved when you realised that each poppy was a person; the moat did indeed become a 'Sea of Red'

Where have all the soldiers gone,
Long time passing,
Where have all the soldiers gone,
Long time ago,
Where have all the soldiers gone,
They've gone to graveyards everyone,
When will they ever learn?
When will they ever learn?
Pete Seeger

It is time to explore new destinations, I have already taken you many times to Portugal and Greece, we've visited Hong Kong and Thailand too as well as the USA and South America, but some very different voyages became the stations on my journey. The problem is that I should be living by the sea. Just a few years in Aden and I realised how much I needed the sight, sound and smell of the sea in my life, and what happens, I end up living in the middle of Africa and then in the middle of England, as far away from the sea as possible. Any holidays that took me to the coast were special - remember Kynance Cove - so this latter part of my journey took me towards the oceans!

Sylvia and Dermott had taken the Hurtigruten Norwegian coastal voyages several times so Jean and I decided we would venture forth in the depths of winter and follow the coast of Norway round to the Russian border and hopefully see the Northern Lights. This is no holiday cruise but a voyage on a working vessel completing a round trip of 12 days from Bergen to Kirkenes on the Russian border and return. A vessel leaves Bergen every day supplying a lifeline to the small harbours and fjords along the coast. We visited 34 ports and more than 100 fjords and the scenery was beyond description, it was so beautiful and awe-inspiring.

When we arrived in Bergen we found that the ship we should have been embarking on was in dry dock for a mechanical problem so instead we were accommodated on *MV Finnmarken* due to sail the following day. For the inconvenience of having an extra night added to our holiday we had a complimentary tour of Bergen and an upgraded cabin! Bergen is a tourist destination itself especially the Bryggen, the old wharf and centre of the Hanseatic League's trading area, did ships really go from here to King's Lynn and Kingston-upon-Hull?

Our ship of 15,690 tons had the capacity for 35 cars and 1000 passengers, but being the depths of winter there were less than 300 on board. The cabin was comfortable and the public rooms excellent. You may remember on the first morning of the Palace on Wheels journey in India when I opened the curtains of my compartment and had a memory making moment seeing the brightly coloured saris of women working in the fields? I had another memory making moment on the Hurtigruten - I came up the staircase to go to breakfast on the first morning and there, in the large window was a snow-covered mountainside right by the ship, it was a frightening sight but we soon became accustomed to the narrowness of many fjords where you felt you could reach out and touch the mountainsides.

The ship called into so many ports, sometimes just for half an hour to off load or upload cargo and take on passengers who may be continuing their journey for a couple of days or just until the next port of call later in the day. To cater for them were several cafes as well as the main restaurant. Jean and I found a patisserie on one of the upper decks which was always deserted and which produced delicious coffees and cakes and gave a view of all the stunning scenery that we passed by. The ship had a very good system for purchasing coffee which was invaluable to coffeeholics like us. A cup in the café cost £5, but we purchased an empty mug for £25 which could be filled as often as you wanted.

The excursions were very expensive but we chose to do two. At the port of Kirkenes the coach took us on a tour of the countryside before approaching the border with Russia and an opportunity for historic photos and purchases from tiny souvenir shop. The border was hardly worth a visit but the journey there and back was worthwhile just see to the countryside.

The best excursion was a day's touring of Vesterålen. We left the ship at Harstad and travelled by coach across Hinnøya Island where even though the landscape was deeply snow covered it was still possible to see the outlines of fields. At first glance Arctic Norway appears untouched, narrow fjords, soaring snow-capped mountains with small settlements clinging to the water's edge. The island of Kvaeoya that we passed by consists of seven square kilometres, mostly of mountains and infertile land but when the ice age retreated the fifty metres of sea-bed that was exposed became rich farming soil. Fish farms in the off- shore waters along this Arctic coastline are the result of the growing local population's requirement for food but also for the export markets. So even in this apparent wasteland of ice and snow farming of one type of another exists both in winter and summer.

The coach then brought us to Gullesfjord where we joined an ordinary passenger ferry which took us along Sigerford to Sortland. The highlight of this day was visiting the 750year old church at Trondenes. The church is painted white but it sat in a twilight, late afternoon, white world. The snow surrounding the church was very deep, the church was also snow covered and the adjacent fjord was all snow and ice. By contrast the interior was brightly lit with candles and the pulpit painted in many colours.

In spite of the short daylight hours every moment was filled with snow covered mountains - the Seven Sisters particular favourites and fjords wide and narrow, we even passed the entrance to the fjord for Mosjoen where I had holidayed years ago. In the most isolated places seemingly away from any other habitation there would be a brightly painted house by the edge of the water, how harsh life must be for the owners in winter.

We had the most dramatic seas in a force 12 storm as we passed around the North Cape, the northern most point in Europe, reminiscent of that awful storm in the Bay of Biscay when we were en route to Santander on the ferry. However, spectacular sunsets brought each day to a close - and we never saw the Northern Lights!

The 'on the sea' experience continued when my sister Mary and I decided to explore the Scottish Islands and the Faroe Islands. Our transport this time was *MV Astoria*, a modest sized vessel of 16,000 tons and taking only 550 passengers although on this voyage she was not full. The thought of travelling on a vessel that takes 2000-3000 passengers is an anathema to me. Even though I have travelled extensively in the UK, the Western Isles, the Orkneys and the Shetlands are too remote for tourists unless you fly, ferry or cruise and the Faroes, part of Denmark, are far north in the middle of the Norwegian sea between Iceland and Norway.

Following in the footsteps of Flora MacDonald and Bonnie Prince Charlie we went 'over the sea to Skye'. In 1746 Flora aided the Stuart Young Pretender's escape from the Outer Hebrides to Skye and thence to France where he later died. She spent many years in America and then returned to Skye where she died in 1790 and was buried at Kilmuir. She has a simple grave with a tall white Celtic cross and the memorial reads *Her name will be mentioned in history and if courage and fidelity be virtues, mentioned with honour*.
An interesting snippet to link Skye with Oxford, tradition has it that the main gates of Trinity College must never be opened until a Stuart ascends the throne of England.

Near the cemetery is the *Museum of Island Life* with its re-created stone and thatched cottages similar to those that would have been inhabited on the island in the 18th and 19th centuries. I found them particularly interesting as examples of vernacular architecture. The stones used to create the walls were more like small boulders than building stones, the thatched roofs came well down over the walls protecting the tops of the window openings, and the roofs were held down with ropes weighted by stones. It was in a cottage/croft like this that Flora and her Prince would have hidden.

There are some striking rock formations on Skye called Kilt Rocks, the cliffs rise out of the sea and the rocks appear to form regular pleats as you would see in a Scottish kilt. Occasionally a waterfall breaks the symmetry of the formation. Skye seemed to me a calm and peaceful island with gentle scenery.

The ship headed further north to the Shetland Islands where there is more dramatic scenery with high cliffs and mountainous seas coming in from the North Atlantic. The Eshaness Cliffs are part of an ancient volcano (not at all like Crater in Aden!) and here we were fortunate to see the start of the nesting season for fulmers. Pairs of the birds were creating their nests in the crevasses of the near vertical rocks and from a distance the grey rock face appeared covered in white dots.

After leaving Eshaness we passed the oil terminal at Sullom Voe with its continuous flame (a remembrance of the Little Aden oil refinery) and then came to a narrow strip of road at Mavis Grind connecting the Shetland mainland to the peninsula of Northmavine. The scenery was bleak and barren all around and surrounded by water, the information board gives the details of the area.

MAVIS GRIND

(Old Norse meaning gate of the narrow isthmus)

Mavis Grind is possibly the only place in the United Kingdom where you can stand on the edge of the Atlantic Ocean and throw a stone overland into the North Sea. As such the narrow strip of land has often been used as a shortcut from one side of Shetland to the other. Various cargoes have made the crossing but the route is perhaps best known as a 'boat draa' where mariners avoided the long, and at times dangerous journey around the north mainland by hauling their vessel overland instead. The crossing was used regularly until the 1950s.

We now went even further north through huge seas to Torshavn, capital of the Faroe Islands where we docked in a heavy snowstorm. It was obvious that we had left Spring far behind in the Shetlands and arrived into the depths of winter. The houses lining the harbour were brightly coloured, very like those in Bergen but also many had the yellow that I had seen in Finland, Stockholm and Russia, a warm colour in a cold climate. The day's excursion took us through the most sensational scenery, all snow covered, dramatic mountains, hairpin bends to the roads, tunnels through the mountains - my comment in the photo album says 'the long and winding road on the edge of mountains and through many tunnels'. There seemed to be no space for agriculture but at the base of the mountains and surrounding an isolated house could be seen the outlines of small fields now snow covered. En route to our lunch stop at Gjogv we travelled across the Atlantic Bridge connecting the islands of Streymoy and Eystruroy, said to be the only bridge in the world over the Atlantic Ocean although I think there is one in Scotland too! Here are the highest mountains on the Faroes, six peaks ranging from 2000 to 3000 feet, all snow covered and all very menacing! In one of the valleys by the water's edge lies the village of Funningur reported to be where the first Norsemen landed in the 9thC. There were just a few houses and a church to be seen scattered along a curve of the small bay. Our guide preferred to use the term Norsemen to Vikings.

And so to Gjogv, the northernmost village on Esturoy so colourful amid the snow and ice. The houses are situated along a gorge that runs to the sea, the two arms of the gorge form a natural safe harbour and a watercolour of the harbour is my latest travel purchase. The population is only about 50 and the few houses have combinations of red, yellow and green wooden walls and roofs and some of the properties are roofed with turfs. It is starkly beautiful but living here must be hard, the guesthouse and restaurant cater for tourists which provide a source of revenue for this small community. I understand walking and birding are popular in the summer months. I was sorry to leave the Faroes, they are strange awe-inspiring islands, so foreign compared to our Western Isles but with a compelling beauty in their winter coverings.

Returning southwards to Lewis and Harris in the Outer Hebrides. Winter was still clinging to the mountains here and I won't give you more scenic details except to mention Horgabost Bay on Harris. Transport Kynance Cove from Cornwall to Harris and you have Horgabost Bay, in the bright sunshine miles of the palest golden sands, quiet seas ranging from turquoise to emerald green and not a soul to be seen except for those of us from the coach. But it was cold, very, very cold.

On to Tarbert in Harris where all signs of winter had disappeared and where the tweed factory provided a riotous display of colour in the rolls of tweed available for purchase. When I think of tweed I think of browns and greens with perhaps a dash of red, not in Harris, here are pinks and purples, green and lime, turquoise and yellow, many colours in unusual combinations that would make the most gorgeous clothes. We were told that weavers are allowed no more than two looms in their homes and to be eligible for the Orb Mark which is Britain's oldest surviving Certification Mark a tweed must have been "hand-woven by the islanders at their home in the Outer Hebrides and made from pure virgin wool dyed and spun in the Outer Hebrides". The weaving is carried out on either a single width loom or the more modern double width loom. Both are powered exclusively by the weaver's own leg work. Single width costs £20 per metre and double width £40 per metre. The Harris Tweed shop had a mouth-watering display of things to buy, bags and purses, dog collars and dinner mats but I tried not to be tempted!

There is a very poignant sculpture on Lewis in the form of a teardrop made from stones, it must stand about 10 feet tall and it commemorates the failure of Bonnie Prince Charlie to take the English throne for the exiled Stuarts.

Our visits to the Scottish Islands ended here, on arrival in Mull the fog and snow prevented a landing at Tobermory so we didn't get to see the colourful houses that were the setting for the children's' TV programme Balamory. Whilst we were anchored offshore there was a heavy snowstorm, some of the crew who came from sunnier climes had never seen snow and this resulted in them making two fine snowmen on the upper deck. Then the weather and exceptionally high seas prevented a visit to the Orkney Islands. This part of my journey certainly fulfilled my need for being by the sea!

Having rounded the Northern Cape in stormy seas, it was time to return to the Southern Ocean of the Cape in South Africa and at what better time of the year than the whaling season at Hermanus in Walker Bay. It is said to be one of the best whale watching destinations in the world and it is here that the Southern Right Whale comes to mate and breed in the winter and spring months. I was there in August so did not expect to see the huge numbers that can be seen later in the year but nevertheless I was rewarded with sightings of several out in the bay, sometimes just a hump in the sea at other times the whale would arise from the waters as it breached at other times the tail would be lifted aloft and give a playful flick. One morning two whales were close in shore and talking to each other, such an eerie sound, the watery equivalent of a lion's roar, a deep, long, echoing sound, almost other worldly.

The name Southern Right has a chilling origin, as whalers identified them as the right whales to hunt and kill. Walker Bay is a Whale Sanctuary Marine Protected Area between July and November and no unauthorised boats are allowed within the bay during that period so it is good to know that the whales can safely raise their young before going out to join the estimated 10,000 Southern Rights in the southern hemisphere.

The southernmost point in Africa is at Cape Agulhas (not the Cape of Good Hope) and the commemorative plaque below the lighthouse points in each direction to the Indian Ocean and the Atlantic Ocean. It is the meeting of the warm water of the Indian Ocean and the cold Benguela current from the Atlantic. Unlike in Brazil where you can see the meeting of the different coloured waters of the Solimoes and Amazon rivers here there is nothing to see but waves breaking on the very rocky shoreline.

On the day of my visit the seas were deceptively calm, unlike the storms to the north but one has to remember the shipwrecks for which this coast is notorious. At the Danger Point lighthouse is a memorial to the troopship *H.M.S.Birkenhead* that foundered here in 1852.There are many shipwrecks but this one deserves a special mention for its long lasting legacy. The memorial says:

IN MEMORY OF THOSE WHO PERISHED
in
H.M.S. BIRKENHEAD
26th February 1852
THE SHIP CARRYING REINFORCEMENTS
FOR THE EIGHTH KAFFIR WAR, STRUCK
A SUNKEN REEF APPROXIMATELY
1 1/3 SEA MILES SOUTH-WEST by SOUTH
FROM THIS POINT
NINE OFFICERS, THREE HUNDRED &
FORTY-NINE OF OTHER RANKS AND
EIGHTY-SEVEN OF THE SHIPS
COMPANY LOST THEIR LIVES.
EVERY WOMAN AND CHILD WAS SAVED.

The legacy of this disaster is known as the *Birkenhead Drill.* The commanding officer of the soldiers on board ordered them not to rush to the lifeboats but to 'stand fast' and allow the 'women and children first'.

The Shipwreck Museum at Bredasdorp is the repository of items found along the shores from the many ships that have foundered along this treacherous coast. At the entrance to the museum is a reminder: *Before entering this Shipwreck Hall, take a few seconds and give your thoughts to the many men, women and children who lost their lives during these shipwrecks.*

On display is a fine set of Delft tableware from the Dutch Indiaman *Haerlem* that was wrecked in March 1647. This wreck changed the course of history, the crew and cargo landed on the shore of Table Bay, bartered with the local Khoi population and grew vegetables during their enforced stay. They were later rescued by Jan van Riebeeck who then returned to Table Bay in 1652 to establish a refreshment station for the ships of the Dutch East India company. From one shipwreck was born a nation!

There are many artefacts from the *Birkenhead* and also from the East Indiaman *Arniston* that was wrecked near Cape Agulhas in May 1815. She was being used as a troopship and 372 lives were lost, only six survived. A wreath of poppies is laid each year on 30 May and an everlasting light shines beneath a memorial to the all who died on the *Arniston*, placed there by the regiment of the fallen soldiers.

The Cape of Good Hope, the Cape of Storms, however you describe this southern edge of the African Continent it is still as Sir Francis Drake said in1580 *The fairest Cape we saw in the whole circumference of the earth.*

And so dear friends, as Jane Austen would say, the time has come for you to leave me. There is no more past to return to, there are no more photograph albums to delve into, no more passport stamps as reminders of past stations on this journey. It has been an experience to revisit places long since forgotten and to meet again the many friends that I made on my journey and especially to dig deep into the storage space of my memory bank and allow the memories to flow out, the good, the bad and the long forgotten too.

But the past is past and my journey now continues into the future but there is a sharp bend ahead on the track so I cannot see how much further it goes. I will take the journey slowly as there is more studying to be done, more places to visit. Richelle Mead perfectly expresses my thoughts.... *Sometimes it's worth lingering on the journey for a while before getting to the destination............*

Ann
Not a good mother
Eventually a good wife
Always a good friend

AND FINALLY

Thank you to my sister Mary for doing her best with my ancient photographs, if you cannot see them clearly the fault is mine.

22323173R00172

Printed in Poland
by Amazon Fulfillment
Poland Sp. z o.o., Wrocław